THE MOST
EXTRAORDINARY
LIFE

DISCOVERING
THE
REAL JESUS

BOB ROGNLIEN

Editor: Robert Neely
Cover Design: Timothy J. Bergren
Interior Design: Amit Dey

ISBN: 978-0-9815247-6-4

Published by GX Books

DEDICATION

To my five granddaughters,
Eleanor, Abigail, Celeste, Vivian, and Riley.
I pray this book will one day help you find your way
as you learn to follow the Way of Jesus
and live the extraordinary lives he is calling you into.
I love you very much.

AKNOWLEDGEMENTS

I want to express my gratitude to all those who supported me, prayed for me, and made the writing of this book possible. Specifically, I want to thank Matt Switzer and Julie Dirkse for giving me invaluable and insightful feedback on the first draft. Thank you to Pam Rognlien and Chris Pudel for carefully rooting out my many mistakes and to Amit Dey for designing the interior pages. Special thanks to Tim Bergren for designing another great book cover and to Robert Neely for editing another of my manuscripts and making it eminently more readable. Above all I give thanks to Jesus, the most extraordinary man who ever walked the face of this earth, who continues inviting us all to follow him in learning to live extraordinary lives as well. To him be all the glory!

CONTENTS

INTRODUCTION

WHY JESUS?

THE QUEST

My friends Mark and Hani had already disembarked as my wife Pam and I stepped off the dusty bus into the dry morning heat of the Jordan Valley. The four of us caught the early bus from Jerusalem to Tiberias and asked the driver to drop us off at this unposted road leading east toward the Jordan River. I had our six-month old son Bobby strapped to my chest, and he was squinting as I tried to shield his eyes from the desert sun. Pam and I were living in the Old City of Jerusalem where I was conducting a year of post-graduate study in New Testament archeology and sociology at the Ecole Biblique et Archeologique, the famous French school of biblical archaeology. Mark and Hani, post-graduate archaeology students conducting research at the Albright Institute, had agreed to join us on a little adventure to see how close we could get to the site of Jesus' baptism.

I was on an obsessive quest to visit every site mentioned in the Gospels in which Jesus carried out his ministry and only had a few left to check off my list. Ever since I had become a follower of Jesus in my teens, I felt the urge to actually see the places where biblical events took place. Spending my formative years living overseas in several different cultures imbued me with a love for travel and cross-cultural experiences. Based on the way I grew up, I knew that, if I could visit the places where Jesus lived out his mission, I would gain a clearer understanding of who he really is. But at that time, in 1990, the traditional site of Jesus' baptism in the Jordan River, just east of Jericho, was strictly off limits because the river formed the border between the Israeli-controlled West Bank and the country of Jordan on the east bank. Since Israel and Jordan were technically still "at war" with each other, this was an understandably sensitive military area. In fact, a wide swath of land leading up to the river was still laden with land mines meant to prevent an invasion. But I still wanted to see how close we could get to this fascinating site.

As the bus pulled away, we started hiking east down the unmarked road which ran alongside a date palm plantation. The sun quickly climbed higher in the sky and, although it was January, we could all feel the temperature rising. We settled into a steady rhythm, chatting as we walked and enjoying the desolate beauty of this biblical desert. It was here that the people of Israel had crossed into the land of Canaan under the leadership of Joshua over three thousand years ago. I could almost hear John the Baptist's voice echoing off these arid ridges, warning the Sadducees and Pharisees of the unquenchable fire that was soon to come. Eventually we saw the double rows of electrified fencing marking the beginning of no-man's land. As we drew closer, we observed the bright yellow signs warning us of land mines ahead. The Jordan River was carved deep into the arid furrows beyond, so we couldn't actually see it, but I could tell it was close and my heart began beating faster.

Just then, out of the corner of my eye, I saw a cloud of dust rising to the south and realized an Israeli military vehicle was racing toward us. It was a drab olive truck with an open flatbed on which was mounted a large machine gun manned by young Israeli soldiers. And it was pointed straight at us! Since our friend Hani came from a Palestinian family that has lived in Jerusalem for countless generations, we were immediately concerned he might fall under undue suspicion. So we pushed him to the back of our little group, and I stepped forward to do the talking. I was quick to show my U.S. passport as I tried to explain why we were out there wandering around the desert. After their initial concerns were addressed, the soldiers were courteous but stern in informing us that we couldn't be in this area. Then they loaded us onto the open bed of the truck and drove us a mile or two south to the ancient monastery of St.

Gerasimus. The monks there received us warmly and were kind enough to call a taxi for our return to Jerusalem.

You might think me reckless or irresponsible for undertaking such a journey. I could blame it on my 26-year-old lack of judgment, but the truth is I would do it all over again today! I feel a pull inside of me toward the person of Jesus. Not the plastic Jesus glued to a dashboard, or the flannel Jesus stuck to a Sunday school wall, or the romanticized Jesus of sappy hymns, but the real flesh and blood, sweat and tears Jesus who walked this earth. That tug is what drew me into the desert that day with my fledgling family and newfound friends. I have a deep desire to see Jesus as he really is, to know him more fully, and to follow him more closely. This quest has called me back to the Holy Land again and again for more than three decades. This quest has moved me to invest my entire adult life in researching all the information I can find that illuminates his life, his death, and his resurrection. This quest is why I have chosen to write this book. Perhaps a desire to know more of the real Jesus is the same impulse drawing you to read this book.

But what is it about Jesus that draws us so?

ONE SOLITARY LIFE

I love history because it is our story, the human story. I spend many late nights lying in bed reading about some obscure chapter of that human story. Even more than the wars and empires and discoveries that have defined our world, I am fascinated by the people who have shaped this human story. Aristotle and Alexander the Great. Cleopatra and Julius Caesar. Augustine and Genghis Khan. Mozart and Mao Zedong. Martin Luther and Martin Luther King, Jr. Extraordinary people who changed the world with armies, adventures, ideas, and art.

The story of our human race is told in the insights and discoveries, the accomplishments and heroics, the callings and crimes of men and women who rose above the rest by blind accident, sheer effort, or brave sacrifice. I love reading biographies of these heroes and villains because their examples teach me so much about myself and show me how to live a more significant life. But one person in history stands out above all the others, not just for his accomplishments and influence, but also because his unparalleled impact on human history is so disproportionate to his social standing and political position. About a hundred years ago James Allan Francis, pastor of the First Baptist Church of Los Angeles, described him this way:

> Here is a man who was born in an obscure village. He was brought up in another obscure village. He worked in a carpenter shop until he was thirty, and then for three brief years was an itinerant preacher. He never wrote a book. He never held an office. He never raised an army. He never owned a home. He never had a family of his own. He never went to college. He never traveled two hundred miles from the place where he was born. He never did one of the things that usually accompany greatness.
>
> He gathered a little group of friends around him and taught them his way of life. While still a young man, the tide of public opinion turned against him. His friends forsook him. One denied him, another betrayed him. He was turned over to his enemies. He went through the mockery of a trial. He was nailed to a cross between two thieves. When he was dead, he was taken down and laid in a borrowed grave by the kindness of a friend. He rose from the dead.
>
> Today we look back across nineteen hundred years and ask, what kind of mark has he left across the centuries? When we try to sum up his influence I am far within the mark when I say that all the armies that ever marched, and all the navies that ever sailed, and all the parliaments that ever sat, and all the kings that ever reigned, put together have not affected the life of man upon this earth as powerfully as has that One Solitary Life.[1]

While Pastor Francis may not have had all the cultural details correct, he brilliantly captured what makes Jesus of Nazareth unique in all of history. Lacking all the trappings of what we normally call greatness, on one level Jesus seems a very ordinary first-century Jew. And yet Jesus lived a life unlike any that has ever been lived in human history. His self-giving love was matched only by his transforming power. His tender compassion was extended to the vulnerable and privileged

---

[1] James Allen Francis, *The Real Jesus and Other Sermons* (1926, reprint edition, Dauphin Publications, 2018), pg. 119, adapted by author.

alike. His revolutionary insights transcended normal categories of learning and knowledge. He rejected both political and religious positions of control. His profound intimacy with God as Father drew others into God's presence as well. He healed and set free those he touched. He trained and empowered others to do everything he did. He redefined the family and cast a vision for a whole new kind of world. Most remarkable of all, he suffered unjust torture and execution, but then physically rose from the dead, giving birth to an indestructible new kind of life. This is the real Jesus. His incomparable life has informed, inspired, empowered, and transformed billions of people ever since. As we get to know who he really is, by simple historical comparison we can confidently say Jesus lived the most extraordinary life. But what is the source of this incomparable life?

AN INVITATION TO THE ABUNDANT LIFE

Jesus said, *"I came that they may have life and have it abundantly."* (John 10:10) Some have assumed Jesus was speaking of strictly material abundance, but it is clear from his example and teaching Jesus was pointing to something much more important. Contrary to popular assumption, Jesus grew up in a family with possessions and means, but he chose to keep nothing for himself and lived a simple life, living with and relying on the support of others.

So, what is this abundance of which he spoke? Jesus also said, *"I am the vine; you are the branches. Whoever abides in me and I in him, he it is that bears much fruit, for apart from me you can do nothing."* (John 15:5) The abundant life Jesus offers is the fruitful life. It is not about an abundance of possessions for which we need to build bigger barns—it is the abundance of life itself; a richer, fuller, more impactful life that multiplies the goodness God has intended since the beginning of creation. Jesus said this fruitful life of multiplying goodness flows through a deep personal connection with him.

What made Jesus' life so extraordinary is that he chose by faith to abide deeply in his heavenly Father, and so his life produced an abundance of good fruit unlike the world has ever seen. The fruit of his life was not material wealth, but a rich treasure of spiritual truth, joyful relationships and transforming power. And Jesus' fruit was not seedless. His fruit contained seeds and so the goodness of his life was planted and multiplied in the lives of others. By learning to abide in Jesus, the men and women who followed him also bore good fruit containing seeds, which in turn multiplied this reproducing abundant life in the lives of others. And so on and so on. This abundant fruitfulness produced a movement of love and power that changed the world and continues to do so two thousand years later! This movement is what Jesus called the *"Kingdom of God"* in which God's will is done on earth as it is in heaven, with increasing impact for good. So how do we abide in Jesus and multiply the good fruit which he produces in order to see his Kingdom come?

Jesus gave two primary invitations: *"believe in me"* and *"follow me."* (John 14:1-11; Mark 1:15) To believe in Jesus is to trust him, to exercise faith in him. Believing is not only agreeing with the words he spoke and the words written about him. It is about putting your life in his hands the way you trust a doctor who is anesthetizing you for a life-saving operation. Believing in Jesus means much more than just agreeing with him; it means surrendering yourself to him.

You cannot manufacture faith in Jesus. Faith is a gift of God produced by his Word through the work of the Holy Spirit. But you can read God's Word and listen for Jesus' voice speaking to you along with others who are on the same journey. This plants the seeds of faith in your heart. Even now the Holy Spirit is speaking faith to your heart. Stepping out in this faith is what it means to believe in Jesus. You can't create faith, but you can exercise the faith you are given one step at a time. This is how we come to know Jesus and live in a relationship with him. His Spirit begins to fill us and change us from the inside out. Believing is how we abide in him and he in us.

Jesus also said, *"follow me."* To follow Jesus is to live in a particular kind of relationship with him: the relationship of disciples to their rabbi. Disciples live in such close proximity to their rabbi that they can not only hear what the rabbi says, but also see what the rabbi does. Disciples walk so closely behind the rabbi they are literally walking in his footsteps, learning to imitate his way of life. In this way, the disciple not only comes to know what the rabbi knows, but also learns to do what the rabbi does, ultimately becoming like the rabbi.

The life of discipleship is a journey made up of many steps of faith. All you need is a tiny seed of faith to take the next step. Jesus said, *"For truly, I say to you, if you have faith like a grain of mustard seed, you will say to this mountain, 'Move from here to there,' and it will move, and nothing will be impossible for you."* (Matthew 17:20) As you read God's Word and listen for the voice of Jesus as a member of his family, the Holy Spirit will give you the mustard seed of faith you need to take the next step to follow in his footsteps. Not alone, but with your brothers and sisters. This is what it means to answer Jesus' invitation to believe in him and follow him. This is what it means to be part of the Kingdom of God. Jesus is extending this invitation to you right now.

To those who answered Jesus' invitation to believe in and follow him as a part of his family, Jesus also gave a commission, *"Make disciples."* (Matthew 28:18) Every disciple is meant to become a rabbi who in turn calls disciples. This is the seed in the good fruit that Jesus produces. Making disciples is not reserved for an elite few, nor does it require a special degree or title. Every person who follows Jesus is being equipped and empowered to make disciples. As we become more like Jesus, we learn to set an example for others to follow. By inviting people into our homes, our families, and our lives, we give others access to the abundant life of Jesus that is growing in and among us through the Holy Spirit. By meeting people where they are and entering their lives, we embody the Good News of Jesus for them. This is how spiritual families on mission grow. This is how the everyday women and men who first followed Jesus fulfilled the great commission, and it is how we are called to live today if we want to be part of God's coming Kingdom.

HELP FOR THE JOURNEY

If this sounds intimidating, the good news is you are not meant to go on the journey of discipleship by yourself. Jesus invited a houseful of men and women to be his extended spiritual family of followers and called twelve of them to be his full-time disciples. Together they believed in him, followed him, and learned to make disciples the way he did. They couldn't do this alone, and neither can we. We need others to help us learn how to follow Jesus. Because we don't have the privilege of physically following the historical Jesus, we need those ahead of us on the journey to show us the way. Jesus is our perfect historical example, but we also need imperfect living examples to become Jesus-shaped disciples. The apostle Paul was painfully aware of his imperfections, but he understood that a disciple is called to become a living example for other disciples to follow. He told the Corinthian believers, *"Be imitators of me, as I am of Christ."* (1 Corinthians 11:1)

We all need someone to imitate. We need an imperfect but living example to show us what it means to trust and follow Jesus. Each of us are called to become these imperfect but living examples to help others learn to trust and follow Jesus. This is our mission. This is how the Kingdom of God comes. As a young man, I came to know Jesus personally and began the journey of following him one step of faith at a time. But it wasn't until many years later as a seasoned pastor that I finally came to understand discipleship is this process of imitating those who are following Jesus and then inviting others to imitate my imperfect example of a Jesus-shaped life. When someone explicitly invited me into a discipling relationship, it changed my life forever. Now, having invested my life in many men and women who in turn are investing their lives in many others, I see so clearly this is the good, reproducing fruit we are meant to bear as we abide in Jesus. There is no greater joy than seeing the life of Jesus multiplied in the lives of others through your investment in them. This is the abundant life Jesus offers. This is how the Kingdom of God comes!

If we are going to follow the perfect example of Jesus so we can become imperfect examples for others to follow, we need to be sure we are clear on what the perfect example is. If you use a photocopier to make a copy of an original document and then make a copy from that copy, and then keep making copies from copies, the text becomes degraded and distorted. This is how we lose our way. No matter who is setting an example to help us follow Jesus, we must always keep our eyes on the perfect example to make sure we are following his way. This is why the Bible is so important in the life of a disciple. Reading, studying, and discussing the Gospel accounts of Jesus' life gives us a clearer picture of the Jesus-shaped life we are called to live. Reading, studying, and discussing the book of Acts and the letters of the New Testament gives us a clearer picture of how the first followers learned to live that Jesus-shaped life.

What makes this more challenging is that we live in a completely different time and culture than Jesus and his first followers. It is easy to read the Bible and misunderstand its meaning. We need help to gain an accurate biblical picture of the real Jesus so we can be sure we are actually following his way. If our image of Jesus is a distorted copy of a copy and we can't read the original, we will also become distorted versions who lead others astray. Peeling back the layers of history and learning the culture in which Jesus lived and carried out his mission cleans our lens and gives us a more accurate picture of the Original. This book is written to help you gain a clearer image of the real Jesus, which will give you a clearer vision of the life you are meant to live.

Following the Footsteps of Jesus in the Holy Land

As I mentioned earlier, when I became a follower of Jesus in my teens, I found myself wanting to travel to the places where Jesus carried out his mission so I could gain a more accurate understanding of who Jesus really is in his original historical and cultural context. I made my first trip to the lands of the Bible when I was 21 years old and have been going back ever since. I have spent my entire adult life studying the history, archaeology, and culture of the New Testament in order to gain a clearer picture of the real Jesus. For over thirty years, I have led trips that follow the footsteps of Jesus, visiting the actual places where Jesus' life unfolded and helping others gain a clearer picture of him as well. I see it happen over and over and over again—as people see the real Jesus more clearly, they are changed, learn to follow him more closely, and become more like him. This is my prayer for you as you read this book.

If you are confused about who Jesus really is, I pray this book will give you a more accurate picture of the man and his message so you can come to know and trust him personally. If you are still getting to know Jesus, I pray this book will help you trust him more and to follow him more closely in your daily life. If you already know Jesus and are following him, I pray this book will equip you to more effectively set a Jesus-shaped example for others to follow. We will trace the public life of Jesus from his baptism to his resurrection. I will share with you some of the latest archaeological discoveries and historical research that illuminate his life. Each chapter begins with a dramatized version of a Gospel story in which I color in the background of the account with relevant cultural details. Each chapter ends with a few questions meant to help you discern what God is saying to you and what step of faith he wants you to take. Remember, the journey of discipleship is made up of one small step of faith after another. Come with me and let's take the next step together...

CHAPTER ONE

BECOMING THE BELOVED

DOWN BY THE RIVER

Andrew sat down on the soft bank of the river and leaned back against the rustling reeds. The cool water flowed past his feet as he watched his rabbi wade back out into the Jordan River for what seemed to be the thousandth time. *Doesn't he ever get tired?* Andrew thought to himself. He heard his rabbi call out, "Repent, for the kingdom of heaven is at hand. For this is he who was spoken of by the prophet Isaiah when he said, 'The voice of one crying in the wilderness: Prepare the way of the Lord; make his paths straight.'"

Weeks ago, when the fishing season had ended, Andrew and his brother Simon had traveled south from their homes on the north shore of the Sea of Galilee to hear John the son of Zechariah preach his firebrand message of repentance and preparation. They were accompanied by their buddy John the son of Zebedee, a cousin related through their mothers, whose family was in a business partnership with theirs. The three fishermen from Capernaum were so gripped by John's call to repentance they decided to follow him. Every day they sat on the riverbank, as Andrew was now, listening to John's challenging message and watching people from every walk of life come to hear him and be baptized. People just kept coming—farmers, shepherds, potters, even hated tax collectors and Herodian soldiers!

The Ministry of John the Baptist

Now some of the leading Pharisees and Sadducees from Jerusalem arrived at the river. John the Baptist, as he was coming to be called, began again with his booming voice. "You brood of vipers! Who warned you to flee from the wrath to come? Bear fruit in keeping with repentance. And do not presume to say to yourselves, 'We have Abraham as our father,' for I tell you, God is able from these stones to raise up children for Abraham. Even now the axe is laid to the root of the trees. Every tree therefore that does not bear good fruit is cut down and thrown into the fire." Andrew could see the religious leaders bristle at John's words, knowing they were the objects of John's rebuke. But they didn't leave. It was as if they were transfixed by the Baptist's voice. As John paused, people began wading into the river, responding to the Baptist's call.

Just then John the son of Zebedee approached and sat down beside Andrew, handing his friend some figs. Smiling at him gratefully, Andrew felt the growing warmth of the desert sun on his neck as it climbed higher in the sky. He knew they would need to retreat soon to the shade of their tent to escape the blistering afternoon heat. Their rabbi was done baptizing the latest batch of listeners and then started in again. "After me comes he who is mightier than I, the strap of whose sandals I am not worthy to stoop down and untie. I have baptized you with water, but he will baptize you with the Holy Spirit and fire." Andrew's heart stirred at the thought of the one who would baptize with holy fire!

They had often heard the Baptist talk about the Messiah for whom he was preparing, but it was hard to imagine what it would be like when the "anointed one" finally arrived. The Jewish people had been waiting for this Davidic king so long it had come to seem like a wishful dream. But even the Gentiles spoke of a coming powerful Jewish king whom they referred to as "the Christ." Andrew squinted up at the brilliant blue sky and began to mull over these messianic promises. *Would he come with a conquering army ready to defeat the Roman soldiers who occupied their land, as the Pharisees taught? Would he descend from the sky, as Daniel had predicted, a heavenly king reigning with supernatural power?* Andrew had heard about the esoteric Essenes who lived in Qumran on the Dead Sea, not far from where he sat, and how they taught there would be two Messiahs, a royal conquering Messiah and a heavenly priestly Messiah.

Suddenly Andrew was shaken from his thoughts by a sharp elbow to the ribs from his friend John. "Look what's happening!" Andrew looked out at the river and saw the Baptist standing in the water talking with a Jewish man about thirty years old. John said, "I need to be baptized by you, and do you come to me?" They had never seen their rabbi refuse to baptize someone. The man responded, "Let it be so now, for thus it is fitting for us to fulfill all righteousness." At that the Baptist bowed his head and the two went down under the water together. When they came up something happened that Andrew would never forget.

First, he heard a sound from above like fabric being torn. Looking up he saw something brilliantly white descend on the man in the river. It reminded him of the white doves which frequented that place, but this was no bird! Then he heard a deep voice from above, resonating as if spoken from an unfathomable distance, "You are my beloved Son; with you I am well pleased!" Andrew turned to his friend with an uncomprehending look. The son of Zebedee looked back with equal amazement. *What could it all mean? Who is this man?*

By now it was time to retreat to the shade of their tents, and the Baptist withdrew from them for the rest of the day. Andrew and John spent the afternoon arguing with Simon about what happened in the river. That evening they sat around the fire eating their simple supper, saying nothing. The next afternoon the Baptist summoned Andrew and John back to the riverbank. As they approached the river, a man passed by on the road. They recognized him as the one who had stirred such excitement and interest the day before. The Baptist pointed and said, "Look, the Lamb of God!" Andrew and John stared at the man, who looked nothing like a sheep to them. But before they knew it, they found themselves walking behind the man. When he saw them, he turned around, looked straight into their eyes, and said, "What are you seeking?" And they said to him, "Rabbi, where are you staying?" He said to them, "Come and you will see."

Andrew's heart pounded as they followed in the stranger's footsteps. Something told him that everything was about to change. As they passed near their camp, Andrew saw his brother stoking the fire. He ran to Simon and told him what had happened. "We have found the Messiah" he blurted out, not knowing if that were in fact true. Simon's eyes narrowed skeptically, but he dropped his stick and came to see what his brother was so wound up about. Little did Simon know that was his first step along a path that would not only change his life, but the history of the whole world.[2]

THE STORY BEGINS

John the Baptist was one in a succession of first-century prophetic figures who ignited Jewish passions with talk of the coming Messiah. One by one these revolutionary leaders were swiftly crushed by the occupying Roman army, and their scattered movements came to nothing. John himself would soon be arrested and beheaded by Herod Antipas. Several years after John's ministry, when the first followers of Jesus were starting to cause a stir in Jerusalem, a religious leader named Gamaliel pointed out the passing nature of these so-called messianic movements when he said, *"before these days Theudas rose up, claiming to be somebody, and a number of men, about four hundred, joined him. He was killed, and all who followed him were dispersed and came to nothing. After him Judas the Galilean rose up in the days of the census and drew away some of the people after him. He too perished, and all who followed him were scattered."* (Acts 5:36-37) Gamaliel assumed the messianic movement which began with the preaching and baptizing of John would fizzle out in the same way.

As crowds of people came out to the Jordan River to hear John preach fire and brimstone, he must have seemed to be another Theudas or Judas from Galilee, but there was something different about him. John's clothing and lifestyle were reminiscent of the great prophet Elijah who did not die but was taken to heaven in

---

[2] Based on Mark 1:1-11 and John 1:19-42

a fiery chariot. The prophet Micah foretold Elijah's return to prepare people's hearts before the messianic age was to begin, and John seemed to fit the bill. (Micah 4:5-6) John declared his mission to prepare for the coming of the Messiah by quoting Isaiah 40:3-4, *"The voice of one crying in the wilderness: 'Prepare the way of the Lord; make his paths straight.'"* (Matthew 3:3) But unlike so many other revolutionaries, John was not calling people to follow him, but to follow the one who would come after him. Of the coming Messiah, John said, *"He must increase, but I must decrease."* (John 3:30) John was not calling for a political revolution to overthrow the Romans, but was calling people to a revolution of the heart. He was preparing the way for the coming of the true Messiah who would change everything.

The heart of John's message was *"repent,"* which means to allow your perspective to be changed and so to change your life. This was an inner transformation that was meant to transform your outward way of life. To symbolize this change of perspective, John invited people to be immersed in the waters of the River Jordan. Ritual washing and immersion in water were very familiar to the Jewish people. On a regular basis religious Jews immersed themselves in a special bath called a *"mikveh"* in order to be considered ritually purified of any defilement that could separate them from God. They took these ritual baths before bringing a sacrifice to the Temple,

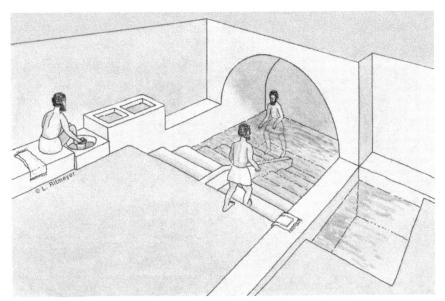

"Mikveh": A Jewish Ritual Bath

after childbirth and times of menstruation, if they had to handle a dead body, and so on. Observant Jews still practice this kind of ritual bathing today.

It is hard to ignore the similarities between John and the esoteric community of Essenes who lived in Qumran on the western shore of the Dead Sea, just south of where John was baptizing. They copied scrolls of the Bible day and night, hiding them in the cliffs above their settlement, which is what led to discovery of the famous "Dead Sea Scrolls" 1900 years later. Like John they quoted Isaiah 40:3-4 as a description of their mission to prepare in the desert for the messianic age. Believing a perfectly pure community in the desert would trigger the coming of the Messiahs, these priestly Jewish separatists were fanatically devoted to ritual purity and observance of the Law. They practiced ritual bathing twice a day, even though they lived in the extreme desert where water was extremely scarce. They were so strict on Sabbath observance they refrained from even defecating on their day of rest!

Some believe John was formerly a member of this exclusive community at Qumran because of the parallels between him and the Essenes. Luke tells us John moved to the desert when he was still young, perhaps after the death of his elderly parents. (Luke 1:80) The first-century Jewish historian Josephus tells us the Essenes sometimes adopted young boys to bolster their membership, so it is possible John was raised in the Qumran community and later expelled over theological differences. This is speculation; we don't know any of these

Dead Sea Scroll Caves at Qumran

details for sure. What we do know is that John's ministry at the Jordan River was something different from the practice of the Essenes at Qumran. John's baptism was not an external cleansing or symbolic purification; it was about an internal change of heart and mind. This was not a slavish obligation to the Law; it was a baptism for repentance. John was preparing the hearts and minds of the people to receive the message of the coming Messiah and to embrace his mission of establishing the Kingdom of God.

Today you can visit the place on the Jordan River where John baptized people and even wade into the waters of the river there to renew your baptism, as we do on each of our trips. Just north of the Dead Sea, east of Jericho, archaeologists have found the ruins of ancient churches and monasteries built on both sides of the river which now forms the border between the country of Jordan and the area controlled by Israel known as the West Bank. Traditionally, this spot was identified as the place where Joshua led the people of Israel into the Promised Land when God miraculously parted the waters of the river in a miniature reenactment of the more dramatic Red Sea crossing forty years earlier. (Joshua 3:14-17) In this place John called people to repent and prepare for the coming of the Messiah. It was as if John knew a whole new chapter in God's story was about to begin right there in the same spot!

Site of Jesus' Baptism in the Jordan River

While John was preaching fire and brimstone in the Judean desert just outside Jerusalem, Jesus came of age in a small Galilean town in the north of Israel called Nazareth. Jesus and John were related through their mothers, which means they must have known each other growing up, as Jesus' family came down to Jerusalem for the Passover holiday every year and John's family lived just outside of Jerusalem. When he was about 30 years old, Jesus abruptly left the successful family construction business in the hands of his younger brothers and headed south to the Jordan River where John was baptizing.

A NEW COVENANT

Despite his family connection with John, it seems curious that Jesus began his public ministry by submitting to an act of repentance. We would expect him to head straight to the huge courts surrounding the Temple in Jerusalem where he could draw large crowds and gain instant notoriety. Instead he went to the desert and asked his cousin John to baptize him in the Jordan. John found this curious as well and protested, *"I need to be baptized by you, and do you come to me?" But Jesus answered him, "Let it be so now, for thus it is fitting for us to fulfill all righteousness."* *Then he consented.* (Luke 3:14-15)

To make sense of Jesus' answer and John's acceptance of it, we need to understand the biblical word *"righteousness."* Both the Hebrew and Greek words in the Bible we translate "righteousness" describe a covenant relationship. In the biblical world people related to each other by making promises to one another and then trusting those promises. A family might promise to look after their neighbor's livestock if they wandered onto their land, and the neighbors would reciprocate that promise. They trusted each other to live up to those promises and the result was a "righteous" relationship between neighbors. In ancient societies, and in many cultures still today, covenants shaped nearly all relationships. When we live up to our covenantal promises and trust others to do the same, we are living in right relationships.

In the modern western world, we have largely lost the concept of covenant except in marriage. Thirty-four years ago, I stood up before family and friends and promised to love and be faithful to my beloved Pamela, even unto death. She made the same promises to me, much to my relief! Trusting each other to live in those promises is what has bound our lives together for three and a half decades. This is how covenants work—making promises and trusting those promises. When Jesus came to John for baptism, John was confused because he knew Jesus didn't need to repent. Jesus' explanation that he was doing it to *"fulfill all righteousness"* pointed to the establishment of a new kind of covenant relationship inaugurated by baptism. Jesus wasn't baptized for his own sake, but to set an example for those who would follow him into the New Covenant.

Some 700 years earlier the prophet Jeremiah had foretold,

> *"Behold, the days are coming, declares the Lord, when I will make a new covenant with the house of Israel and the house of Judah, not like the covenant that I made with their fathers on the day when I took them by the hand to bring them out of the land of Egypt, my covenant that they broke, though I was their husband, declares the Lord. For this is the covenant that I will make with the house of Israel after those days, declares the Lord: I will put my law within them, and I will write it on their hearts. And I will be their God, and they shall be my people. And no longer shall each one teach his neighbor and each his brother, saying, 'Know the Lord,' for they shall all know me, from the least of them to the greatest, declares the Lord. For I will forgive their iniquity, and I will remember their sin no more."* (Jeremiah 31:31-34)

When Jesus went to John at the Jordan, he was announcing the establishment of this long-awaited New Covenant. By being immersed in the Jordan River, he demonstrated that baptism is the entry point into this new kind of relationship with God and with God's people. When the skies were torn open and the Holy Spirit was poured out upon Jesus, the Father said, *"This is my beloved Son, with whom I am well pleased."* There could be no clearer or more powerful statement of Jesus' identity. When we are baptized in the name of the Father, Son, and Holy Spirit, this is exactly what God is saying over us. "This is my beloved daughter. I am so pleased with her. This is my beloved son. I am so proud of him." God is making us a promise in our baptism and inviting us to trust that promise. This is how we enter into a New Covenant relationship with God. Jesus shows us the way.

Many voices in this world will try to tell you who you are, but there is only One who can tell you the whole truth. The God who made you in his own image claims you as his precious child through the New Covenant that Jesus established. In the waters of baptism this intimate relationship with God as your Father is publicly declared. We can live in this relationship every day by faith, by trusting the promise God has spoken over us. Five hundred years ago, the famous Reformer Martin Luther modeled the practice of reclaiming his baptismal identity every morning when he woke up and every evening when he fell asleep. What a wonderful way to start and end each day, hearing the Father say, "This is my beloved son. I am so pleased with him. This is my beloved daughter. I am so proud of her." Can you hear his voice speaking over you right now?

THE FREE GIFT

It is easy to forget that at this point Jesus had not done anything remarkable deserving of special praise from the Father. When he was twelve years old, the boy Jesus astounded teachers at the Temple in Jerusalem with his insights, but for the eighteen years that followed Jesus submitted to his parents and worked as a stone cutter and builder in the family business in Nazareth. Jesus had not earned any advanced degrees. He had not preached any powerful sermons. There were no miracles or dramatic prophetic declarations. He was simply a working-class artisan living with his family. Why is the Father so pleased with Jesus? What is he so proud of? Why is Jesus so beloved by the Father?

Parents can answer these questions quite easily. Why do you love your children? Why do they bring joy to your heart? A good father will say it is simply because she is his daughter. A good mother will say it is simply because he is her son. This gift of unconditional parental love seems to grow exponentially in the hearts of grandparents. I remember holding my granddaughter Eleanor in my arms for the first time. She was born with a congenital heart defect and had already endured two open heart surgeries by the time she was six months old. As I held her close with no more tubes and needles in the way, I thought my heart would burst with love for her! I was so pleased with her, not because of anything she had done for me, but simply because of who she is. She is my beloved granddaughter, and I am so pleased with her!

This is how it works in the New Covenant of grace. Jesus has made it possible for us to know God as our very own Father. His unconditional love is poured into our hearts through the Holy Spirit as a freely given gift, because Jesus has washed away all the obstacles that stand in the way. God has spoken the truth of who you are in your baptism. If you are not yet baptized, you can decide to receive this great gift by faith and be baptized. Baptized or not, this is your true identity. God loves you and is pleased with you simply because he is your Father and you are his child! You don't have to do anything to deserve it. You could never work hard enough to earn it. It is a gift of pure grace. Just as my five beautiful granddaughters whom I try to spoil on a weekly basis cannot earn my love but can certainly enjoy it, all you can do is receive and enjoy the Father's great love for you. All you can do is trust that God's promise is true. He really does love you, he is so proud of you, and he invites you to live in this intimate relationship with him. Will you believe him? Will you promise him your love in return?

REFLECT AND DISCUSS
Read Matthew 3:13-17

1. What voices are trying to tell me who I am?

2. How much opportunity do I give my heavenly Father to tell me who I am?

3. (If you are baptized) What does my baptism mean to me?

4. (If you are not baptized) How would I be different if I chose to be baptized?

5. God, what are you saying to me and what step of faith do you want me to take in response?

CHAPTER TWO

PREPARING FOR BATTLE

A SOLITARY JOURNEY

Jonah tugged on the leather straps one more time and patted his old donkey affectionately. "We don't want to lose another load over the edge like we did last fall, now do we Daisy?" he said, knowing full well she couldn't understand a word he said. Talking to his donkey always made the journey from Jericho to his home in Jerusalem feel a little less lonely. Normally Jonah traveled with a group of other merchants, but three days ago he fell sick and missed their departure. This time he had to make the trip alone. He felt a knot in his stomach thinking about those caves in the cliffs and wondering who or what might be lurking in them. His wife Sarah would be furious when she found out he made the journey by himself, but what could he do? He couldn't stay in Jericho forever!

The sun was just starting to peek over the Jordanian highlands to the east, but Jonah still felt the lingering cool of the night on his face. He knew it would take the whole day to get to Jerusalem and wanted to make sure he was home well before dark. Long ago Jonah lost track of how many trips he had made to Jericho to pick up merchandise for the family shop in Jerusalem. Like his father and grandfather before him, Jonah made the round trip four or five times a year to stock up. Making his way along the Roman road from Jericho as it curved to the

Reconstruction of Herod's Palace in Jericho

right and began its climb into the mountains of the Judean desert back toward Jerusalem, Jonah spied Herod's luxurious winter palace off to the right across the dry stream bed, sparkling in the glint of the morning sun. He scowled and muttered under his breath. *Those imposters! Those dirty thieves! Traitors all of them...*

Jews like Jonah all hated the Herodians for usurping the Jewish throne, working for the pagan Romans, and filling their coffers through exorbitant taxation. Gigantic fortresses and exorbitant palaces like this one were glaring reminders of the excesses of the so-called Herodian royal family which had ruled for over 70 years now. *At least that toad Herod Archelaeus is no longer in charge of Judea!* About twenty years earlier Herod's son Archelaeus had been deposed by the Romans for flagrant incompetence, and Judea had fallen under the direct rule of Roman governors ever since. *But now we have that spineless Pontius Pilate to deal with instead. At least the threat of zealot rebellion keeps his worst impulses in check!*

Jonah and Daisy passed beyond the palace and began the steep climb into the desert mountains. The Roman road wound along the southern ridge of the deep valley known as Wadi Kelt. The sun continued its daily climb in the sky above and soon Jonah was fully engulfed in the desert wilderness. It was such a barren and dangerous place that this stretch of road was called the Ascent of Adumim, meaning "the red ascent." *Was this a reference to the blood red stone of the mountains or the bloody threat of bandits and predators who loved to hide out in the many caves lining these dry valleys?* Jonah was never quite sure which meaning was intended.

Just then he heard a noise up ahead, and every hair on his body stood on end as he tightened the grip on his walking stick. He had a double-edged knife tucked in his belt, but the walking stick was his first weapon of defense. If it came to close combat, then he would pull his knife. He felt a trickle of sweat moving down his spine. As they came around the corner, Jonah realized the noises were coming from the deep valley down below to his right. Pulling Daisy to a stop, he crept to the edge of the cliff and looked down into the wadi. There he made out a man in ragged clothes who seemed to be highly agitated. He shouted, "'Man shall not live by bread alone, but by every word that comes from the mouth of God!'" The words echoed off the red rock cliffs. Jonah recognized it as a verse from the Torah he had heard read in the synagogue.

Fascinated, Jonah leaned out for a better view, and just then some rocks below him gave way, clattering down into the wadi. The man suddenly looked up at him, and Jonah saw a gaunt, sunburned face. His lips were cracked and his eyes fixed on Jonah with a piercing gaze. Startled, Jonah pulled back from the edge, grabbed Daisy's lead, and pulled hard. *Faster, come on, faster you old nag!* Jonah's heart was beating double time, and all he could think about was those piercing eyes. As they got further and further away, Jonah's pulse normalized, but still he heard those words ringing in his ears, "'Man shall not live by bread alone, but by every word that comes from the mouth of God.'"[3]

DESERT BOOT CAMP

Just to the west of the place where John baptized Jesus lies the ancient city of Jericho. It is the oldest continuously inhabited city in the world, dating back over 11,000 years. It was infamous for the dramatic collapse of its walls when Joshua led the people marching around it for six days blowing trumpets, but by the time of Jesus it was renowned for its plentiful freshwater springs and fruitful date palms. (Joshua 6:1-27) Just beyond Jericho, the Judean mountains begin rising up from the Jordan Valley, forming innumerable steep desert valleys called wadis. This mountainous desert stretches west all the way up to the city of Jerusalem. It was into this formidable desert wilderness that the Holy Spirit led Jesus after his baptism.

---

[3] Based on Matthew 4:1-11

Remains of Herod's Palace in Jericho

The Roman road that ran south from Galilee and passed through Jericho then turned west and climbed the hills of this mountainous desert on its way to Jerusalem. No wonder Jesus set his parable of the Good Samaritan here, as it was a place where travelers were attacked by thieves on a regular basis. (See Luke 10:25-37.) The Roman road passed next to the ancient palace of Herod the Great, which he had built just south of Jericho with a bridge spanning one of the dry stream beds that flowed out of the mountains. On one side of the wadi was the palace with huge banquet halls and lavish spas. On the other side were lush sunken gardens, a huge swimming pool, and a raised dining platform boasting a 270-degree view over Jericho and the mountains.

Following his baptism, the Holy Spirit led Jesus past this lavish palace and into these dangerous desert mountains where he would spend the next forty days in training and preparation. Wadi Kelt is the name of the dry desert valley straddled by Herod's palace. It contains a unique feature for that area: three large freshwater springs that flow year round. In order to supply his swimming pool and spa, Herod built two aqueducts to channel that fresh water from two of the springs to his palace. One of these springs still runs today. It is the only water supply of its kind for many miles in every direction. For this reason, we can be confident this dry valley is where Jesus spent his forty days, because even while fasting from food he would have needed a source of water. The rock walls of Wadi Kelt are lined with countless caves which undoubtedly served as shelter for Jesus during these challenging weeks. Mark tells us that Jesus was there *"with the wild animals,"* which would have included Arabian wolves, Dorcas gazelles, Hyrax badgers, and Griffon vultures. (Mark 1:13)

What was Jesus doing in this harsh environment for forty days? The Gospel writers simply tell us it was a time of fasting, culminating in a mighty clash with the devil himself. Fasting is a spiritual discipline designed to help us learn to rely more fully on God rather than on our own strength and wisdom. Jesus spent forty days fasting from food, praying, and listening to the Father in order to prepare for the great challenges that lay ahead. It was like his spiritual boot camp. In that time Jesus made it crystal clear that his calling was to his Father's mission not his own, and that he would fulfill his calling by his Father's power and not his own.

Saint George's Monastery in Wadi Kelt

THE TESTING

Surely one of the great understatements of the Bible is when Matthew writes, *after fasting forty days and forty nights, he was hungry.* Obviously, it is no accident that it was in this moment the devil launched his attack on Jesus. The devil will always look for our weak spot and pick the most vulnerable moment to strike, because he is a coward! And so, in Jesus' moment of greatest hunger, the tempter suggests Jesus turn stones into bread. The slopes of Wadi Kelt are still littered with innumerable bread-sized stones today. With the hunger of forty breadless days gnawing at your ribs it would be easy to hallucinate and see those hillsides covered with fresh loaves!

But notice the way the devil words this temptation, *"If you are the Son of God, command these stones to become loaves of bread."* (Matthew 4:3) Can you recognize the devil's strategy? After Jesus received the clear declaration of his true identity from the Father, now Satan was trying to call that promise into question. *"If you are the Son of God…"* This is what the devil always does. He finds our moment of vulnerability and then feeds us lies about our identity. "You are not worthy. You don't matter. You don't deserve it. You don't belong. You don't have a future. You are all alone." As Jesus said sometime later to his disciples, *"The thief comes only to steal and kill and destroy."* (John 10:10) The devil was trying to steal Jesus' identity, because he knew it was the only way he could keep him from exercising the authority that would empower the fulfillment of his mission. The tempter will try to do the same thing to you and me.

In the baptism of Jesus, we see a clear demonstration of our Covenant identity as sons and daughters of our heavenly Father. In Jesus' spiritual battle in the desert wilderness we see a demonstration of just who our Father is—the King of the universe! As the all-powerful and all-knowing Creator of the universe, our Father the King holds all authority and exercises all power in heaven and earth. This has earth-shaking implications for those of us who come to know we are his daughters and sons. If you are a child of the King, you are royalty. If you are a son or daughter of the King, you intrinsically bear his authority and power by virtue of your identity. The source of Jesus' authority and power was his identity as the Son of his Father the King. The devil attacked Jesus' identity because he wanted to prevent Jesus from exercising the authority and power that would enable him to fulfill his mission.

It is significant that Jesus responded to the devil's attack by quoting Scripture: *"It is written, 'Man shall not live by bread alone, but by every word that comes from the mouth of God.'"* (Matthew 4:4) Jesus made a deliberate decision. He chose not to respond to the devil with his own words, but by speaking the words his Father had given him. This means Jesus acted as an authorized representative of his Father the King. When we act on behalf of an authority greater than ourselves, the power of that greater authority flows through us to accomplish their will. This is exactly what Jesus was doing! Rather than speak on behalf of himself, Jesus was speaking on behalf of his Father the King in order to do his will on earth as it is done in heaven. Jesus explained this to his disciples in the upper room on the eve of his arrest when he said, *"The words that I say to you I do not speak on my own authority, but the Father who dwells in me does his works."* (John 14:10)

Of course, the devil does not give up easily, he is persistent in his efforts to derail us. And so he attacked Jesus a second time, this time trying to co-opt the Word of God, *"If you are the Son of God, throw yourself down, for it is written, "'He will command his angels concerning you,' and 'On their hands they will bear you up, lest you strike your foot against a stone.'"* (Matthew 4:6) We know the devil is a deceiver. Going all the way back to the garden of Eden we see him trying to twist what God said to Adam and Eve: *"Did God actually say, 'You shall not eat of any tree in the garden'?"* No, God had told them: *"You may surely eat of every tree of the garden, but of the tree of the knowledge of good and evil you shall not eat, for in the day that you eat of it you shall surely die."* (Genesis 2:16-17 and 3:1) Here we see the deceiver at work again, trying to twist God's Word and trick Jesus into jumping off the pinnacle of the Temple in order to gain instant notoriety when angels would supposedly catch him.

Because the point of this temptation was for Jesus to seek the recognition of others, it was set in a prominent place. The "pinnacle" described here is likely the southwest corner of Herod's massive Temple Mount complex, which towered more than 180 feet above the wide street below. This was a primary shopping street that led to the main Temple entrances and would have been constantly filled with throngs of pilgrims. Interestingly, extensive archaeological excavations in that area have not only uncovered the beautifully paved street, shops, and bridge, but also the place where the trumpeters stood at the top of that pinnacle to announce the beginning and end of the Sabbath. Perhaps this is the very spot envisioned in this second temptation of Jesus.

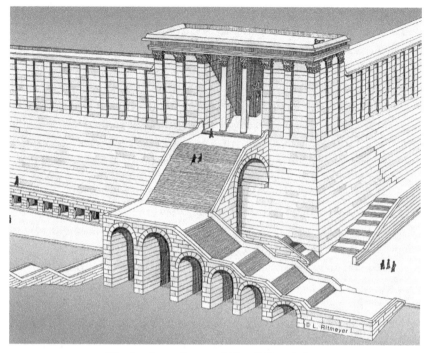

The Southwest Corner of Herod's Temple Mount

Jesus authoritatively responds to this temptation by once again speaking on behalf of his Father rather than himself, *"Again it is written, 'You shall not put the Lord your God to the test.'"* (Matthew 4:7) Finally the devil tipped his hand to reveal what he was really after. Taking Jesus to a high mountain, he showed him all the kingdoms of the world and said, *"All these I will give you, if you will fall down and worship me."* (Matthew 4:9) The devil was afraid Jesus would step into the fullness of his authority as Son of the King, because he knew at that point Jesus' power would be infinitely greater than his own. The devil was willing to give Jesus all his temporal authority if he would just serve a worldly kingdom rather than his Father's heavenly Kingdom. Of course, this is exactly the goal the devil has for each one of us. He knows if he can call into question our identity and get us to serve his worldly kingdom before God's heavenly one, he will be able to manipulate us and keep us from fulfilling our true purpose.

Jesus' response is a model for us to follow: *"Be gone, Satan! For it is written, '"You shall worship the Lord your God and him only shall you serve."'"* (Matthew 4:10)

Jesus shows us that, by virtue of our true identity as daughters and sons of the King, we carry divine authority. When confronted with the power of the devil we can exercise the authority we have been given, speak the Word the Father has given us, and command the devil to *"be gone."* And just as the devil left Jesus, so he will leave us too, even if it is *until an opportune time.* (Luke 4:13) James says it this way: *Submit yourselves therefore to God. Resist the devil, and he will flee from you.* (James 4:7) If we hope to live in the New Covenant Jesus began in his baptism and learn to follow Jesus as his disciples, we will also need to learn how to confront the enemy of our soul who desperately wants to keep us from fulfilling our Kingdom calling. When by faith we exercise the authority given to us as sons and daughters of the King and submit to his purpose in our lives, we find the power we need to overcome the obstacles that stand against us.

THE POWER TO FOLLOW

I am so grateful I grew up in a family where my worth was clearly communicated in word and deed. I came to faith in a church family that emphasized the New Covenant of love and grace that Jesus came to establish. For that reason, it was easy for me to trust and believe I am a beloved child of God and that God is pleased with me, not because of anything I have done, but because of what Jesus has done for me. I was well grounded in my Covenant identity from an early age.

However, I was not very well equipped to operate in the Kingdom authority and power of Jesus. As I grew into adulthood and sought to live in the calling God had for my life, I found it increasingly difficult to fulfill. I assumed people would be receptive and want to partner with me. I expected those who claimed the name of Jesus to be on board with what I was trying to accomplish for God. But it wasn't true. In fact, I was shocked by the amount of pushback I faced and deeply hurt by the betrayal of people I trusted. I needed to learn how to operate in Jesus' authority so I could access the power I needed to fulfill God's purpose in my life.

The simple fact is that we do not live in a neutral world; it is not a level playing field. God's good design in creation has been broken by human rebellion and sin. Ever since Adam and Eve decided they didn't need God and could manage things quite well on their own, things in this world have gone from bad to worse. That same worldly brokenness has invaded our souls and if we are honest, we must admit that many things inside of us do not reflect the goodness of God's design and purpose. To top it all off, a fallen angel named Satan is intentionally working against God's good purpose in this world, and he has worldly authority and power, not to mention a legion of fallen angels to work with him in his mission to steal, kill, and destroy. This is the sobering reality in which we find ourselves.

It would be easy to let this intimidate us and fill us with fear and despair, but this is exactly why the Spirit led Jesus into the desert for those forty days. Jesus was showing us how we can learn to overcome the enemy in this fallen world where the deck is stacked against us. Out of our Covenant identity, Jesus is showing us how to operate in his Kingdom authority, so we have access to the same power he did. A roadblock for many of us is that we often assume Jesus was able to overcome the devil and do miracles and change lives because of his divinity. Since we are clearly not divine, we conclude what Jesus did in the wilderness does not apply to us. This is a critical mistake.

It is true Jesus is fully God. John begins his account of Jesus' life by making that crystal clear that *In the beginning was the Word, and the Word was with God, and the Word was God.* (John 1:1) Jesus is the Word and the Word is God. Jesus pointed to his own eternal divinity when he applied the Old Testament name of God, I AM, to himself. (John 8:58) Jesus' full divinity is central to a biblical understanding of who he is. However, because of this we often assume Jesus sort of floated around Galilee magically carrying out his mission by operating in his divine nature, almost like he had a superhero suit on underneath his robe! This works in the movies, but it is a profoundly unbiblical view of Jesus.

John went on in the first chapter of his Gospel to fill out his description of Jesus: *And the Word became flesh and dwelt among us, and we have seen his glory, glory as of the only Son from the Father, full of grace and truth.* (John 1:14) Now we are starting to see the real Jesus. He is fully divine but at the same time fully human. If it were a math formula it would be 100% God + 100% Human = 100% Jesus. All the mathematicians are protesting, wait a minute, that doesn't add up! Of course it doesn't, because if the infinite is going to become finite it is not going to fit into the finite box of human logic. We have to hold in tension the truths that Jesus is fully human and fully divine at the same time. The problem is, because Jesus' divinity stands out as unique, it is often the part we emphasize, while we tend to forget about his full humanity.

But when God became fully human in Jesus, he specifically chose to set aside his infinite power for a period of time so he could show us the way life is meant to be lived in this broken world. Jesus was still fully God, but for thirty-some years on this earth he chose to live in his full humanity to show us the way we are meant to live. When the Apostle Paul wrote a letter to the followers of Jesus in Philippi, he quoted one of the earliest descriptions of Jesus recited by the early church. It says, *Have this mind among yourselves, which is yours in Christ Jesus, who, though he was in the form of God, did not count equality with God a thing to be grasped, but emptied himself, by taking the form of a servant, being born in the likeness of men.* (Philippians 2:5-7) In order to become fully human, God *"emptied himself"* and took on human form. Jesus repeatedly tells us he lived his life in complete dependence on his heavenly Father: *"Truly, truly, I say to you, the Son can do nothing of his own accord, but only what he sees the Father doing. For whatever the Father does, that the Son does likewise."* (John 5:19)

The point here is that Jesus did not overcome the devil because he was divine. He overcame the devil by relying on his heavenly Father the King and speaking his Father's Word, not just his own. The main reason for fasting is to learn how to depend on the Father and not on ourselves. This is exactly what Jesus did. He set an example for us to follow. In the wilderness Jesus showed us how to overcome the devil by depending on God rather than ourselves, by speaking God's Word and not just our own. He was showing us this is how we are to operate in the authority and power of our Father the King! This is why we don't need to be afraid of the devil or intimidated by the opposition we face. Because our Father is the King of the universe, as his kids we have been given divine authority and power to overcome the infinitely lesser power of the enemy.

As a young man I had to face the reality that there were forces at work in this world opposed to the purpose to which God had called me. I could see the world was broken and basically at odds with God's purpose. I could see the brokenness in my life and the lives of others that often stood in the way of God's will being done. But at that time, I wasn't sure if the devil was real because I had never actually met him. I thought maybe the many New Testament passages referring to the devil and demons were just an ancient way of talking about how evil is at work in the world generally. But then I came face to face with demons and discovered the truth that actual spiritual beings are actively at work trying to thwart the good purposes of God.

At first this realization was unsettling, but when I experienced the power of God flowing through me to overcome the works of the devil, I learned firsthand that we have nothing to fear if we learn to walk in our identity and exercise the authority we have been given to do God's will. In fact, I discovered the power of the devil is literally laughable compared to the power of God! John said it this way in one of his letters: *The reason the Son of God appeared was to destroy the works of the devil.* (1 John 3:8) Ever since I have been slowly learning how to live a life that looks more like Jesus, which includes operating in the authority and power he has given us. I have been learning to speak and act on behalf of my Father the King rather than on my own behalf. The result has been so much more and better fruit in my life, by the grace of God. I have seen so many lives changed, so much brokenness healed, so many captivities released, not because of my strength but because of the power of Jesus flowing through me.

When Jesus sent his disciples out on mission, Luke tells us *he called the twelve together and gave them power and authority over all demons and to cure diseases, and he sent them out to proclaim the kingdom of God and to heal.* (Luke 9:1, 2) At the end of his life in this world the risen Jesus gave us our commissioning: *"All authority in heaven and on earth has been given to me. Go therefore and make disciples of all nations, baptizing them in the name of the Father and of the Son and of the Holy Spirit, teaching them to observe all that I have commanded you. And behold, I am with you always, to the end of the age."* (Matthew 28:18-20) Just before he ascended into heaven Jesus told us, *"But you will receive power when the Holy Spirit has come upon you, and you will be my witnesses in Jerusalem and in all Judea and Samaria, and to the end of the earth."* (Acts 1:8)

Do you believe Jesus has given you the authority to speak and act on his behalf? When you trust that he has authorized you to represent him and you submit by doing whatever you see him doing, the power of the Spirit will flow through you to do God's will, just as it did through Jesus. You will receive the strength and confidence you need to be his witness even in the face of great opposition. If the devil himself comes against you he will not prevail if you stand by faith in your identity as a son or daughter of the King and exercise by faith the authority he has given you. Like Jesus you can say, *"be gone Satan"* and he will most certainly flee!

REFLECT AND DISCUSS

Read Matthew 4:1-11

1. What are the obstacles I face in trying to do God's will?

2. In what ways has Jesus authorized me to represent him and speak on his behalf?

3. How am I submitting myself to God's purpose and power?

4. How can I learn to fight spiritual battles and win?

5. God, what are you saying to me and what step of faith do you want me to take in response?

CHAPTER THREE

COMING HOME

FAMILY TIES

Jude rolled over on his straw bed for what seemed like the thousandth time. Why couldn't he get to sleep? The house and the village beyond had long since fallen silent and Jude couldn't hear anything. Well, except for the heavy breathing of his brother Simon and the occasional rustling of the animals out in the courtyard. Ever since he could remember, he had shared a room with all four of his brothers. But then James got married and moved into another room of their house with his new wife Hannah. A year later Joses married Esther and moved into the new upstairs room he built for her. Then it was just three brothers sharing a room until Jesus shocked everyone by announcing he was leaving home and heading south to Judea. Now Jude and Simon had the room all to themselves. As Jude lay there, he began mulling over the tumultuous events of the recent past.

As the oldest brother, they all assumed Jesus would marry, take leadership of the family business, and eventually become the head of the family. When their father Joseph died six years ago, this expectation became a reality, and the pressure on Jesus to accept a wife started to grow. Every year that went by without an engagement announcement put his mother Mary a little more on edge. In a small conservative village like Nazareth, people know your business, and gossip is the norm. James' and Simon's weddings took some of the attention off him, but as Jesus approached his 30th birthday the pressure started mounting for him not to bring shame on the family. His uncle Boaz took Jesus aside and tried to talk sense into him, but to no avail. Even the engagement last summer of their eldest sister didn't do much to distract their mother from possible matches for Jesus. Then he told them all he was leaving, and the family was thrown into chaos.

Things had not been the same since Jesus left. He turned over leadership of the extended family and the family business to his next oldest brother James, but the turmoil wasn't just about leadership. It was about his presence. Jesus was an outstanding builder, a consummate craftsman, and had an uncanny way of making everyone he did business with feel like they were getting the best deal of their lives. But it was more than that. Something about Jesus always made everyone around him feel better... unless they were threatening someone in his family—then they were afraid of him! As the youngest son, Jude felt he had a special place in his eldest brother's heart, but now he realized that was how nearly everyone felt about Jesus.

Jude thought his mother would have a breakdown when Jesus left, but strangely she was the one who handled it the best. Not that it wasn't hard for her, but it was as if she had finally remembered a long-forgotten secret and it all made sense to her at last. When she hugged Jesus goodbye, she had tears in her eyes, but a sly smile stole across her lips. They heard reports Jesus had gone to their cousin John who was baptizing at the Jordan River, but then there was no word for over a month. *Where could he be? What was he doing? Why did he leave us?*

Suddenly Jude sat straight up in his bed rubbing his eyes. The morning light was streaming through the window, and he heard the whole household bustling with activity. *How did I oversleep? Today is the wedding!* Jude leapt up from his bed and walked blinking into the sunlight of the courtyard. His mother and aunt were raking coals from the clay oven in the corner and cleaning up what was left of breakfast. His two oldest brothers were loading packs onto the donkey to carry the essential supplies. "Were you guys planning to leave me behind?" Jude quipped as he sat down next to his sister Sarah and grabbed some dates and a piece of bread before it all disappeared. She smiled at him, punching him affectionately, and asked, "Where have you been all day, sleepy head?!"

By the second hour of the day, the whole family was on their way to Cana. It was just over a half day's journey across the Netofa Valley, but they wanted to arrive well before sundown when the celebrations would begin. Naomi, his cousin on his mother's side, was marrying some guy from Cana, and they had been invited to join in the celebration. They were all to gather in the courtyard of the bridegroom's family home and wait for the groom and his entourage to bring Naomi and her attendants to the party sometime after sundown. Jude wasn't much of a romantic, but he loved family weddings for the great food and dancing!

The sun was already starting to drop lower in the sky as they made their way up the hill on which Cana was built. Jude had fallen to the back of the line, and as he looked at his mother and brothers, sisters, sisters-in-law, uncle, aunt, cousins, and other members of the family winding up the road ahead of him into the town, he felt a pang in his chest. *Why isn't Jesus with us? Where is he? It won't be the same.* In the distance he heard the sound of a crowd gathering. As they rounded the last corner, they saw the walls of the wedding home decorated with olive branches and wildflowers. The musicians were starting to tune their instruments and the cooks were carrying baskets of food into the house. But then Jude heard a sound that stood out among all the others. It was a laugh. It was unmistakable. It was Jesus! *What is he doing here?*

They each hugged and kissed Jesus until it seemed he would collapse. Jesus introduced them to some new friends he had made down at the Jordan River, including the groom's cousin Nathanael. They staked out a spot in the far corner of the courtyard and settled in to wait for the wedding party to arrive. As the sun set, the smell of olive oil lamps and sizzling meat filled the air. Suddenly the shouting and singing erupted when the wedding attendants came through the doorway leading into the courtyard, followed by the bride and groom. By the time the moon had climbed overhead, Jude had lost track of how many lamb meatballs he had eaten, though his stomach was trying to remind him. Just then he noticed a commotion among the servants. They were checking the pitchers of wine at each table, obviously looking for more. *Looks like this celebration is going to come to a premature end!* Jude contemplated his empty cup and felt bad for the family. *Nothing worse than letting people down on one of the most important nights of your life!* Just then he noticed his mother and eldest brother disappearing into one of the rooms with the master of ceremonies.

Before Jude realized what was happening, the host raised his voice to get everyone's attention, the servants filled every cup with wine, and the master of ceremonies made a toast to the wedding couple. Jude joined the rest in raising his cup, shouted *l'chayyim*, and took a drink of the best wine he could ever remember drinking. *Wow! Usually they serve the best wine first to set the tone. But this wine puts the rest to shame!* By then Jesus and Mary had rejoined the family and Jude noticed his mother was beaming with joy and pride. *Does she know something we don't? Will Jesus be moving back home?* Jude hoped his eldest brother would never leave home again.[4]

BEGINNING WITH JOY

The Gospel writers all agree that following his baptism and time of testing in the desert, Jesus returned north to his home region of Galilee uniquely empowered. Luke describes the transition this way: *And Jesus returned in the power of the Spirit to Galilee, and a report about him went out through all the surrounding country. And he taught in their synagogues, being glorified by all.* (Luke 4:14-15) After his baptism he had gone into the desert *full of the Holy Spirit* and now he emerged from the desert *in the power of the Spirit.* (See Luke 4:1.)

John the Baptist testified that this filling and empowerment of the Spirit was not a fleeting spiritual experience but a permanent condition: *"I saw the Spirit descend from heaven like a dove, and it remained on him."* (John 1:32) He also testified that this was not a limited filling, but a continually overflowing presence: *"For he whom God has sent utters the words of God, for he gives the Spirit without measure."* (John 3:34) As we have seen, Jesus' baptism was an affirmation of his <u>identity</u> as the beloved Son of his heavenly Father, and his testing was an exercise of his <u>authority</u> as Son of his Father the all-powerful King. From this point on, people who encountered Jesus consistently recognized in him a unique authority and power, to which some were drawn and by which others were threatened.

John tells us Jesus met five of his soon-to-be disciples at the place of his baptism: Andrew, Simon, Nathanael, Philip, and apparently John the son of Zebedee. (John 1:35-51) I like to call them the "Five Guys," but that's just because I love hamburgers! Like Jesus, these new friends all came from towns in Galilee

---

[4] Based on John 2:1-12

and they traveled with Jesus as he made his way north, teaching in various synagogues along the way. Jesus was not formally trained as a rabbi; rather, he had spent the last 18 years working in the family construction business. From the age of five to twelve he would have attended *Beth Sefer*, the primary school held in the synagogue where the rabbi taught Jewish boys to read the Torah, the Old Testament Law. But apparently, Jesus did not continue studying with the rabbis at secondary school (*Beth Midrash*) or post-secondary school (*Beth Talmud*), where he could have been formally recognized as a rabbi.

When people in his hometown of Nazareth talked about Jesus, they referred to him as a *"carpenter."* (Mark 6:3) Those of us who come from a northern European cultural perspective naturally picture a woodworker in his shop cutting boards. However, the Greek word *tekton* usually translated "carpenter" is best translated "builder." In the Middle East nearly all building is done with stone. While a *tekton* could build some things with wood, the vast majority of their work was cutting stone. Somehow the authority and power of this unschooled stonemason was so compelling that the leaders of various synagogues wanted him to speak in their Sabbath services! John specifies that Jesus taught in the synagogue in Capernaum, the town where his new friends Simon, Andrew, and John all lived on the north shore of the Sea of Galilee. Philip lived in nearby Bethsaida, just a few miles further along the shore of the lake. Perhaps Jesus was purposely visiting the hometowns and synagogues of these five guys he met at the Jordan River.

John also tells us Jesus went to Cana, the hometown of Nathanael. This visit was not for him to teach in the synagogue, but to attend a wedding. (See John 2:1-11.) Jesus' mother was also there, which implies it was the wedding of a relative or family friend. Cana was a Jewish town built on a hill overlooking the Netofa Valley, just 14 miles north of Nazareth. The exact location of Cana has been uncertain for over 700 years, but archaeologists recently discovered an ancient cave with a Christian shrine which had contained replicas of the six stone water jars Jesus used to turn water into wine, likely confirming the correct location.

At this wedding in Cana Jesus saved the host family one of the most shameful episodes imaginable in first-century Jewish culture. As Pam and I experience regularly in our travels through the Holy Land, hospitality is one of the highest values in Middle Eastern culture and was even more so in biblical times. Failing to provide gracious hospitality by running out of wine, especially at an event as important as a wedding, would have been a social disaster for this extended family. When Mary the mother of Jesus found out about the family's crisis, she told Jesus about it, implying he should do something. To clarify that he was now following the leading of his heavenly Father rather than his earthly mother, Jesus pushed back against her implied request, saying *"Woman, what does this have to do with me? My hour has not yet come."* (John 2:4) But then he solved the problem anyway!

Large First-Century Water Jars for Ritual Washing

As we mentioned in Chapter 1, ritual washing was very important in religious Jewish culture at the time of Jesus. This family had six large storage jars which were designed to hold water for purification. John specifies they each held 20-30 gallons and were made of stone. Jars matching this description have been found in a number of archaeological excavations of first century Jewish sites. Most storage jars were made of clay, but in the complex practices of ceremonial purity the rabbis taught that clay vessels could not be purified while stone vessels could be ritually washed clean of ceremonial impurities. For that reason, these more expensive stone vessels were sought after by religious Jews, especially for storing the water used for these cleansing rituals. After all, if your water for ritual purity was kept in tainted storage vessels, then everything you tried to purify actually became impure!

The water in these large stone jars is what Jesus transformed into over a hundred gallons of the most delicious wine any of them had ever tasted. John tells us this was Jesus' first miracle. (John 2:11) Jesus saved this family from public humiliation, multiplied the joy of the wedding celebration, and demonstrated for the first time the supernatural power of God that flowed through him to help others. The water in these jars was used in rituals that divided those who were considered "clean" from those considered "unclean." How ironic that Jesus transformed this water into a source of joy and blessing for all those who had gathered for the wedding celebration regardless of their religious status! It is a beautiful picture of the way he joyfully welcomed the outcasts of his society and transformed their shame into joy, while criticizing the legalistic religious leaders who judged and ostracized them.

This became one of the unique characteristics that set Jesus apart from other religious leaders of his time. Although he modeled and taught the highest of ethical standards, even calling on his followers to love their enemies and forgive seventy times a day, he did not promote a burdensome religious system weighed down by complex ritual requirements as the Pharisees did. Instead, like the water in those jars, he transformed legalistic religion into a life-giving relationship as joyful as that wedding celebration in Cana. Not surprisingly the dour religious leaders of his time criticized him for his generous welcome and accused him of being a *"glutton and a drunkard, a friend of tax collectors and sinners."* (Matthew 11:19) But Jesus didn't seem to care. Still today he shows us a generous way of life filled with blessing and fruitfulness. He invites us into a family celebration where the joy is multiplied!

Later in his ministry Jesus told a story about a father who had two sons. The younger son broke the father's heart by taking his share of the inheritance and squandering it in immoral living. Meanwhile the elder son dutifully worked the family farm. When the younger son hit rock bottom, he came home ready to apologize, and the father threw a huge party for him, celebrating the return of his lost son. However, the elder son was so angry he refused to join in the celebration. Already in Cana Jesus wanted to show his followers that he came to bring us into a more abundant life where the joy and blessings miraculously overflow. The question is whether or not we will join the party.

I have been following Jesus for over forty years now, and deeper joy has been my consistent experience of learning to walk in his footsteps. As I trust Jesus and follow him by the power of the Spirit, unexpected blessings and overflowing joy are the result, even in the midst of difficult circumstances. Jesus wants to multiply his joy in your life as well no matter what your story might be. Whether you are the rebellious child or the dutiful one, your Father is inviting you to celebrate with him that you have come home to your family!

HOME BASE

After visiting the hometowns of Simon, Andrew, John, and Nathanael, among others, Jesus arrived in his own hometown of Nazareth. Apparently, his new friends had returned to or stayed in their hometowns as Jesus returned home with his family. Nazareth was a conservative religious Jewish village perched on the northern ridge that overlooks the fertile Jezreel Valley. Today it is the largest Palestinian city in Israel, with over 70,000 people living there. It is hard to determine the exact population of Nazareth in the first century, but it was probably between 600 and 1500 residents, perhaps 40-80 extended families. These families made their living by farming the surrounding land, keeping flocks of sheep and goats, making wine, pottery, leather goods, and pressing olive oil. As mentioned earlier, Jesus' family had a thriving construction business. Nazareth was founded only a couple of centuries before Jesus' time, so is not mentioned in the Old Testament. It is also not mentioned in any sources outside of the New Testament until a couple hundred years after Jesus. This explains what Nathanael meant when he first heard of Jesus and said, *"Can anything good come out of Nazareth?"* (John 1:43) He was not indicting Nazareth as a center of immorality, rather he was casting aspersions on Nazareth as a town of insignificance.

Modern Nazareth

It is obvious that by coming to his hometown, Jesus was coming back to his family. In the modern West, when we think of a family, we tend to picture a mom, a dad, and two to three kids living on their own in a single-family dwelling. However, in biblical culture as well as most cultures throughout history and still today, family was primarily thought of as an extended family. Grandparents and parents, aunts and uncles, siblings and cousins, business partners and slaves all lived together in multi-room compounds, sharing life together and working in the family business. The Old Testament uses the Hebrew word *beth* and the New Testament uses the Greek word *oikos* to refer to both the extended family and the multi-room house in which they lived and worked. The rooms of their *oikos* houses were built together around a central courtyard where meals were shared and the family business was carried out. The doors and windows of these rooms all faced in toward the courtyard, only one strong door in a wall of solid stone gave access from the outside. This structure created a kind of secure family compound where multiple generations of an extended family could find both protection and provision.

Jesus came home to an extended family that lived in a multi-room compound like this, where they shared their lives together and based the operations of their construction business. Recently archaeologists examined the remains of a first-century Jewish house that was rediscovered in 1880 when the Sisters of Nazareth built their convent in the heart of the ancient town of Nazareth. Underneath the Convent you can see the remains of a doorway and a room from this house, over which were built a series of churches dating from the Byzantine and Crusader periods. All the evidence points toward the conclusion that this was the actual house in which Jesus and his extended family slept, shared their meals, and carried out the family construction business. It is amazing to know we can still visit the very house in which Jesus grew up!

We know Joseph and Mary had five sons including Jesus, and at least two daughters. (Matthew 13:55-56) We do not know exactly how many others were part of their extended family, but it would be unusual for them not to live with more relatives and friends making up a larger *oikos*. The nearby city of Sepphoris was Herod Antipas' capitol of Galilee and was undergoing a massive rebuilding process through most of Jesus' life. This means the building trade would have been booming at that time and may be what had brought Joseph's family to Nazareth from Bethlehem in the first place.

The First-Century House of Joseph in Nazareth

This means Jesus did not grow up in a poor family, as many assume, but in an extended family with a busy and thriving family business. As we mentioned earlier, from the age of about five to twelve, Jesus would have attended *Beth Sefer*, the primary school taught by the rabbis in the synagogue. Luke tells us at the age of twelve the boy Jesus amazed the leading rabbis with his wisdom and insight as he dialoged with them in the courtyards of the Temple in Jerusalem. When his distraught parents found him there, Jesus said to them, *"Did you not know that I must be in my Father's house?" And they did not understand the saying that he spoke to them.* (Luke 2:49-50) Since Mary and Joseph didn't understand him and his calling, Jesus chose not to launch his public ministry right then and there, but instead *he went down with them and came to Nazareth and was submissive to them.* (Luke 2:51) This means that for the next 18 years Jesus patiently submitted to his parents and worked in the family business. For her part, *his mother treasured up all these things in her heart. And Jesus increased in wisdom and in stature and in favor with God and man.* (Luke 2:52) Although it must have required tremendous patience on Jesus' part, this was not wasted time. The Father was preparing Jesus for what lay ahead.

During those years Jesus apprenticed as a stone mason in the family business. His father and his uncles trained Jesus to cut and lay stone, to build walls and arches, and to construct the mud and straw roofs that were common in that day. Since Joseph is never mentioned again in the Gospels after Jesus was twelve years old, we can assume he must have died when Jesus was in his teens or twenties. Surprisingly, in the ruins underneath the Sisters of Nazareth Convent, archaeologists also found a beautifully constructed rolling-stone tomb cut into the bedrock underneath this house. The design and execution of this tomb are of exceptionally high quality, normally reserved for the wealthy. A local tradition says this was the tomb of "the just (or righteous) man," which is exactly how Joseph is described in the Gospels. (Matthew 1:19) This may in fact be the family tomb built by Jesus and his brothers when their father Joseph died. If so, we can see physical proof of just what a fine craftsman Jesus really was!

First-Century Tomb Under Joseph's House

At the age of twelve, Jesus already knew God was his Father and he was called to be about his Father's business. (Luke 2:49) It is startling to realize that, although he could amaze the rabbis with his teaching as a boy, he waited and worked for another 18 long years in the family business before launching his public ministry. Perhaps he was waiting until the other brothers were old enough to take over leadership of the family in Joseph's absence. Perhaps he knew he needed to continue to grow and mature before he was ready for the challenging call that lay ahead. The writer of Hebrews tells us Jesus *"learned obedience through what he suffered"* in order to be made fully ready for his calling. (Hebrews 5:8-9)

There is a powerful lesson here for us. God's Spirit is at work in us, preparing us to fulfill a purpose greater than ourselves. The question is whether we will submit to the process of apprenticeship and training. Will we trust the Father's timing? Will we answer the call when the time is right? At the age of 30, Jesus knew it was his time and he went to the synagogue in Nazareth to launch his public ministry. What will we do when the time is right?

REFLECT AND DISCUSS

Read John 2:1-11

1. In what ways have I experienced religion as a heavy burden?

2. How can I accept Jesus' invitation to come home to him and join in the celebration?

3. How can I allow Jesus to multiply his joy in my life?

4. In what area do I need to wait for God's timing and allow him to prepare me for what lies ahead?

5. God, what are you saying to me and what step of faith do you want me to take in response?

CHAPTER FOUR

A NEW KIND OF FAMILY

SOMETHING HAPPENED AT THE SYNAGOGUE

Somewhere a rooster was crowing and the animals out in the courtyard were starting to stir. James stretched his sore arms and groaned. He had hauled a lot of stone in the past week, and he could feel it in every muscle. But Shabbat had started the night before, and he was looking forward to the day of rest ahead. Ever since Jesus had showed up at the wedding in Cana last week, his whole extended family was wondering what he would do next. *Is he sticking around or will he just leave us again?* James was now running the family business, but Jesus' attention seemed to be drawn to more spiritual matters.

The household was waking up, and James saw his sisters and his wife out in the courtyard starting to serve food for the morning meal. Soon they would all go to the synagogue together for Shabbat prayers, so everyone was getting ready, but with greater excitement than usual, because Jesus had been invited by the synagogue rulers to speak at the service that morning, even though he had never been trained as a teacher by the rabbis.

By the time the household was all seated on the floor in the synagogue, James could feel the anticipation rising in the room. *The other families are all looking*

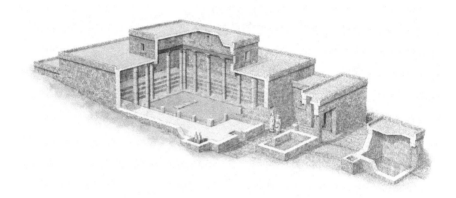

Reconstruction of a First-Century Synagogue

at us. He knew they had heard reports of "Jesus the builder" teaching in various synagogues around Galilee. The whole family beamed with pride at the thought of Jesus being recognized as a rabbi! Meanwhile, James pondered the change he saw in his older brother. Jesus had always been confident, but there was a joyful authority about him now, as if he had stepped into a role for which he was perfectly suited.

The synagogue attendant took the large Isaiah scroll from the protective *genizah* cabinet and carefully handed it to Jesus, who walked to the middle of the room, laid the roll of leather on the scroll table, unrolled it almost to the end, and read in a loud voice, "*The Spirit of the Lord is upon me, because he has anointed me to proclaim good news to the poor. He has sent me to proclaim liberty to the captives and recovering of sight to the blind, to set at liberty those who are oppressed, to proclaim the year of the Lord's favor.*" Jesus rolled up the scroll, handed it back to the attendant, moved to the platform at the front of the synagogue and sat down on the Moses' Seat.

The room went still. It was as if everyone in the synagogue was holding their breath. All eyes were fixed on Jesus, waiting to see what he would say next. They had been waiting their whole lives for this Messianic promise from Isaiah to be fulfilled. Their people had been waiting a lifetime of lifetimes for this liberation to arrive. They had suffered at the hands of the Assyrians, the Babylonians, the Persians, the Greeks, and now the Romans. The Zealots thought they could make this day come by provoking rebellion. The Essenes thought they could make it come by living a perfect life in the desert. Many ordinary Jews like James had simply forgotten the promise, assuming it would never happen in their lifetime. But now he found something was stirring inside of him. His heart was beating faster. *What will Jesus say about this Messianic vision?*

Then Jesus broke the deafening silence. *"Today this Scripture has been fulfilled in your hearing."* You could hear a collective gasp. *Today? Right now? Is that true? Is it finally here? What does it mean?* The dizzying questions ricocheted through James' mind. The crowd started to murmur approvingly, but Jesus quieted them down and continued to speak. He began to tell stories from the Bible about Gentiles like the widow of Zarephath and Naaman the Syrian whom God chose to bless even though they weren't part of God's covenant people. *What was Jesus saying? Isn't the Messiah coming for Jews? Is he saying the pagans will also receive the blessings of Messiah when he comes?!*

Suddenly James saw the Pharisees in the front row stand up. "Blasphemer! Unschooled heretic! How can you say the Messiah is for the Gentiles?" They began tearing their robes in protest. What followed was so chaotic James wasn't sure if it was real or some kind of waking nightmare. The whole room erupted in shouts. Several men grabbed Jesus and dragged him outside. The crowd followed, shouting as they pushed and shoved him toward the nearby cliffs that dropped down into the Jezreel Valley. James felt a cold pit growing in his stomach. He knew they were taking Jesus to the Stoning Place. He had only seen it used once before in his life, but he would never forget it. The religious leaders had tied a man's hands behind his back, taken him to the top of a large rock, and pushed him off. James thought the fall must have killed him, but then they dropped large rocks down on him from above just to make sure. James had never been able to erase that sickening sound from his mind.

James was outside now, getting pushed along with the crowd. He looked around wildly for his brothers and cousins, but they were doing nothing. Abruptly the crowd stopped in front of the Stoning Place. He looked at his mother, but she was just staring, a look of shame frozen on her face. *Shouldn't we do something?*

James was so confused, so conflicted. His feet felt like they weighed a thousand pounds, and all he could do was watch. *Why did Jesus say those things? Doesn't he love our people?* He wanted to scream, but it was as if his mouth was sealed shut. Just then someone shoved him hard from behind and he went down in the dirt. Scrambling to his feet he saw the ringleaders gesturing wildly and shouting, "Where is he? Where did he go? Who is hiding him?" But Jesus was nowhere to be found. Then pandemonium broke out with shouting and pushing and mass confusion.

Slowly the crowd dispersed, and James found himself sitting at the base of the rock where they were going to stone his brother. He could see Simon and Jude arguing. Joses was leading his wife and sisters back toward the house. But Mary was bent over with her face in her hands. James went to console her, but his mother pushed him away. "How could he do this to us?" she snapped in anger. "And after what happened at the wedding! This was his golden opportunity…" Her voice faltered as a faraway look crept into her tear-stained eyes. As they made their way back home, James wondered if he would ever see his older brother again.[5]

REJECTED BY HIS OWN

Ever since the Babylonians had destroyed the Jerusalem Temple in 587 BC and hauled their people off into exile, Jews had developed the tradition of gathering for worship on the Sabbath in the *beth knesset*, Hebrew for "house of assembly." Originally if ten or more Jewish men gathered in a home it was considered such an assembly, but eventually Jews built public spaces dedicated for these and other gatherings. In Greek they were called *sunagoge,* from which we get the English word "synagogue." By the time of Jesus most Jewish towns and all cities had one or more synagogues which were used for the Sabbath prayer service, while also serving as a school and a civic center during the week. Although archaeologists have identified and excavated many ancient synagogues in Galilee dating from the third to the sixth centuries AD, only a handful of first-century synagogues have been discovered so far. This is partly because the later more ornate synagogues were often built over the simpler first-century synagogues, obliterating them.

---

[5] Based on Luke 4:14-30

First-Century Synagogue of Magdala

The synagogues that have been discovered from the time of Jesus measure 40-60 feet wide by 53-80 feet long (1220-4200 square feet) and are generally rectangular in design. Typically, they have a single doorway and feature rows of stone benches or built-in seating around the perimeter, creating a slight stadium effect. Some include a small vault-like closet called a *genizah* (Hebrew: "hiding place") where the highly valuable Torah scrolls were locked away for safe-keeping. Each synagogue had a group of community leaders called the "synagogue rulers" or "elders" who oversaw the synagogue and scheduled rabbis to teach at the Sabbath services. They also supervised the "synagogue attendant" who was responsible for cleaning and maintaining the building, meting out punishment to those convicted of breaking the Law, and most of all, guarding the costly scrolls. The most recently discovered first-century synagogue in Israel was uncovered in the ancient city of Magdala on the northwest shore of the large freshwater lake known as the Sea of Galilee. This was the hometown of Mary Magdalene and was a prosperous center for the drying and processing of fish caught in the lake. The synagogue excavated in Magdala is the most ornately decorated of any first-century synagogue discovered so far, boasting colorful fresco panels on the walls and intricate mosaic floors. It also featured an ornately carved limestone scroll table which sat near the center of the building and was covered with symbols representing the Temple in Jerusalem.

On the Sabbath day, extended families entered the synagogue through the main door, found a place on the floor, turned around to face the entrance, and sat down. The seats around the perimeter were probably reserved for the elderly, the synagogue rulers, and other prominent members of the community. When the time came for the rabbi to read the Scripture passage at the Sabbath prayer service, the synagogue attendant carefully took the appropriate scroll from the *genizah* and handed it to the teacher. The teacher then placed the scroll on the scroll table and unrolled it to the place where the reading was found. After completing the reading, the teacher rolled up the scroll, handed it back to the attendant, and then went to the front of the synagogue and sat down in a special chair called "the Moses seat" to teach the people. (See Matthew 23:2.)

When Jesus returned to Nazareth following his baptism and time of testing in the wilderness, Luke tells us he attended the Sabbath service at the synagogue *"as was his custom."* (Luke 4:16) This reflects both the conservative religious culture of first-century Nazareth and the pious faith of his family. (See Luke 2:41.) Luke assumes we understand Jesus would be attending the synagogue with his extended family. Although Jesus had not been formally trained as a rabbi, reports of his uniquely authoritative teaching had convinced the synagogue rulers to recognize him as a teacher and invite him to teach from the Law at the weekly gathering. When the time came for him to teach, Jesus followed the exact procedure described above, taking the scroll of Isaiah from the attendant, unrolling it, and reading the passage from the Isaiah scroll which we refer to as Isaiah 61. Then he returned the scroll to the attendant and sat down on the Moses Seat.

The passage Jesus read expresses the deepest hopes and prayers of the Jewish people at the time of Jesus. It is *"good news"* because it describes the *"year of the Lord's favor"* that the Messiah will bring to God's people. For centuries the Jews had been occupied and oppressed by foreign pagan superpowers, but through it all this promise of an anointed Messiah whom God would send to liberate his people and establish his Kingdom kept their hope alive. Over the centuries their unfulfilled hope had dissolved into bitterness and entitlement. They prayed for God to destroy the Gentile nations and prided themselves in being better than the rest of the world because they were chosen by God and followed his Law. When Jesus sat down and said, *"Today this Scripture has been fulfilled in your hearing,"* every heart in that synagogue skipped a beat at the idea that this promised Messianic jubilee was beginning. Finally, the Messiah would come and destroy the enemies of Israel and vindicate his chosen people! At that moment Jesus was the most popular man in Nazareth.

But Jesus' interpretation of this passage was not what they were expecting. As he went on to lift up the biblical stories of the widow of Zarephath and Naaman the Syrian, jaws began to tighten and faces began to scowl. (1 Kings 17:8-24; 2 Kings 5:1-14) The people of Nazareth who had known Jesus since he was a boy were filled with rage at the suggestion that God's promise of favor and blessing was for their oppressors as much as for them. The charge of blasphemy and heresy that were levelled against Jesus came with the penalty of stoning to death in the Old Testament law. (Leviticus 24:17; Deuteronomy 13:6-10) The rabbis explained that stoning entailed tying a man's hands behind his back, taking him to a height at least twice the height of a man, and pushing him off. If the fall did not kill him, then you were to drop stones on him from that height until he was dead. A number of cliffs drop down into the Jezreel Valley just south of Nazareth, so it is easy to picture this scene. Luke's description of the crowd taking Jesus to a cliff to throw him down is not a random act of mob violence, but a very deliberate act of judgment. It is hard to imagine a more complete rejection of Jesus and his vision by the people of his hometown.

Jezreel Valley from the cliffs outside of Nazareth

Modern western readers, like me, often miss the role of Jesus' family in this account, because we have such an individualistic mindset. But once we realize Jesus' extended family is present in the synagogue, it raises important questions. Where was Jesus' *oikos*? If extended family is meant to provide protection, why weren't Jesus' brothers and uncles and cousins standing up to the crowd? Why wasn't Jesus' mother pleading for his life? Apparently, they were so shocked by Jesus' inclusion of the Gentiles that they weren't prepared to stand with Jesus in his moment of greatest need. From John's account of the wedding in Cana shortly before this, we get the impression that Mary was anxious for Jesus to step into his

Messianic calling. But her assumptions about what the Messiah would say and do were a far cry from what Jesus actually did. Jesus said, *"A prophet is not without honor, except in his hometown and among his relatives and in his own household."* (Mark 6:4) John describes it this way, *He came to his own, and his own people did not receive him.* (John 1:11) This rejection by those closest to him must have been one of the most painful moments in Jesus' life.

We don't know exactly how Jesus escaped the stoning, but Luke simply says, *passing through their midst, he went away.* (Luke 4:30) Was this some kind of Jedi mind-trick? "This is not the Messiah you are looking for!" We don't know exactly how this happened, but in the very next verse Luke tells us Jesus *went down to Capernaum, a city of Galilee.* (Luke 4:31) Why would Jesus leave his hometown and go to Capernaum? Remember the five guys whom Jesus met down at the Jordan River? Three of them lived in Capernaum. It seems clear Jesus was going there to see if these guys would be more open and receptive to him than his hometown and his own family.

Later Jesus taught his disciples a very simple but powerful principle when training them for mission: *"Whatever house you enter, first say, 'Peace be to this house!' And if a son of peace is there, your peace will rest upon him."* (Luke 10:5-6) Jesus was telling his disciples to carry out their mission by extending friendship to people and looking for those who are open and will reciprocate friendship. Jesus went on to say when you find a *"a son of peace,"* someone who is open and responsive to you, *"remain in the same house, eating and drinking what they provide, for the laborer deserves his wages. Do not go from house to house. Whenever you enter a town and they receive you, eat what is set before you. Heal the sick in it and say to them, 'The kingdom of God has come near to you.'"* (Luke 10:7-9) Jesus is telling us that, when we find a "person of peace" we are to spend time with them, invest in the relationship, show them the power of God, and explain the truth of God's Kingdom.

This is exactly how Jesus lived. He offered his "peace" by welcoming people, listening to them, and serving them. Then Jesus built close relationships with those who responded by welcoming him, listening to him, and serving him. These were his "people of peace." Down at the Jordan Jesus had welcomed Andrew, Simon, and John, spent the whole afternoon with them, and probably served them a meal as the culture would have demanded. He was offering his peace to them. When he came to Nazareth, he did the same with his town and his family, but they did not reciprocate. And so, Jesus decided to go to Capernaum and see if Andrew, Simon, and John were "people of peace" to him. Would they reciprocate his offer of friendship?

Who are the people in your life who seem far from God but are open to you? Perhaps these are your people of peace. What would it look like to offer your friendship to them? How could you invite them in closer to see if they will reciprocate? How could you invest in those friendships if they do reciprocate? When you listen to God and take these steps of faith you are following the example of Jesus. You are living as his disciple.

A NEW OIKOS

Capernaum, literally "the village of Nahum," was a thriving fishing town on the northern shore of the Sea of Galilee, some six miles east of Magdala. Like Magdala, it was located on the ancient trade route known as the Via Maris which connected Egypt to Damascus. In Jesus' time this was a significant part of the system of Roman roads that connected Palestine to the rest of the Roman Empire. Capernaum was smaller than the city of Magdala, but larger than some of the surrounding villages, probably about 1500-2000 people. This northern shore of the Sea of Galilee has always been the best fishing in the lake because the River Jordan enters just to the east, bringing a continual flow of nutrients that attract fish. In addition to fishing, Capernaum was a center for the production of olive oil, flour, and glass.

The first-century town has been extensively excavated and the most prominent feature of the ancient remains is the large, ornately carved white limestone synagogue at the center of Capernaum. This white limestone building dates to a few hundred years after the time of Jesus, but it was built directly on the walls of a black basalt synagogue from the first century. Luke tells us, surprisingly, this earlier synagogue was built with money donated by a wealthy Roman centurion who commanded the nearby garrison of soldiers. (Luke 7:5) This may explain why it is the largest first-century synagogue discovered so far.

When Jesus arrived in Capernaum, once again he was invited to teach in the Sabbath service, and so he went to this very synagogue which we can still visit today. When Jesus got up to teach, the people were amazed, not only at the content of his teaching but the impact his words had on them. Luke writes, *they were astonished at his teaching, for his word possessed authority.* (Luke 4:32)

Ancient Synagogue in Capernaum

Normally rabbis in Jesus' time quoted the interpretation of another rabbi. Then they quoted the interpretation of a second rabbi. Then they drew a derivative conclusion from these opinions. Jesus' teaching was radically different. Just as we saw during his time of testing in the wilderness, Jesus spoke as an authorized representative of his heavenly Father. He was not offering a derivative human interpretation but was speaking for God directly to the people.

It wasn't only what Jesus said that impacted people, but also what he did. In reaction to his authoritative teaching in the synagogue that day an unclean spirit began to manifest in a man who was under demonic influence. The demon identified Jesus as *"the Holy One of God."* Exorcists in Jesus' time used complex secret spells and dramatic rituals to try and drive out demons. By contrast, Jesus simply rebuked the demon, saying, *"Be silent and come out of him!"* When the demon left this man, the people reacted with amazement saying, *"What is this word? For with authority and power he commands the unclean spirits, and they come out!"* (Luke 4:34-37) Recalling Jesus' baptism and time of testing in the wilderness, we see Jesus was simply living in the authority he had received from his Father by virtue of his identity as Son of the King. As a result, the power of the indwelling Spirit who continued to fill him flowed through him to carry out his Father's will.

Simon and Andrew's Extended Family House

Simon, his brother Andrew, and their extended family were in the synagogue that day and witnessed all that took place there. Following the service Simon invited Jesus to their home for the midday Sabbath meal. As was the custom, Simon and Andrew lived together with their extended family in a multi-room house where they shared life and carried out the family business together. In this case, archaeologists have identified and excavated the actual house of Simon and Andrew, which is remarkable! Their house was just one block south of the synagogue, near the waterfront. It consisted of seven rooms arranged around a central courtyard with an animal pen along one side. There was a single door leading from the street into the courtyard, and all the rooms opened up into that central space. It is a classic *oikos* house and the largest discovered in Capernaum. In these rooms Simon and his family, Andrew and his family, Simon's mother-in-law, their relatives, and other partners in the family business lived and carried out their work.

When Jesus accepted Simon's invitation to come to the house after the synagogue service, everyone in the family would have been thrilled. In that culture you didn't invite just anyone into your home. The *oikos* existed for the sake of the *oikos*. You invited people of good standing in the community who would bring honor to your family. A family of good reputation would never invite people of a lower class or questionable character in their home because such an invitation would cast shame on the family. Since Jesus was already considered a famous rabbi, his presence in their home brought great honor to their family. But suddenly his presence created a crisis. Like many men, Simon did not think through the implications of his invitation. One of the highest values in first-century culture was to provide generous hospitality, particularly through food and drink. But Simon's mother-in-law normally organized the meals, and she was sick with a fever. The Gospels tell us Jesus solved the dilemma himself by rebuking the fever and healing her! Then she immediately began to serve them the sabbath meal.

It is interesting to note Jesus was demonstrating the very steps he would later train his disciples to follow with their "people of peace." Jesus told them when they were out on mission and found a person who reciprocated their offer of friendship, they were to *"eat what is set before you. Heal the sick in it and say to them, 'The kingdom of God has come near to you.'"* (Luke 10:8-9) This is exactly what Jesus did with Simon and Andrew's family. This is the missional strategy of Jesus; look for friends, spend time with them, eat meals with them, show them the power of God, and then tell them about his Kingdom. Sounds pretty simple, doesn't it? Well, except for the healing part! As usual, Jesus was showing his future disciples a new way of life even before telling them about it.

So far Simon and Andrew's family must have loved having Jesus in their home. But then, after dinner he did something no one could have expected. He invited everyone in the whole town to come over. This was simply not done! You don't just give an open invitation. Unacceptable people might bring shame to the family. As we read on, we discover that a very mixed group indeed gathered in their home that night, and even demonized people came. *Now when the sun was setting, all those who had any who were sick with various diseases brought them to him, and he laid his hands on every one of them and healed them. And demons also came out of many, crying, "You are the Son of God!" But he rebuked them and would not allow them to speak, because they knew that he was the Christ.* (Luke 4:40-41)

This was a night none of them had expected. They met a man who spoke with the authority of God unlike anyone they had ever heard before. They saw the power of God flow through this man to touch, heal, and deliver people. They heard him describe a whole new coming reality called the Kingdom of God in which the will of God is done on earth as it is in heaven. And it was all happening right in their own home among their family, friends, and neighbors! In fact, Jesus was showing them a whole new way to be a family.

Mark tells us after this night Jesus took some of them out with him on a mission trip to the neighboring towns and villages. When they returned, Mark says Jesus was *at home* (Greek: *oikos*). Already Simon and Andrew's extended family home was considered Jesus' home and family! The courtyard of the house was filled with people while Jesus was teaching and healing. (Mark 2:1-12) In the next chapter Mark describes how Jesus chose his core group of twelve disciples and then *went home* (Greek: *oikos*). Again, the house of Simon and Andrew was filled with people. But when Jesus' natural family back in Nazareth heard about this, *they went out to seize him, for they were saying, "He is out of his mind."* (Mark 3:20-21) The reports of Jesus' teaching and miracles were so unlike the Jesus they had known they assumed he had gone crazy.

And so, they did what any loving family would do if their loved one was on the streets and out of his mind; Mary and her four other sons went to Capernaum, stood outside the door of Simon and Andrew's house, and knocked. When the door opened, the courtyard was so full of people they couldn't reach Jesus. The message was passed through the crowd to Jesus, *"Your mother and your brothers are outside, seeking you."* When Jesus received the message inside the house, he said, *"Who are my mother and my brothers?" And looking about at those who sat around him, he said, "Here are my mother and my brothers! For whoever does the will of God, he is my brother and sister and mother."* (Mark 3:31-33)

This was a truly radical thing for Jesus to say! There was an incredibly strong cultural expectation for even adult children to honor their parents by obeying their wishes. Those who heard Jesus say this would have been shocked. They also would have understood Jesus was redefining what family means in the Kingdom of God. This new kind of family was not just a nuclear family, but an extended family. It was not just a biological family, but a spiritual family. It was not just a family focused on protecting and providing for its own, but a family that was oriented toward others. Jesus was showing them how to be a family that is defined by doing the will of God; a family that lives together on mission.

Pam and I both grew up in nuclear families where we lived at a distance from grandparents, aunts, uncles, and cousins. When we became adults, we moved far away from home and raised our children at a distance from their grandparents, aunts, uncles, and cousins. We saw our home primarily as a refuge where we could retreat from the challenges of our calling to protect and provide for our nuclear family. Most of our friends and church members lived the same way. Only the closest of friends were typically welcomed into our home. But about fifteen years ago we started to realize this was not the way of Jesus. As we studied the Gospels and researched first-century culture, we began to see Jesus lived a very different kind of lifestyle and formed a very different kind of family. We also got to know some people who had decided to intentionally model their lives after Jesus. They decided they would form their family in the same way Jesus formed his. When we were around them, we saw that their way of life looked healthier and more fruitful than ours. So, Pam and I decided we would do the same; we would learn to follow Jesus in our family life.

As we followed Jesus in this way, we started to see our family not only in biological terms, but also in spiritual terms. We started to define family not just as a nuclear family of parents and children, but as a multigenerational extended family. We started to see our home not as a refuge where we could withdraw from the world, but a place where others were welcomed in, particularly those outside the family of God. We started to see our purpose was not just protecting and providing for ourselves, but being and sharing the Good News of Jesus with the world. As we learned to let Jesus shape our family life, we found our family life was becoming healthier and our marriage was becoming stronger. There was a deeper sense of joy as more people became truly brothers and sisters to us. We also found we now had a place to invite our "people of peace," our neighbors and friends who were not interested in church but were interested in spending time with us and our new spiritual family. We were learning to live as a family on mission.

Now, fifteen years later, we would never want to go back to the way we used to live. We have seen God change lives and bring people to himself in this setting. Learning to build a more Jesus-shaped family and live on mission together is the most abundant life we could ever live! What about you? How do you define your family? What would happen if you let Jesus shape your family life more intentionally?

REFLECT AND DISCUSS
Read Mark 3:31-35

1. Who or what am I letting define my understanding of family?

2. What would it mean to let Jesus shape my family life?

3. How can I actively look for "people of peace," people who are open to my friendship?

4. How can I intentionally invest in people of peace who are open and responsive to me?

5. God, what are you saying to me and what step of faith do you want me to take in response?

CHAPTER FIVE

THE INVITATION TO FOLLOW

A NEW KIND OF FISHING

Simon poked his stick at the last embers of the cooking fire in the clay oven. Looking around the dimly lit courtyard, he saw that most of the family had gone to bed. His brother Andrew and their two hired men were on the other side of the courtyard playing a game of "Dogs and Jackals," laughing as they rolled the dice. Simon could hardly believe all they had seen over the past few weeks. Jesus had entered their home and their lives, and it seemed everything was changing. They heard Jesus say things they had never heard before. They saw Jesus do things they had never seen before. He slept in their home, ate at their table, and taught in their synagogue. And he took them with him when he taught in other synagogues. He welcomed people no one would welcome. He touched people no one would touch. He healed people no one could heal. Everywhere they went, people were talking about Jesus. Crowds gathered whenever they stopped. The synagogues couldn't hold all the people who wanted to hear his teaching, so they had started gathering on hillsides and in open spaces.

Simon shook himself from his thoughts and realized it was now fully dark. He lit his torch from the coals in the oven and picked up a bundle of nets. "Come on guys, it's time!" Andrew and their hired men picked up bundles of nets, and they all headed out to the nearby wharf. The family boat was tied to the stone pier, bobbing in the moonlight. It had first belonged to his grandfather and then his father, and now it was Simon's pride and joy. Just then their partner Zebedee appeared on the adjacent dock with his sons James and John and their hired men. Nodding, they began to load their boat, tossing in nets and climbing aboard. Simon stepped into his boat and lit the lamps while the others loaded the gear. Pushing off from the pier, they pulled hard on the oars heading east. There was no wind tonight, so they would have to row to the best fishing spots nearer the mouth of the river.

They typically fished at night because that was when the fish came closer to the surface to feed, and darkness hid the white flax of their nets from the wary prey. As two of them rowed the boat, the other two let out the nets parallel to the shore. Wooden floats held up the top edge while stone weights pulled down the bottom edge. If they were close enough to the shore, the net formed a wall in the water stretching from the surface down to the lakebed. The net had two layers, one with bigger openings and one with smaller openings, so that fish would swim into it and then get trapped. Working together with another boat, they were able to set their nets so the fish

The Sea of Galilee

couldn't swim around them and escape. Most nights they caught more than they needed to support two extended families, even after Herod's tax collectors took most of the profits. *Life is good,* Simon thought, almost as if to convince himself. They had a successful business and lived in one of the largest houses right on the waterfront in the heart of Capernaum. *So why am I feeling so restless?*

Simon had always loved being out on the water, setting the sails, drawing the oars, and the thrill of pulling in nets full of teeming fish. But something had changed. If he was honest with himself, he had to admit that compared to what Jesus was doing, catching fish now seemed rather dull! *Especially tonight.* As the long night wore on, still they had caught nothing. *What is going on? We never get skunked like this. After all, we are pros!* Simon could feel the frustration rising in him like the sun that was just beginning to peek over the eastern hills. As dawn broke, they rowed their boats into a little cove just west of town, where they could wash their empty nets and nurse their wounded pride.

Slumping down on a big black rock, Simon stared out at the steely ripples fanning across the lake, catching the glint of the rising sun. *All that effort and nothing to show for it!* Coiling up lines and scrubbing nets, Simon wrestled with frustration and other feelings he couldn't quite put his finger on. He used to love running the family fishing business with his brother Andrew and the rest of their extended family. Their partnership with Zebedee and his sons allowed them to take full advantage of the plentiful fishing along that northern shore. *We have a thriving business and I have a good life. I should be satisfied with that.* But he wasn't. Simon realized this dissatisfaction had been gnawing at him for months and catching nothing that night was bringing it all to the surface.

The sound of hundreds of feet shuffling through the grass roused Simon from his thoughts and moved him off his stone seat by the water's edge. He was surprised to see Jesus coming, followed by a crowd of people who began sitting down on the steep hillside that rose up from the rocky beach there. The sun climbed in the sky, and the deep blue waters of the Sea of Galilee sparkled. It was already mid-morning. Jesus stood at the edge of the lake and began to address the crowd, but still more people came and were pushing to get closer. Simon realized things could get out of hand quickly as he saw Jesus motioning for him to bring his boat. Jesus climbed in and Simon rowed out just a short way from the beach, so Jesus could speak to the crowd without being overwhelmed.

Jesus Teaching from Simon's Boat

Jesus' voice carried across the water to the crowd now seated on the natural amphitheater of the hillside around the cove. Time seemed to stand still as Jesus told parables about the Kingdom of God, but when he finished Simon realized the sun was now well overhead. As the crowd began to disperse, Jesus turned in the boat and said the last thing Simon ever expected to hear, "Put out into the deep and let down your nets for a catch." A thousand angry thoughts flashed through Simon's mind. *Is he mocking me for our terrible night of fishing? Who does this Nazarene stonecutter think he is to tell me where and when to fish? Doesn't he know my grandfather's grandfather fished these waters? Doesn't he know no one fishes in the middle of the day? Doesn't he know our nets won't reach the fish in the deep water?* Shocked by the strength of his feelings, Simon realized something more was going on inside of him. Maybe he didn't really want to be a fisherman anymore.

Simon took a deep breath, swallowed his pride, and against all reason answered, "Master, we toiled all night and took nothing! But at your word I will let down the nets." As the two hired men rowed, he and Andrew let out the nets and, to their shock and surprise, felt the ropes snap tight with a powerful jerk. The water was roiling with fish and the gill net overflowed. They could barely hoist the net and heard the knots starting to tear. "Hey John! James! Quick, we need your help!" The Zebedee brothers leapt into action and rowed their boat out to help. Pulling the ropes from either side, they emptied the nets until both boats were filled to the gunnels and starting to take on water. It was a catch like they had never seen. No fish story here—this was nothing short of a miracle!

As they reached the shore, Simon turned to Jesus and fell down before him in the boat. He didn't care that fish were flopping in his face; all he felt was unworthiness in the presence of Jesus. "Depart from me, for I am a sinful man, O Lord." Andrew and James and John stood in stunned silence, nodding in agreement. Jesus said to Simon, "Do not be afraid; from now on you will be catching men." At that moment Simon felt the shame melt away and was filled with a new kind of joy. He finally understood what was going on inside of him. It wasn't that he was to give up fishing, it was that he was going to learn a whole new kind of fishing! His heart leapt inside of him. When they landed on the beach the four fishermen stepped out of their boats and into a whole new way of life.[6]

THE FAMILY BUSINESS

Every extended family in the first century was built around a family business. Simon and Andrew's *oikos* was built around a fishing business. In modern culture our working life is usually disconnected from our family life, so it is easy to imagine Simon and Andrew kissing their wives goodbye in the morning and going off to work as fishermen. In fact, every member of the *oikos* was involved in the family business. Some knotted nets. Some carved stone net weights and anchors. Some cleaned and dried the fish on the rooftop. Some sold the fish to local fishmongers. Some repaired the fishing boat. And Simon and Andrew went out in that boat to do the actual fishing. This is how ancient families worked. Interestingly, when they excavated the house of Simon and Andrew, the archaeologists uncovered exactly what you would expect to find in the home of an extended fishing family, including anchors, net weights, and fishhooks.

---

[6] See Luke 5:1-11

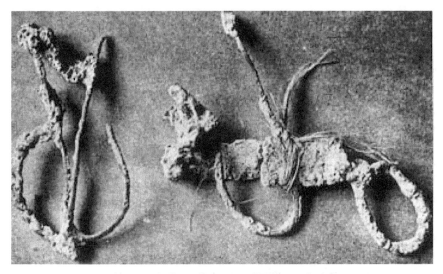

Fishing Hooks from the House of Simon and Andrew

Archaeologists have also discovered a first-century fishing boat from the sea of Galilee. Unearthed from the lakebed not far from Capernaum, it is exactly the kind of boat Jesus' disciples would have used nearly every day. It is 28 feet long, 8 feet wide, had a removable mast and sail, and was outfitted with four oars for rowing. A boat like this would be a fishing family's most important possession because it allowed them to do large scale fishing, which was a very lucrative business on the Sea of Galilee in the first century because the fish were so plentiful. Beyond feeding the local population, this fish was dried, salted, and shipped all over the Roman empire. Although individuals might use a line and hook to catch fish to eat with their family, commercial fishing was done with nets. Net fishing was normally done at night when the fish are more active and when the nets are less visible. Three primary types of net fishing were used on the lake in Jesus' time.

A single man by himself could use *a casting net* which was circular, about eight feet in diameter with weights around the perimeter. The net was gathered together and then flung out over the water so that the weights pulled the net out into a circle, like a pizza chef spinning a fresh crust overhead. When the casting net hit the water, the weights around the perimeter sank to the bottom, trapping any fish below it. The fisherman then dived down, gathered together the edges of the net, and pulled it up like a sack with the fish inside. This is the kind of fishing Simon and Andrew were doing on the shore when Jesus called them to follow him. (Mark 1:16, 17)

First-Century Fishing Boat

The dragnet was a long net with floats along the top edge and weights along the bottom edge. Fishermen in a boat pulled the net out into the water from the beach and then looped back to shore, forming a semicircular wall in the water. A crew of men then dragged the net up onto the beach, trapping a large number of every kind of fish. This is the type of net envisioned in Jesus' parable about sorting different kinds of fish after they are caught. (Matthew 13:47-50)

The primary mode of commercial fishing in first-century Galilee was with *gill nets*. This was a three-layer net consisting of two larger looped nets and a finer looped net in the middle. With floats on the top and weights on the bottom, the gill net formed a wall in the water like the dragnet, but in this case the fish swam through the loops in the larger net and got caught in the smaller looped net as they tried to escape. This net

Reconstruction of the Galilee Boat

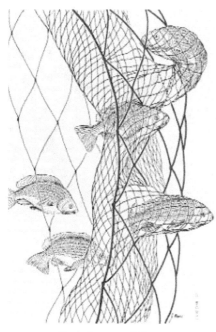

First-Century Gill Net

was let out behind the boat as it was rowed parallel to the shore, forming a wall stretching from the surface to the bottom. Then the fishermen disturbed the water on the shore, driving fish into deeper water where they were caught in the net. This was the type of net the disciples of Jesus used most often and is the kind of net Jesus told Simon to *"Put out into the deep and let down your nets for a catch."* (Luke 5:4)

Because the family business was intergenerational, it is not surprising that the younger members of the family were trained by the older members. When boys reached the age of twelve, they generally left *Beth Sefer* (Hebrew for "house of the book"), the primary school at the synagogue, and began working in the family business. The boys began to help their fathers, uncles, and older brothers or cousins, while the girls helped their mothers, aunts, and older sisters or cousins. At first, they watched what their more experienced relatives were doing, then they began to actively help. As time went on, they took on more and more responsibility, learning new skills from their mentors as they progressed. The more experienced did not just *tell* their charges how to do it, they *showed* them so the younger ones could imitate their techniques.

In this way the younger members of the family were apprenticed until they were fully functioning partners in the family business. This is how Jesus learned his family's trade and became a builder. This is how Simon, Andrew, James, and John all became fishermen. This is also how Jesus was going to show them a whole new way to fish; he was about to transform their successful family business into a Kingdom business.

JESUS-SHAPED DISCIPLESHIP

If a student showed special promise in his studies at *Beth Sefer* and his parents were ambitious, rather than enter the family business at the age of twelve, he could apply to continue his studies with the rabbi in *Beth Midrash* (Hebrew for "house of study"). Having learned to read and memorize Torah, the Old Testament Law, now the students began to study its interpretation. They learned the rulings of different rabbis who had come before and debated how those rulings applied to various situations. Around the age of eighteen most of those students left *Beth Midrash* and entered the family business, perhaps also working on the side as a scribe, writing marriage contracts, bills of sale, and other legal documents.

The best of those students could apply to continue their studies in *Beth Talmud* (Hebrew for "house of learning"). If accepted, they left home and moved into the rabbi's *oikos*. These disciples now spent all their time with the rabbi. They listened to the rabbi's teachings. They observed the rabbi's actions. Over time they began to share the rabbi's teachings with others and imitate the rabbi's actions. Their goal was to learn to know what the rabbi knew and do what the rabbi did so they could become like the rabbi. The rabbi was apprenticing his disciples into his family business. Around the age of thirty, if the disciple had in fact mastered the rabbi's way of life, he could then be recognized as a rabbi in his own right. This meant he began teaching in the synagogue and accepted disciples to come live with him and learn his way of life so they could also become rabbis someday.

A Rabbi Teaching His Disciples

As we noted in Chapter 3, apparently Jesus did not go beyond his studies in *Beth Sefer* but from the age of twelve apprenticed as a builder in the family business. The authority of Jesus' teachings and the power of his healings were what caused people to recognize him as a rabbi, although his authority was quite different from the Pharisees and other rabbis of his time. Jesus didn't base his teachings on the interpretations of other rabbis, but on the Hebrew Bible itself and the revelation he received directly from his heavenly Father. His teaching was not focused on the minutiae of legal rulings, but rather on the practical living of daily life. Jesus didn't use complex technical language that only the well-educated could understand; he spoke in simple terms and told stories taken from everyday life that people could remember and pass on to others. Jesus didn't use elaborate techniques or esoteric formulas to try and heal or deliver people, he simply rebuked sickness and they were made well. He simply commanded demons to leave and they left. He was a rabbi unlike any other!

While normally only the best of the best students could apply and hope to be accepted as a disciple of the rabbi, Jesus invited people of every background to follow him, people who never would have dreamed of applying to be a disciple. He called blue-collar workers, like the fishermen Simon, Andrew, James, and John who had only the most basic education. He called Matthew the tax collector, who would have been one of the most hated men in Capernaum because he was a traitor working for the enemy to line his own pockets. He called Simon the Zealot, likely a former member of the revolutionary group who had sworn themselves to overthrowing the Romans and killing tax collectors. It is hard to imagine a more socially diverse and politically divergent group of disciples, and this was his core group!

In addition to this core group of the twelve full-time disciples who left their jobs to travel with Jesus, the Gospel writers refer to the wider group of people who gathered in the house of Simon and Andrew and believed in Jesus as his *"disciples."* (Luke 6:17) These were the 72 disciples that Jesus trained and sent out on mission in addition to the 12 disciples. (Luke 10:1-12) This was an even more diverse group of men and women whom Jesus counted as his spiritual family. (Mark 3:35) When Jesus was in Bethany at the home of his friends Mary, Martha, and Lazarus, he confronted Martha for trying to pressure Mary to join her in the kitchen and instead affirmed Mary for sitting at his feet, the unmistakable posture of a disciple. (Luke 11:38-42) A female disciple was unheard of in ancient Judaism and yet the Gospel writers tell us *"many"* women, such as Mary Magdalene, Joanna, Suzanna, Mary the mother of James the younger and of Joses, and Salome, *"followed"* Jesus. (Mark 15:40-41)

Although Jesus quickly became a famous rabbi, he welcomed every kind of person into his family and gave them full access to his life. That is why every time we read of Jesus coming back to his new home in Capernaum, the courtyard of Simon and Andrew's house was filled with people. When Jesus returned "home" in Mark 2, we read of the four men who carried their paralyzed friend to Jesus. They couldn't get to Jesus through the crowded courtyard, so they used the stone steps near the door to take their friend up on the flat rooftop, dug a hole in the mud thatched roof above Jesus' head, and let down their friend to be healed! (Mark 2:1-12) When Jesus returned home in Mark 3, we read that the house was so full they couldn't use the clay oven in the courtyard to cook the meal. This was when Jesus' mother and brothers thought Jesus had gone crazy, so they traveled to Capernaum to bring him back to Nazareth. When they arrived at the door of the house it was so full of people, they had to pass the message to Jesus that his mother and brothers were asking for him. (Mark 3:20-21, 31-33)

In these passages we can see the way Jesus made disciples was by inviting them into his life as part of an extended spiritual family. The way we often try to make disciples is by inviting them to a church service, or a Bible study; we give them a book to read or send them a video to watch. That is not enough if we want to follow the way of Jesus. He was the most amazing teacher who ever lived, and he taught his disciples the greatest wisdom and insights this world has ever seen. But Jesus offered them more than just information. He also invited them into a relationship of imitation. Jesus' disciples got to hear what he said, but they also got to see how he lived. Jesus said, *"believe me"* and he also said, *"follow me."* (John 14:11; Mark 1:17) Jesus challenged them to believe his words and to follow his ways. They were invited into a spiritual family made up of disciples who got to spend so much time with their rabbi and have such access to him that their lives began to be shaped by his.

When Jesus calls us to follow him, he invites us into the kind of relationship where we not only listen to what he says, but we also watch what he does. He calls us to learn the information he is teaching us, the truth that sets us free, but he also calls us to imitate his singular way of life. When Jesus said, *"I am the way, the truth, and the life"* he described this kind of discipleship. (John 14:6) It is in practicing the *way* of Jesus and believing the *truth* of Jesus that we begin to live the *life* of Jesus, the fruitful, abundant life we were created to live!

A FAMILY OF DISCIPLES

You might be wondering how we can become these kinds of Jesus-shaped disciples today when we live 2,000 years after Jesus in a completely different time and place. After all, we are not among those first men and women who got to share life with Jesus on a daily basis, so how are we supposed to imitate his way of life? This is an important question. It is a reminder that disciples are meant to grow up and become rabbis who make disciples of their own. Discipleship is a Jesus-shaped way of life which is passed down from generation to generation within the family of God.

Thankfully we have four reliable eyewitness accounts of Jesus' life, death, and resurrection in the four Gospels. In the book of Acts, we have a carefully documented account of how the Holy Spirit guided and empowered the first disciples to become apostles who made more disciples and formed new spiritual families on mission. In the New Testament, we also have various letters to guide us, written by apostles who were discipled directly by Jesus and those who received direct revelation from Jesus. Together this biblical witness gives us a beautiful description of the perfect example of Jesus to which all disciples in every age can look for guidance and inspiration.

However, this is still only information about the life we are called to imitate. As rich and valuable as it is, we need something more. We have a perfect example in the Jesus of history, but we also need a living example in our present-day lives that we can see with our eyes and with whom we can interact on a regular basis. We need an imperfect but visible example of Jesus to help us learn his way. We need a spiritual family of disciples who can help us learn to follow Jesus in our time and place.

The Apostle Paul understood this very well. Although he was painfully aware of his shortcomings, not the least of which was persecuting the first followers of Jesus, he was also bold enough to offer his own imperfect life as an example for his disciples to follow. He wrote to the Corinthians, *"Be imitators of me, as I am of Christ."* (1 Corinthians 11:1) This wasn't because he thought his life was perfect, but because he knew the perfect Jesus was alive in him through the Holy Spirit. As he wrote to the Galatians, *"I have been crucified with Christ. It is no longer I who live, but Christ who lives in me."* (Galatians 2:20) Paul offered his Jesus-shaped life to others as an imperfect example of the perfect way of Jesus.

It wasn't only his life he lifted up for people to imitate, but also the lives of those he was discipling, such as Silas, Timothy, Titus, and Luke. He wrote to the Thessalonians, *"For you yourselves know how you ought to imitate us."* Then he went on to say that they were trying *"to give you in ourselves an example to imitate."* (2 Thessalonians 3:7, 9) The truth is we don't need another perfect example. We have one already and his name is Jesus. What we do need are generations of real-life examples who can help us learn to follow the way of Jesus in our time and place.

It is crucial for us to remember that all of this is meant to take place in an extended spiritual family which is living on mission together. All through the Gospels and the book of Acts, we hear how Jesus and his first followers *"made disciples."* (Acts 14:21) But a fascinating shift takes place in the letters of the New Testament. Not once do the apostolic letters mention the word "disciple." What happened? Did the followers of Jesus forget about discipleship? Not by a long shot! As the movement of Jesus began to spread across the Mediterranean world, more and more non-Jews were trusting Jesus and following his way. But Gentiles did not understand the language of disciples and rabbis, so the apostles translated discipleship into the language of extended family.

Ancient Gentiles lived in *oikos* just like ancient Jews did, so they completely understood the role of parents in training their sons and daughters into the family business. The apostles realized parenting was a vivid picture of what Jesus-shaped discipleship is all about. Those who seek to follow Jesus need spiritual parents who will apprentice them into the mission of God's family. That means spiritual parents show their spiritual children what it looks like to follow Jesus, then this "younger" generation begins to participate in that way of life, until finally they are living the way of Jesus. That means now they have become spiritual parents who can raise up new spiritual children and train them to follow the way of Jesus as well. This extended spiritual family of disciple-making disciples living together on mission is what the writers of the New Testament refer to as *"the church."*

When Paul wrote to the church in Philippi, he described his discipling relationship with Timothy this way, *"you know Timothy's proven worth, how as a son with a father he has served with me in the gospel."* (Philippians 2:22) When writing to the church in Corinth, Paul used this familial language to describe the process of discipleship by which he was helping them learn to follow Jesus: *"I do not write these things to make you ashamed, but to admonish you as my beloved children. For though you have countless guides in Christ, you do not have many fathers. For I became your father in Christ Jesus through the gospel. I urge you, then, be imitators of me. That is why I sent you Timothy, my beloved and faithful child in the Lord, to remind you of my ways in Christ, as I teach them everywhere in every church."* (1 Corinthians 4:14-17)

Paul had discipled Timothy and now he sent Timothy to further disciple the Corinthians. This is how a spiritual family of disciples is meant to function. One generation of disciples invests in the next, training them in the way of Jesus and raising them up to invest in yet another generation of disciples and so on. In this way we are called to grow up in Christ so that we become spiritual parents who are raising up spiritual sons and daughters who will also train yet another generation of disciples to carry out the family business. This is what it means to be the church. Of course, this is exactly what Jesus had in mind when he said to Simon and Andrew, *"Follow me, and I will make you fishers of men."* (Matthew 4:19) Although they had a beautiful home and a successful business, he invited them into something that was so much greater. Instead of simply catching fish to provide for their natural family, they would save people and invite them into a family of disciples where they would learn how to truly live an abundant life, bearing good fruit that lasts forever! This is the church Jesus said he was building.

I had been a full-time pastor for nearly 20 years before I understood how Jesus-shaped discipleship was meant to function. I had committed my life to making disciples, but I thought of discipleship primarily as information: preaching sermons, teaching Bible studies, and providing good devotional materials. I was able to disciple some people, but they were not equipped to effectively disciple others because I was not inviting them into my life and my family; I was not showing them the way of Jesus; I was not giving them the opportunity for imitation. Everything changed for me when someone invited me into their life and family where they challenged me to follow them as they followed Jesus.

They weren't perfect, but I could see in them and in their family more of the way of Jesus. As I learned to follow Jesus' way more closely, I was able to do the same with others. Pam and I learned how to form an extended spiritual family of disciples where one generation was raising up the next generation. The result is that the people I was discipling were empowered to disciple others. Their disciples were able to do the same. And so on.

Now I have so many generations of disciples that I have lost track of my spiritual grandchildren and great-grandchildren! By building a spiritual family where Pam and I can offer our imperfect lives as Jesus-shaped examples for others to follow, God has multiplied the fruitfulness of our lives and we have found the inexpressible joy of watching our spiritual grandchildren follow Jesus, reach the lost, and make disciples. What about you? Are you a disciple of Jesus? Do you have a spiritual family? If so, who is the spiritual parent who is discipling you in the family business? Are you growing up in Christ to become a spiritual parent yourself? If so, who are your spiritual children that you are discipling into the way of Jesus? I encourage you to keep reflecting on these questions as we continue to explore the way and the truth of Jesus' life.

REFLECT AND DISCUSS

Read Matthew 4:18-22

1. Have I heard and answered Jesus' call to discipleship?

2. Who are the spiritual parents that are helping me to follow Jesus?

3. How can I begin to make disciples the way Jesus did?

4. Who are the spiritual sons and daughters I am raising up to work in the family business?

5. God, what are you saying to me and what step of faith do you want me to take in response?

CHAPTER SIX

WHERE ALL ARE WELCOME

AN UNEXPECTED PARTY

Matthew swatted at a fly as he absentmindedly ran his fingers through the bronze coins in the tray on the countertop in front of him. Most of his day's take was safely locked in the strong box underneath the cushion he was sitting on, but he liked to keep a good amount of change handy in case anyone tried to pay the toll with a large coin. The trade caravans that moved south along the Via Maris from Damascus to Egypt had to cross over the river from Herod Philip's territory in the east to Herod Antipas' territory to the west. Matthew's tax collection booth was positioned near the bridge east of Capernaum in Antipas' territory so that no one could escape paying him the toll fees. There was always the threat of robbery, but he wasn't worried about bandits because of the armed guards stationed on either side of his tax booth. *Besides, everyone knows we tax collectors are under the protection of the Roman army and no one wants to mess with them. Well, except maybe the Zealots!* Matthew chuckled to himself, pretending not to be nervous.

He loved studying the different designs of the coins that came in. Matthew was often paid in Roman prutahs with palm trees and victory wreaths and occasionally with one of Herod's bronze coins with the pomegranate or the battle helmet. The pagan magician's auger on Pilate's prutahs was offensive to most Jews, but Matthew just thought they were oversensitive. Occasionally he would get a silver shekel from Tyre with the dramatic eagle or a Greek drachma with the stoic figure of Zeus seated on his throne. Matthew's favorites were the silver denarii, a standard day's wage, with the resolute image of Caesar Augustus or Tiberias staring back at him, flanked by the title "son of god" or "highest priest." He liked to think of Caesar as his boss and would sometimes talk to him when no one else was listening.

Just then five farmers approached on the road. They were heading out to their fields and gave him a steely stare as they passed by. He glared back, his face set like flint toward them, pretending not to care. Matthew had long since gotten used to the disdain and outright hatred the local people expressed for him on a daily basis. *They are just jealous!* He knew he was considered a traitor because he colluded with the enemies of Israel by collecting taxes to help fill the coffers of Rome. He was considered an oppressor because of the heavy tariffs the Herodians added to support their lavish lifestyles. And he was considered an extortionist because his income came directly from collecting even more than the Romans and Herodians charged. If he was honest, the hatred of his neighbors gnawed at him daily, but he tried to push those thoughts from his mind. *Working for the Romans and Herod is definitely a double-edged sword!* Matthew puffed out his cheeks and let the air out slowly.

He couldn't complain. He and Priscilla had a good life. Their house in Magdala was among the finest in the area. Their children lacked for nothing. They had slaves to tutor the children, handle all the hard work, and cater to their every need. Priscilla kept their social calendar full, especially since Herod Antipas decided to move his capital from Sepphoris and build a new capital city on the western shore of the lake. *Tiberias! With its grand theater and fancy shopping streets, soon it will eclipse Magdala as the leading city of the area.* He thought about their well-connected Herodian "friends" like Chuza and Joanna, knowing they were looking for status and influence more than real friendship. *I do miss the family though.* Matthew found himself wondering how his brothers and their kids were doing back at the extended family home in Cana. Although it was an easy day's journey, he hadn't been back for over a decade. Ever since he decided to put his mathematical skills to work as a tax collector, his entire family had disowned him and refused to receive him. That's when he decided to start using his "professional" name Matthew rather than Levi, the name his father Alphaeus had given him. *Their loss, not mine!* Matthew put on a brave face and pretended he didn't care, but he did. Deeply. Sometimes he sat in his big fancy house and felt so empty inside.

Suddenly a noise snapped Matthew out of his daydream, and he instinctively put his hand on the handle of the dagger in his belt. Looking down the road, he saw a crowd coming on foot, led by the controversial new rabbi Jesus who had moved into Capernaum a couple of months ago. Matthew had heard rumors of him for weeks. Not welcome in the synagogue, Matthew had to wait for an opportunity to hear Jesus out in the open fields. Two weeks ago, he had gone up on the hillside above Capernaum to hear the rabbi from Nazareth for himself. Jesus said it is the poor who are blessed in God's Kingdom. *How can that be? They have no money!* Jesus said it is the meek who will inherit everything. *The meek end up with nothing!* He said it is the peacemakers who are blessed, not the war mongers. That made no sense to Matthew. It was as if Jesus was trying to turn everything upside down. He didn't understand what Jesus meant by all of it, but it stirred something deep inside him.

Ever since Matthew had been mulling over the words of Jesus. *What is the Kingdom of God? Does it really change everything?* He suddenly clutched his chest. It was as if he could feel a weight pressing down on him, making it hard to breathe. The weight had always been there, but now Matthew was desperate for it to be lifted. He was desperate to be released from this prison of his tax booth, his fancy house, his powerful friends. Just then Jesus and the crowd with him stopped right in front of Matthew's booth. Matthew's heart was beating so hard he wondered if they could hear it. Jesus looked directly into Matthew's eyes. Holding out a hand, Jesus simply said, *"Follow me!"* In an instant Matthew knew what Jesus meant. Jesus was inviting him into his extended family. He was inviting Matthew to join in Jesus' family business. He was inviting him to become a disciple. *Impossible!* Matthew could see the people around Jesus were thinking the same thing. In fact, they looked downright angry that Jesus would even suggest such a thing. But Jesus kept looking into Matthew's eyes and holding out an unwavering hand.

Matthew's head was spinning with questions. *Can he be serious? What would this mean? How will we live? What will Priscilla say?* But for the first time in memory, he felt the weight lifting from his chest as his heart slowed down. He felt lightheaded as he stood up. Then he lifted up the countertop and stepped out of the tax booth. The crowd murmured, but Jesus just started to laugh! The joyful laugh washed over Matthew like a brook running with cool spring water. A grin started to creep across Matthew's face and before he knew it, he was laughing too! Jesus pulled him into a bear hug that Matthew thought would crush him. And when he was released, it felt like he was floating on air. Before he knew what he was saying, Matthew blurted out, "Rabbi, it would do me a great honor if you and your friends would dine in my home tonight!" Jesus just smiled and nodded and began to walk. Matthew could hear his guards calling out to him, asking what to do with the strong box full of coins. He just ignored them and kept his eyes fixed on the back of Jesus' head. There was no turning back now...[7]

CLEAN OR UNCLEAN?

Jesus was different from any rabbi anyone had ever seen. He broke all the religious rules about who he was supposed to avoid and who he was supposed to spend time with. Ancient Jews had developed a very complex system of purity laws governing how they were to interact with people and the world around them. This tradition was rooted in God's call for Israel to be holy as he was holy. God meant for his people to be distinct from the pagan cultures surrounding them so they could live according to his intent and design. However, somewhere along the line the Jewish people lost sight of their mission to the wider world.

Instead of being different in order to invite people of other cultures into the way of God, increasingly they came to see their difference as a special status to be protected from the world around them. This led the rabbis to develop a system of rituals and rules separating Jews from Gentiles and from those among their own people who were considered "unclean." In the second century BC an Egyptian Jew named Aristeas expressed this when he wrote that the law "surrounds us with unbroken palisades and iron walls, to prevent our mixing with any of the other peoples in any matter being thus kept pure in body and soul, preserved from false beliefs, and worshiping the only God omnipotent over all creation."[8]

---

[7] Based on Matthew 9:9-13

[8] "The Letter of Aristeas," Apocrypha and Pseudepigrapha of the Old Testament in English by R. H. Charles, Christian Classics Ethereal Library, (Oxford: The Clarendon Press, 1913)

The ancient concept of ritual impurity contributed to this Jewish attitude of separation from pagan culture, but it is difficult for modern people to understand. It is not a moral state brought about by sinful actions or attitudes. Nor is it a physical affliction like dirt or disease. It is similar to the way modern people think of germs, but on a spiritual or symbolic level. Modern people know we can pick up germs by touching a door handle or from someone coughing into their hand and then shaking ours. We know we can pass those germs to others without realizing it simply by touching them. We know those germs can make people very sick. In the same way, first-century Jews believed just by touching something or someone they could contract ritual defilement that would stand between them and God. Eating the wrong kind of food or wearing the wrong kind of clothing could likewise contaminate them. They knew this defilement was invisible and could be passed on to others without realizing it. As a result, the rabbis developed elaborate rules about how to become ritually pure and how to avoid being defiled.

This meant entire groups of people were considered unclean, and observant Jews were instructed to avoid any contact with them at all. First and foremost, this meant avoiding any kind of contact with Gentiles, not entering the home of a Gentile, and not touching things that Gentiles could have touched. This effectively divided their entire world in two. Samaritans, their half-Jewish cousins, were also considered unclean as a group and also to be avoided. Even Jews who did not or could not follow all the complex rituals and rules prescribed by the rabbis were assumed to be unclean. This led to the classification of various subgroups as unclean. For instance, because shepherds had to constantly spend time in the fields watching over their flocks, the rabbis doubted they could follow all the proper rules and rituals. As a result, they declared shepherds to be unclean. Other individuals were classified untouchable, such as "lepers" who suffered from various types of skin disease. Menstruating women were also considered unclean, so a woman with an ongoing vaginal flow of blood, no matter how slight, was considered continually unclean.

As we discussed in Chapter 1, the practice of ritual bathing was instituted to deal with the inevitable ritual impurities that everyone contracted through the normal course of everyday life. A person wishing to be freed of ritual impurity would enter the dressing room of the *"mikveh,"* take off all their clothes, and go down the steps into the water until they were fully immersed. A witness was present to assure that not even a hair remained above the water. Then the person would come up the steps out of the water considered ritually pure. These immersion baths are found in practically every excavation of first-century Jewish sites in Israel, a testimony to how deeply entrenched this system was in daily life. The frequency of these ritual baths varied based on a person's exposure to potential defilement and their religious convictions. Some groups, like the Essenes, were obsessed with ritual purity and used the *mikveh* twice a day!

Mikveh, a First-Century Ritual Both

This system resulted in a highly compartmentalized society. Certain people were not allowed to mix with other people or spend time in certain places. It created a heightened sense of suspicion and judgment as people were constantly wondering if the people around them or the things they were touching had become unclean. People became very selective about who they invited into their homes and with whom they shared meals. During the COVID-19 global pandemic, many people experienced a similar suspicion and separation, although on a purely physical level, so it lacked the spiritual implications of ritual impurity. If a Jew were considered unclean in the first century it was assumed he was cut off from God's blessing and protection and that God would not hear his prayers. The result is those who were labeled "unclean" experienced not only rejection but also condemnation.

Ultimately Jesus abolished these categories of ritual purity and pointed his followers beyond an external religiosity to the deeper matters of character and integrity. He explained the difference to his disciples when he said, *"Hear me, all of you, and understand: There is nothing outside a person that by going into him can defile him, but the things that come out of a person are what defile him... Do you not see that whatever goes into a person from outside cannot defile him, since it enters not his heart but his stomach, and is expelled?" (Thus he declared all foods clean.) And he said, "What comes out of a person is what defiles him. For from within, out of the heart of man, come evil thoughts, sexual immorality, theft, murder, adultery, coveting, wickedness, deceit, sensuality, envy, slander, pride, foolishness. All these evil things come from within, and they defile a person."* (Mark 7:14-23) Jesus was calling his followers into a whole new way of seeing the world around them.

It is so easy to slip into the habit of judging people based on external appearance and religious categories. It is so easy to become like the priest and the Levite of Jesus' parable who simply passed by the wounded traveler because they were afraid of becoming religiously impure. (Luke 10:25-37) We can unconsciously build a religious bubble that separates us from the world around us. Jesus calls us to a completely different way of seeing others and interacting with them, particularly those who are different from us. He calls us to see every person we meet as a precious child of God who is meant to be a member of our own family. Those who follow the way of Jesus refuse to shun people who don't follow the religious expectations of our tradition, but instead treat them as our own sisters and brothers.

A RADICAL WELCOME

One of the many things that set Jesus apart was the radical welcome he offered to everyone he met. Because he wasn't bound by external religious categories, he was free to include people from every walk of life in his movement. Although Jesus strategically chose to focus his mission on the smaller Jewish villages of Galilee, his vision of God's Kingdom applied to both Jews and Gentiles alike. (Luke 4:16-30) Jesus periodically took his disciples into the Gentile regions surrounding Galilee where he delivered an "unclean" demonized man from the Greek Decapolis, and he healed a daughter of the "unclean" Syrophoenician woman from the region of Tyre and Sidon. (Mark 5:1-20; 7:24-30) Sometimes Jesus made a point of traveling through Samaria when he could have avoided it and he freely interacted with "unclean" Samaritans. When he met a woman of Samaria at Jacob's well, Jesus asked her for a drink of water, shared the Good News with her and her whole village, then he and the disciples ended up staying with them for two more days. (John 4:7-42) It was completely unheard of for a Jewish rabbi to stay in the home of Samaritans and eat at their table!

It wasn't just Gentiles and Samaritans that Jesus embraced; he also radically welcomed outcast Jews. The reason the home of Simon and Andrew always seemed to be so full of people when Jesus was around is that he invited everyone into his spiritual family, regardless of their social standing or religious classification. The Gospels give account after account of Jesus ignoring the religious rules and interacting with those "sinners" whom the rabbis told "good" people avoid. Those who were possessed by unclean spirits were welcome in Jesus' family and were delivered of their spiritual oppression. Those considered lepers due to a skin disease were required to wear a sign around their neck indicating their condition and were supposed to cry out "unclean!" whenever they saw someone approach, warning them to stay away. Jesus regularly ignored these rules and freely touched lepers, healing them physically and restoring them to their families. (Mark 1:40-45)

Although women were not technically categorized as unclean, because menstruation was considered a source of ritual impurity, rabbis often viewed women as potential sources of contamination. Add to that suspicion the charge that women were seductive and a temptation to sexual sin, and we begin to understand why women were often shunned by religious men outside of their own family. It was considered inappropriate for a man of good standing to interact with a woman in public if she was not part of his *oikos*. Now we see why Jesus' interactions with the Gentile Syrophonecian woman and the Samaritan woman at the well were even more radical given that these "unclean" people were also women! When a hemorrhaging woman was publicly exposed for secretly touching Jesus in the hopes of being healed, the crowd would have expected a terrifying rebuke for transmitting her "defilement" to Jesus. Instead, Jesus publicly affirmed her action and identified her as a member of his own family when he said, *"Daughter, your faith has made you well; go in peace."* (Luke 8:48) The fact that Jesus not only welcomed women into his spiritual family but invited them to follow him on mission trips with the male disciples would have been shocking to the religious sensibilities of the rabbis who, in their waking prayers each morning, thanked God for not making them women. (Luke 8:1-2)

Perhaps the most radical welcome of all was when Jesus invited Matthew the tax collector into his inner circle of disciples. (Matthew 9:10) In addition to being hated as traitors and extortionists, tax collectors were also considered categorically "unclean" because they were in such close partnership with the pagan Romans. Matthew was certainly the last person anyone ever expected Jesus to call into his inner circle of disciples! To top it off, Jesus then accepted an invitation to spend the day in Matthew's *oikos*, sharing a meal with his family and his morally questionable friends in the tax collection business. Even for Jesus' own disciples this must have been a hard pill to swallow, but the religious leaders were outraged. *And when the Pharisees saw this, they said to his disciples, "Why does your teacher eat with tax collectors and sinners?" But when he heard it, he said, "Those who are well have no need of a physician, but those who are sick. Go and learn what this means: I desire mercy, and not sacrifice.' For I came not to call the righteous, but sinners."* (Matthew 9:11-13)

In the first century Jews studied the Torah, the written Law of the Old Testament. But they also memorized and passed on the oral law, the various sayings of rabbis who had come before them. Nearly two centuries after Jesus, these oral traditions were written down and compiled in a book called the Mishnah, which eventually was included in the Talmud, which in turn became the defining document of Orthodox Judaism. Jesus was scrupulous about following the intent of the Torah, the written biblical Law, but he did not consider the oral law, the specific legal interpretations of the rabbis, to be binding or even helpful.

When the Pharisees criticized Jesus and his disciples for not following their elaborate hand-washing rituals which they called *"the tradition of the elders,"* Jesus responded, *"You leave the commandment of God and hold to the tradition of men." And he said to them, "You have a fine way of rejecting the commandment of God in order to establish your tradition!"* After demonstrating how they were hypocritically violating the written Law in order to enforce their manmade oral laws, Jesus told them they were *"making void the word of God by your tradition that you have handed down."* (Mark 7:1-13) Jesus rejected the crushing burden of these layers of religious rituals and legalistic rules when he said of the Pharisees, *"They tie up heavy burdens, hard to bear, and lay them on people's shoulders, but they themselves are not willing to move them with their finger."* (Matthew 23:4)

By contrast, Jesus invited those who were weary and heavy laden to imitate his teaching and way of life, which he described when he said, *"my yoke is easy, and my burden is light."* (Matthew 11:28-30)

A Family Enjoying the Sabbath Meal

This distinction Jesus made between the actual Word of God and human religious traditions often brought him into conflict with the religious leaders who held so closely to the oral law. Jesus' practice of Sabbath is a case in point. God declared the seventh day of the week a day of rest in which no work was to be done. (Exodus 20:8-11) By the time of Jesus layers upon layers of regulations delineated what could and couldn't be done on the Sabbath day. They mandated how many steps you could take, how many letters you could write, what could and could not be carried, and so on. Even touching a tool on the Sabbath was considered breaking the Law. Jesus observed a weekly day of rest and participated in the synagogue prayer services on the Sabbath, but he did not follow the myriad Sabbath rules of the Pharisees. One Sabbath Jesus and the disciples plucked some heads of grain as they were walking through a grain field, and the Pharisees said to him, *"Look, why are they doing what is not lawful on the Sabbath?"* Jesus responded to their made-up rules by pointing to an example from the life of David and then summed up the biblical purpose of Sabbath rest by saying, *"The Sabbath was made for man, not man for the Sabbath. So the Son of Man is lord even of the Sabbath."* (Mark 2:24-28)

Jesus was intent on demonstrating the true intent of the Law which had become obscured by the countless religious rules and rituals added to it.

We need to ask ourselves if we are offering the same welcome that Jesus offered to those who are outside our religious traditions. To what extent are we willing to follow Jesus' example by inviting people into our lives who live according to a different set of values or a different worldview? Are we willing to follow Jesus in his radical welcome of those on the margins of our society? Jesus said we will all be accountable one day for how we treated those who the world sees as worthless. Describing this final separation of "sheep and goats," he said, *"Then the King will say to those on his right, 'Come, you who are blessed by my Father, inherit the kingdom prepared for you from the foundation of the world. For I was hungry and you gave me food, I was thirsty and you gave me drink, I was a stranger and you welcomed me, I was naked and you clothed me, I was sick and you visited me, I was in prison and you came to me.' Then the righteous will answer him, saying, 'Lord, when did we see you hungry and feed you, or thirsty and give you drink? And when did we see you a stranger and welcome you, or naked and clothe you? And when did we see you sick or in prison and visit you?' And the King will answer them, Truly, I say to you, as you did it to one of the least of these my brothers, you did it to me.'"* (Matthew 25:34-40)

A NEW HUMANITY

Ever since the Tower of Babel, human beings have been confused and divided by their differences. The enmity between Cain and Abel has been perpetuated down through the centuries, to which our history of endless wars and generations of senseless violence bear tragic witness. However, Jesus came to change all of that. He demonstrated a completely different way to understand and treat one another. He showed us a new way to be human in which we see one another as brothers and sisters and treat each other as members of the same family. No longer are those who are different to be treated as hated enemies, but as fellow children of God whom we love. (Matthew 5:43-48)

This radical welcome was continued by the earliest followers of Jesus. Imitating the example set by their Rabbi, the early church was a spiritual family where everyone was welcomed. The first churches that met in extended family homes were revolutionary communities composed of men and women, young and old, Jews and Gentiles, rich and poor, powerful and slaves, the religious and outcasts. People of different races worshiped side by side. Women were recognized as leaders, and slaves were given equal status to their masters. The unity and love shared between people of such divergent backgrounds was unlike anything anyone had ever seen before. (Acts 4:23-37; 11:19-26; Romans 16:1-16)

The Apostle Paul, who was part of forming many of these diverse spiritual families, wrote to the followers of Jesus in the cosmopolitan city of Ephesus and explained it was Jesus who overcame their differences and made them one by his self-giving love, *"For he himself is our peace, who has made us both one and has broken down in his flesh the dividing wall of hostility by abolishing the law of commandments expressed in ordinances, that he might create in himself one new man in place of the two, so making peace, and might reconcile us both to God in one body through the cross, thereby killing the hostility."* (Ephesians 2:14-16) Through Jesus God is recreating humanity according to his original intent as a diverse people united in one human family called to bless all the families of the earth. This is one of the most revolutionary and overlooked outcomes of Jesus' life, death, and resurrection.

It didn't take long before the old prejudices and hierarchies started to creep back into the ancient church. As the years went by gradually women began to be relegated once again to second-class status. Slaves were subjugated to their masters, and the rich were given partiality over the poor. Church leadership became tied to social class, and religious categories of "clean" and "unclean" were reinstated. These divisions and prejudices continue in the church today, but this is not the way of Jesus. The Holy Spirit continues to work in the hearts of God's people, calling us back to a better way, a new way to be truly human, where every person on the planet is recognized as a priceless child of God created in his good image and loved unconditionally. By restoring the church as the family of God, we can recover this radical welcome and reclaim our true identity as brothers and sisters in Christ.

A few years ago, Pam and I moved into a new home in a new neighborhood, and we immediately began to reach out to our neighbors and invite them into our extended spiritual family. The first morning I met the neighbors who lived next door. On the one side lived a three-generation family who came from Mexico originally and spoke Spanish in their home. On the other side lived two young gay men who were preparing to get married. Right away we were confronted with the question of whether we would let cultural differences or differences of lifestyle keep us from welcoming them. It was clear that Jesus would welcome them, and so did we. As we shared meals together and got to know each other, we found both of these families were ready to serve us at least as much as we were seeking to serve them. The result has been the development of strong friendships and many opportunities to share the love of God and the way of Jesus in word and deed.

As we continue to learn what it means to follow Jesus and be formed in his image, we will increasingly fulfill that vision which Paul described to the Galatians when he wrote, *"For as many of you as were baptized into Christ have put on Christ. There is neither Jew nor Greek, there is neither slave nor free, there is no male and female, for you are all one in Christ Jesus."* (Galatians 3:27-28) As we learn to live in this kind of Jesus-shaped family where all are welcome, we will start to see heaven coming to earth. This doesn't mean we compromise our values or hide what we believe. It does mean that we show the same grace to others that God has shown to us.

The apostle John described the powerful vision Jesus gave him of what God's family looks like in heaven when he wrote, *After this I looked, and behold, a great multitude that no one could number, from every nation, from all tribes and peoples and languages, standing before the throne and before the Lamb, clothed in white robes, with palm branches in their hands, and crying out with a loud voice, "Salvation belongs to our God who sits on the throne, and to the Lamb!" And all the angels were standing around the throne and around the elders and the four living creatures, and they fell on their faces before the throne and worshiped God, saying, "Amen! Blessing and glory and wisdom and thanksgiving and honor and power and might be to our God forever and ever! Amen."* (Revelation 7:9-12)

REFLECT AND DISCUSS

Read Mark 2:13-17

1. Are there unconscious ways I tend to categorize the people I encounter as "good" or "bad," "clean" or "unclean"?

2. Who are the people who are different than me that God is calling me to welcome into my home and life?

3. How would my life change if I began to see every person as a potential brother or sister?

4. How can I build a spiritual family where everyone is welcome regardless of their background?

5. God, what are you saying to me and what step of faith do you want me to take in response?

CHAPTER SEVEN

INTO THE KINGDOM

ENTERING THE STORY

"Daphne, go ask the neighbors if they have any olives we can borrow. We are running short." As his wife headed next door, Philip set out baskets of bread and motioned for his daughter Iris to bring out another platter of grilled fish. *I want everything to be perfect for the Rabbi!* Philip pulled a towel from his belt to wipe his forehead. Jesus was talking with a Pharisee named Judah who was reclining at the table with Jesus and the other disciples. Just then the door to the courtyard opened, and in walked two of Bethsaida's local tax collectors. Matthew rose to greet them warmly, offering a kiss on each cheek. "I am so glad you could come and meet the Master!" Matthew said as he offered them a cushion at the low u-shaped table Philip had set up for the occasion. Joanna was at the far end of the table talking with two women who were obviously wealthy like her, based on the look of their jewelry. Sitting next to them was a woman known in town as a prostitute.

Philip could see Nahum, a disciple of the Pharisee Judah, fidgeting in his seat. He was obviously and increasingly uncomfortable as he realized who was on the guest list for the evening. Nahum leaned over and whispered in his rabbi's ear, while the Pharisee nodded knowingly. Judah leaned forward and looked straight at Jesus. "What is the meaning of this? You know we can't share table fellowship with these people." Jesus smiled and took a breath. "What 'people' are you talking about, rabbi?" he said, clenching his jaw. "You know who I mean!" Judah retorted. "Tax collectors and sinners. We can't eat with them! How could you put us in this position?" Jesus turned his attention to the whole table and called for everyone's attention. "Do you want to know what the Kingdom of God is like, Judah?"

Simon motioned to the others. "Shhh! Quiet! The Rabbi is going to tell another story." Earlier he had told them stories about a shepherd searching for a single lost sheep and a woman searching for a single lost coin. Now everyone stared at Jesus as he continued. "There was a man who had two sons. And the younger of them said to his father, 'Father, give me the share of property that is coming to me.' And he divided his property between them." There was a quiet gasp at the table. By now Philip was seated at the end of the table, just to the right of Jesus. *What father in his right mind would give his inheritance away before he had died? What kind of greedy son would dishonor his father so disgracefully by wishing his father dead!* Philip looked as shocked as everyone else at the table, but Jesus seemed not to notice their reactions.

He went on to describe how this dishonorable son took half his father's estate, went off to a foreign land, and squandered it all in reckless and morally questionable living. Philip squirmed uncomfortably. *Imagine watching the fruit of a lifetime of hard work evaporate overnight.* Jesus told them a famine hit that land and the younger son became so desperate he took a job feeding unclean pigs. The son was in such poverty he found himself jealous of the pigs for the disgusting slop he was feeding them. Laughter rippled through the group. Philip smiled. *The irony of it. Jealous of an unclean pig! He got what he deserved.* Jesus continued, "But when he came to himself, he said, 'How many of my father's hired servants have more than enough bread, but I perish here with hunger! I will arise and go to my father, and I will say to him, "Father, I have sinned against heaven and before you. I am no longer worthy to be called your son. Treat me as one of your hired servants."'"

By now everyone was on the edge of their seat, waiting to hear what would happen next. As the son approached his home, the father saw him and began to run through the village, past all the neighbors before whom the son had made him a laughingstock. Philip could practically feel the father's embarrassment. *How shameful! Why would he publicly run to this son who made such a mockery of him?*

They were all bracing themselves for the father's vengeful rebuke of his wayward son. But to everyone's surprise, instead of hitting him, the father embraced his son with compassion and smothered him with kisses. As the son began his rehearsed apology speech, the father interrupted and shouted, "'Quickly bring the best robe, and put it on him, and put a ring on his hand and shoes on his feet. And bring the fattened calf and kill it and let us eat and celebrate. For this my son was dead, and is alive again; he was lost, and is found.' And they began to celebrate." All of those listening to Jesus sat there in stunned silence. This was the last thing any of them expected the father to do! Philip could feel his face flushing with emotion and bit his lip. He thought he could see a tear running down Joanna's cheek. But Judah the Pharisee's eyes were flashing with anger.

After letting the deafening silence hang for a few more heartbeats, Jesus continued. He looked straight at Judah as he described the reaction of the older son who had continued faithfully working the fields of his father's farm. When the older son came in from the field, the elder son heard the sounds of celebration and asked one of the servants what was going on. When he learned what his father had done, he was outraged and refused to join the party. His father came out to him and begged him to join the party, "But he answered his father, 'Look, these many years I have served you, and I never disobeyed your command, yet you never gave me a young goat, that I might celebrate with my friends. But when this son of yours came, who has devoured your property with prostitutes, you killed the fattened calf for him!' And he said to him, 'Son, you are always with me, and all that is mine is yours. It was fitting to celebrate and be glad, for this your brother was dead, and is alive; he was lost, and is found.'"

At that moment you could have heard a pin drop, as if everyone in the house was holding their breath. Abruptly standing up, Judah the Pharisee lifted his nose, drew back his eyebrows and scoffed, "This man has no idea what he is talking about!" Jesus smiled broadly and said, "The Law and the Prophets prepared the way until John; now the good news of the kingdom of God is preached, and everyone is heartily welcomed into it." Judah turned to his disciple and said, "Come, Nahum, this is no place for righteous men!" The two men stormed out while the rest of the guests eagerly asked Jesus to tell them another story.[9]

---

[9] Based on Luke 15:1-32

JESUS THE RABBI

Rabbi is the Hebrew word for "teacher" and was both a title of respect and a recognition of authority in the first century. The authority of any given rabbi was derived from their study of the Law and their application of the rulings of teachers who had come before them. Rabbis are often referred to in the Gospels as "the scribes and Pharisees." They had advanced through the educational system and been discipled by a recognized rabbi. Rabbis were not in charge of the synagogues but were invited by the synagogue rulers to teach the Law at the Sabbath services and hired to teach the children there during the week. Jesus recognized the importance of the rabbinical role when he *said to the crowds and to his disciples, "The scribes and the Pharisees sit on Moses' seat, so do and observe whatever they tell you..."* (Matthew 23:1-3)

But Jesus was also highly critical of the established rabbis, not so much because of their theology but because of their blatant hypocrisy and spiritual pride. Unlike Jesus, many rabbis did not practice what they preached and elevated themselves above everyday people. He went on to say, *"The scribes and the Pharisees sit on Moses' seat, so do and observe whatever they tell you, but not the works they do. For they preach, but do not practice. They tie up heavy burdens, hard to bear, and lay them on people's shoulders, but they themselves are not willing to move them with their finger. They do all their deeds to be seen by others. For they make their phylacteries broad and their fringes long, and they love the place of honor at feasts and the best seats in the synagogues and greetings in the marketplaces and being called rabbi by others."* (Matthew 23:2-7)

The problem Jesus had with the Pharisees was not so much the information they taught, but more the example they set. They didn't even follow their own teachings! As we noted in Chapter 2, Jesus had not received the formal training of a rabbi but was almost immediately recognized as such when he launched his public mission. This was based on the unprecedented authority with which he taught and the indisputable power of his miracles. Instead of appealing to the legal rulings of earlier rabbis, Jesus spoke directly on behalf of his heavenly Father as God's representative on earth. And he backed up his teaching about the Kingdom of God by demonstrating that Kingdom in his powerful actions and his generous way of life. Jesus offered both incredible insight through his words and an incomparable example in his actions.

Jesus' teaching ministry began in the synagogues because leaders in various towns invited him to teach there on the Sabbath. His reputation grew quickly as people recounted the unusual authority of his words and power of his actions. Soon the crowds that came to hear him couldn't fit in the synagogue buildings anymore. Even the narrow constraints of the towns were too restrictive. Jesus tried to limit his fame by asking people he healed not to tell others about it. When he told a leper he had healed not to tell anyone except the priest at the Temple, the former leper *"went out and began to talk freely about it, and to spread the news, so that Jesus could no longer openly enter a town, but was out in desolate places, and people were coming to him from every quarter."* (Mark 1:45)

From this point on, most of Jesus' Galilean teaching ministry took place in the open countryside outside of the towns and villages. In Chapter 5 we saw how Jesus was teaching by the shore of the Sea of Galilee and became overwhelmed by the crowd, so he asked Simon to row him out from the shore to teach the crowds from the fishing boat. There is a small cove on the northern shore of the Sea of Galilee just west of Capernaum where the hillside slopes up from the beach to form a natural amphitheater. It is called "Sower's Cove," because it is likely this is the place where Jesus taught the parable of the Sower and the Seed from Simon's boat. (Luke 5:1-3) Tests conducted there using decibel meters have demonstrated a crowd of more than 5,000 people seated on the hillsides around that cove could hear someone teaching from a boat in the water.

Sower's Cove, Possible Location of Jesus Teaching from Simon's Boat

Another example of Jesus teaching the crowds on the open hillsides is one of his most famous teachings from Matthew 5-7, normally referred to as The Sermon on the Mount. We are told Jesus *went up on the mountain, and when he sat down, his disciples came to him.* (Matthew 5:1) Ancient tradition identifies this *"mountain"* as the hillside that slopes up north and west of Capernaum, overlooking the Sea of Galilee. Today there is a beautiful church that stands there called The Church of the Beatitudes, named after the unexpected description of the Kingdom of God with which Jesus opens the Sermon on the Mount. We don't know the exact spot where Jesus gave this sermon, but the natural beauty of this hillside certainly reflects a setting where Jesus pointed out *the birds of the air* and *the lilies of the field* to illustrate his teaching. (Matthew 6:26, 28)

Church of the Beatitudes, Traditional Location of the
Sermon on the Mount

As we have seen, Jesus taught in the courtyard house of Simon and Andrew when he gathered with his spiritual family, or in other homes where Jesus was welcomed. Jesus invited himself into the home of Zacchaeus the chief tax collector of Jericho, and that became a powerful teaching moment. (Luke 19:1-10) Much of Jesus' teaching took place as he was traveling with his disciples from place to place, which allowed him to use the people and places they encountered along the way as illustrations of his teaching. (Mark 10:17-51) Walking was the normal mode of travel, and it was typical for rabbis to take advantage of that time by teaching their disciples as they walked along. This is reflected in the ancient rabbinical blessing, "May you follow your rabbi, drink in his words, and be covered by his dust." It is easy to imagine the disciples following Jesus along the dusty roads of Galilee, listening to their rabbi, and being coated in the fine dust kicked up by his feet! Jesus was a regular participant in the great religious festivals that took place in Jerusalem. There he was able to use the enormous courtyards King Herod had built around the Temple to teach large crowds that gathered for the high holy days. During the final Passover Jesus spent in Jerusalem we are told *he was teaching daily in the temple.* (Luke 19:47) Herod's Temple courts were surrounded by large colonnades which supported a high roof. These porticoes provided shade in the summer and protection from wind and rain in the winter, so it is no surprise that this is where people often gathered to hear the teaching of famous rabbis. The stone wall behind and the solid roof overhead projected the teacher's voice so many people could hear. John recounts how during the Feast of the Dedication Jesus was teaching the crowds while *walking in the temple, in the colonnade of Solomon,* the portico that ran north and south along the eastern edge of the Temple. (John 10:47) Although the Romans destroyed those colonnades in AD 70, along with the Temple and all its associated buildings, the platform on which they were built still remains as the Temple Mount. When we walk in the massive courts of the Temple Mount today, we are seeing firsthand the context of Jesus' teaching ministry in Jerusalem.

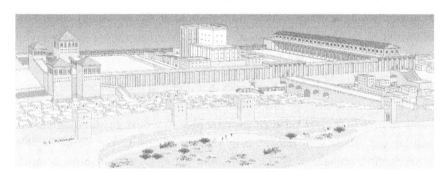

Temple Mount in Jerusalem with Solomon's Colonnade in the Distance

WHEN HEAVEN TOUCHES EARTH

Jesus launched his public teaching ministry by declaring, *"The time is fulfilled, and the kingdom of God is at hand; repent and believe in the gospel."* (Mark 1:15; cf. Matthew 4:17) The Kingdom of God is undeniably the central theme of Jesus' teaching. Unfortunately, it is also the most misunderstood aspect of his teaching. The Kingdom of God is not a geographical place or a doctrinal concept, but a dynamic reality. This Greek phrase can also be translated "the reign of God." Jesus defined this term when he taught the disciples to pray, *"Your kingdom come, your will be done, on earth as it is in heaven."* (Matthew 6:10) God's Kingdom is breaking into the kingdoms of this world when God's will is done here on earth in the same way it is continually being done in heaven. This is incredibly good news, because God's will always produces the greatest good. The reality of heaven is so much better than the reality of a broken earth. The Kingdom of God is what happens when heaven touches earth.

The Beatitudes, which open Jesus' Sermon on the Mount, are eight beautifully constructed verses of a powerful poem describing what life is like when we are living in the Kingdom of God. Each of its eight stanzas begin with the phrase *"Blessed are the…"* which denotes the joyful state produced by living in the fullness of God's goodness. But Jesus went on to say this state of blessing comes to the most unexpected people; *"the poor in spirit… those who mourn… the meek… those who hunger and thirst… the merciful… the pure in heart… the peacemakers… those who are persecuted."* The practical among us will immediately point out these kinds of experiences are not counted as blessings in the world we know. But we discover from the opening and closing beatitudes Jesus was not describing how things work in the kingdoms of this world, but rather how life works in *"the kingdom of heaven,"* which is Matthew's more Jewish way of translating *"the kingdom of God."* (Matthew 5:1-10)

Jesus shows us through these Beatitudes that things in the Kingdom of Heaven operate differently than in this earthly realm. In God's Kingdom those who know they can't manage on their own are able to receive the blessing God is pouring out. Those who feel the pain and loss of this broken world are able to receive the embrace of God's Spirit, who points us to something so much better. Those who do not insist on always getting their own way somehow end up receiving everything they hoped for and more. Those who ache for what is right find the deep satisfaction of healthy and loving relationships. Those who choose not to pass judgement even when they have the right to do so experience forgiveness themselves. Those whose deepest desire is to do God's will see him the most clearly. Those who are able to overcome division and bring people together experience what it means to be part of God's family. Those who suffer unjustly for doing the right things will ultimately be vindicated by God's righteous reign.

Jesus' Kingdom teaching is about learning to live in a completely different way than we are used to operating in this broken earthly realm. That's what he did. What made Jesus so unique was that he carried out his Father's will on earth as it is done in heaven. He shocked everyone by touching lepers and welcoming "sinners" and calling tax collectors and confronting self-righteous hypocrites because he was operating according to the values of a different reality, the reality of the Kingdom of God. That's why he healed the sick, delivered the demonized, made the lame to walk and the blind to see. He announced this new reality when he read Isaiah 61 in the synagogue of Nazareth, proclaiming good news to the poor, liberty to the captives, recovering of sight to the blind, and the release to those who were oppressed, and then said, *"Today this Scripture has been fulfilled in your hearing."* (Luke 4:13-21) He was making the startling declaration that this new Kingdom reality of heaven has already begun breaking into the darkness of our broken world.

This vision of the Kingdom of God was the guiding principle of Jesus' life. He simply did on earth what he saw his Father doing in heaven. Because Jesus' teaching and actions were so unconventional, the religious leaders often accused him of being a lawbreaker. (Matthew 12:1-2) Because he did not follow the specific traditions of the elders and the rabbinical interpretations of the law, he was branded *"a sinner."* (John 9:24) Jesus' practice of healing people on the Sabbath repeatedly caused the religious leaders to accuse him of breaking the Law and ultimately led them to plot his death. Jesus replied to their accusations by explaining, *"Truly, truly, I say to you, the Son can do nothing of his own accord, but only what he sees the Father doing. For whatever the Father does, that the Son does likewise."* (John 5:16-19) This is the essence of living according to the Kingdom of God.

Jesus was crystal clear that he was not a lawbreaker, but quite the opposite. How could doing God's will on earth contradict God's will expressed in the Law? Actually, Jesus was intensifying the moral power of the Law by pointing us beyond human religion and back to the Father's original intention in creation. In the Sermon on the Mount Jesus said, *"Do not think that I have come to abolish the Law or the Prophets; I have not come to abolish them but to fulfill them. For truly, I say to you, until heaven and earth pass away, not an iota, not a dot, will pass from the Law until all is accomplished."* (Matthew 5:17-18)

He then went on to reinterpret various Old Testament laws using the comparison formula, *"You have heard it said... but I say to you."* Jesus demonstrated that the law against murder is ultimately about affirming or denying a person's value. He showed that the law against adultery is ultimately about the way we look at someone of the opposite sex. He pointed out that a man arbitrarily divorcing his wife in order to control or replace her is ultimately a violation of the very covenant of marriage itself. He explained that our calling is not only to love those who are like us and near to us, but also to love those who are different than us and even those who are against us. Jesus was fulfilling the Law by showing us its meaning more completely. As if this were not challenging enough, he summed up his teaching by saying, *"You therefore must be perfect, as your heavenly Father is perfect."* (Matthew 5:21-48)

In one sense Matthew portrayed Jesus as the new Moses whom God foretold would come to represent him and speak his words. (Deuteronomy 18:18) But it would be a mistake to assume that, by intensifying the moral demand of the Law, Jesus claimed obedience to the Law as the basis of his new Covenant. Quite to the contrary, Jesus pointed us to a better way to relate to God. He fulfilled what the prophet Jeremiah had promised, *"Behold, the days are coming, declares the Lord, when I will make a new covenant with the house of Israel and the house of Judah, not like the covenant that I made with their fathers on the day when I took them by the hand to bring them out of the land of Egypt, my covenant that they broke, though I was their husband, declares the Lord. For this is the covenant that I will make with the house of Israel after those days, declares the Lord: I will put my law within them, and I will write it on their hearts. And I will be their God, and they shall be my people. And no longer shall each one teach his neighbor and each his brother, saying, 'Know the Lord,' for they shall all know me, from the least of them to the greatest, declares the Lord. For I will forgive their iniquity, and I will remember their sin no more."* (Jeremiah 31:31-34)

The reason Jesus was so critical of the Pharisees and other rabbinical teachers of his time is that they had externalized the Law into a set of religious rules and rituals categorizing people into good or bad, right or wrong, insiders or outsiders. Jesus established a new kind of Covenant between God and his people. This is not a legal code carved into stone tablets nor is it an externalized set of rules enforced by a religious system. The New Covenant is an internal reality written on the hearts and minds of people. It establishes a familial relationship between us and our heavenly Father in which we come to *"know the Lord."* It establishes relationships between us as brothers and sisters who are part of the same family because we share the same Father. The starting point of these relationships is forgiveness, not condemnation. Their currency is grace, not self-righteousness. Perfection does not come from legalistic effort, but as a freely given gift. That is why Jesus was so free to welcome people of every background into his spiritual family with open arms. He wasn't worried about the legal categories of good and bad; he was demonstrating that all of us are children of God who are invited into our Father's Kingdom because it is a family and a kingdom defined by grace and truth. (John 1:14)

This does not mean Jesus denied the truth of the Law nor condoned sin. He said, *Therefore whoever relaxes one of the least of these commandments and teaches others to do the same will be called least in the kingdom of heaven, but whoever does them and teaches them will be called great in the kingdom of heaven. For I tell you, unless your righteousness exceeds that of the scribes and Pharisees, you will never enter the kingdom of heaven.* (Matthew 5:19-20) The Kingdom Jesus proclaimed is not *less* righteous than the fanatical legalism of the Pharisees; it is *more* righteous because it produces a better kind of righteousness! Slavish religious legalism represents the vain attempt of human effort to produce something that can only come from the One who is the source of life. Jesus invites us into a Kingdom that produces a righteousness exceeding the external righteousness of religious obligation, because it is the result of God's Spirit transforming us from the inside out.

Jesus went on in the Sermon on the Mount to describe this new kind of righteousness as fruit produced by a tree, *"Are grapes gathered from thornbushes, or figs from thistles? So, every healthy tree bears good fruit, but the diseased tree bears bad fruit."* (Matthew 7:16) Religious legalism is a diseased tree that cannot help but produce diseased fruit. Ever since the fall of Adam, human effort has only brought forth thorns and thistles. The Kingdom of God is an invitation into a new kind of Covenant relationship with God that establishes healthy trees who produce good fruit which reproduces to multiply the blessing. It is not that the Law has been abrogated; it is just that God has now brought something even better than the old covenant of the Law—the

New Covenant of grace. This is what Jesus was trying to explain to the Pharisees who condemned him for healing on the Sabbath when he said, *"I tell you, something greater than the temple is here. And if you had known what this means, I desire mercy, and not sacrifice,' you would not have condemned the guiltless."* (Matthew 12:6-7)

Jesus explained it to the disciples of John the Baptist this way: *"No one puts a piece of unshrunk cloth on an old garment, for the patch tears away from the garment, and a worse tear is made. Neither is new wine put into old wineskins. If it is, the skins burst and the wine is spilled and the skins are destroyed. But new wine is put into fresh wineskins, and so both are preserved."* (Matthew 9:16-17) Newly squeezed grape juice was often stored in leather bags made of new goatskins. As the wine fermented and expanded, the fresh leather was able to accommodate it by stretching. But if new wine was put into old stretched out wineskins, they simply could not contain the expansion and would burst. The old stretched out religious systems of the scribes and Pharisees could not accommodate the new Covenant. Jesus' teaching of the Kingdom is an invitation to receive this new wine which calls for a whole new way of living and relating to God and each other.

Jesus' teaching had such a revolutionary impact because it was an invitation into a whole new way of living in right relationship with God that empowered people to do God's will on earth as it is in heaven. It is tempting for people to hear the teaching of Jesus as a new set of religious rules given by a new Moses and then feel the burden of trying to live up to perceived expectations. That is a profound misunderstanding of Jesus' teaching; that is bad news that leads to death. Instead, Jesus called his followers to *"repent and believe."* (Mark 1:15) *"Repent"* means to listen to what God is saying and let him change your perspective. *"Believe"* means to respond to that Word by exercising the faith it produces in us. The reason Jesus' teaching of the Kingdom of God was such Good News to people is that it offers us a new wineskin in which we can receive the new wine of an empowering grace that leads us to live according to the life-giving truth. Jesus offers us a New Covenant that does not contradict the Old Covenant, but it is so much better because it empowers us to do God's will on earth as it is done in heaven. This is what is means to live in the Kingdom of God!

STORIES OF THE KINGDOM

Jesus did not describe the Kingdom of God in abstract terms. He demonstrated it by his example, and he told stories illustrating life in the Kingdom. Jesus' language was very evocative and visual. He often used similes, comparing his hearers to vivid images, *"Behold, I am sending you out as sheep in the midst of wolves, so be wise as serpents and innocent as doves."* (Matthew 10:16) He created provocative pictures like, *"do not throw your pearls before pigs"* and *"It is easier for a camel to go through the eye of a needle."* (Matthew 7:6, 19:24) He used memorable aphorisms to convey his points like, *"Why do you see the speck that is in your brother's eye, but do not notice the log that is in your own eye?"* (Matthew 7:3) Sometimes Jesus used the physical people and places around him as living illustrations of the Kingdom, including birds, flowers, fig trees, little children, and generous widows. But above all Jesus told powerful parables which served as narrative pictures of the Kingdom of God.

A parable is a short story rooted in real life that gives insight and offers wisdom. They are effective tools of communication because they are vivid, memorable, and transferable. Anyone can hear a parable, be impacted by it, and pass it on to someone else. Matthew expressed the importance of parables in Jesus' teaching somewhat hyperbolically when he wrote, *"All these things Jesus said to the crowds in parables; indeed, he said nothing to them without a parable."* (Matthew 13:34) Many rabbis before and after Jesus told parables, but Jesus' parables were markedly different. The point of a typical parable was obvious and often moralistic, kind of like Aesop's Fables. By contrast, Jesus' parables challenged the status quo by featuring unexpected twists and questionable characters. No one expected the Samaritan to be the hero who saved the beaten traveler when there was a priest and a Levite in the story! (Luke 10:25-37) How could a rich man turn out to be a fool? (Luke 12:13-21) Why would street people be invited to the king's wedding reception? (Matthew 22:1-14)

Sometimes Jesus' parables seemed to contradict established moral assumptions. In his parable of the shrewd steward, an incompetent manager ends up being praised even though he uses his position to cheat his boss for his own benefit. (Luke 16:1-13) More often Jesus' parables were subtle and multifaceted, which left some people scratching their heads. Sometimes the disciples asked Jesus to explain his parables when they were alone with him, and Jesus unpacked their meaning. Once the disciples asked him, *"Why do you speak to them in parables?" And he answered them, "To you it has been given to know the secrets of the kingdom of heaven, but to them it has not been given. For to the one who has, more will be given, and he will have an abundance, but from the one who has not, even what he has will be taken away. This is why I speak to them in parables, because seeing they do not see, and hearing they do not hear, nor do they understand."* (Matthew 13:10-13)

Even this answer is hard to understand, isn't it? At first glance it might seem Jesus is trying to keep his teaching hidden from the crowds, but on closer examination we can see his parables were designed to challenge people to go deeper by wrestling with the truth and meaning of the Kingdom of God in their lives, not to systematize it into a legalistic doctrine. Jesus wanted people to ponder what the treasure hidden in a field was for them and to consider what it would mean for them to sell everything and buy the field. (Matthew 13:44) He wanted people to reflect on the impossibly large debt they had been forgiven and consider how that could change their attitude toward those who were indebted to them. (Luke 7:41-43) He wanted them to learn how to persevere in prayer by considering the persistent neighbor who wouldn't give up knocking until he got what he needed. (Luke 11:5-8)

The most important thing about Jesus' parables is that they show us what the Kingdom of God looks like in real life. In the Kingdom of God, everyone gets paid the same wage no matter how many hours in the day they worked. (Matthew 20:1-6) In the Kingdom of God, even a single lost sheep is worthy of the shepherd risking it all to find her and return her to the flock. (Luke 15:4-6) In the Kingdom of God, the repentant prayers of a humble tax collector are more pleasing to the ear of God than the pious petitions of the religiously self-righteous. (Luke 18:9-14) In the Kingdom of God, every kind of person is offered the seed of God's Word, but it only takes root and multiplies in the good soil of a receptive and responsive heart. (Mark 4:3-9) In the Kingdom of God, the wise man whose house withstands the storms is the one who not only hears the words of Jesus but also does them. (Matthew 7:24-27) In the Kingdom of God, the Father runs to embrace his rebellious children who shame him by squandering what he has given them and then celebrates their return by throwing a lavish party. (Luke 15:11-32)

When we read or hear the parables of Jesus, we should not immediately assume we understand what they mean. We are meant to ponder them deeply and wrestle with their implications for our lives. This includes discussing them with others and listening for what God might be saying to us through these deceptively simple stories. This is why disciples need an extended spiritual family living on mission together! Above all, Jesus' parables are meant to prompt us into action. As Jesus said, it is those who both hear his words and do them whose house will endure the inevitable storms of life. (Matthew 7:24-27) In the end, the parables are an invitation to take another step of faith on the journey of following Jesus into the Kingdom where God's will is being done here on earth as it is in heaven.

Jesus was clear about the absolute centrality and priority of God's Kingdom in our lives. After describing all the things that cause anxiety and fear in our hearts, all the things we look to for security and fulfilment, Jesus said, *"For the Gentiles seek after all these things, and your heavenly Father knows that you need them all. But seek first the kingdom of God and his righteousness, and all these things will be added to you."* (Matthew 7:32-33) Jesus has shown us the Kingdom in his life and described the Kingdom in his teaching. By following Jesus we learn to live in that Kingdom. This is the journey that leads us to everything we need and everything we hope for. As Jesus said, *"Fear not, little flock, for it is your Father's good pleasure to give you the kingdom."* (Luke 12:32) If we have the Kingdom, we have everything!

Many of us who believe in Jesus have focused so much on the message of salvation through his death and resurrection that we have neglected the rich teaching Jesus has given us, which is meant to shape our way of life on this earth. When we do focus on Jesus' teaching, we sometimes inadvertently turn it into another list of religious rules and regulations which we then try to obey by our own strength and wisdom. It is time for those who follow Jesus to embrace his vision of God's Kingdom, digging into his teaching to flesh out what it means for us to live according to that Kingdom today, and relying on his Spirit to lead us into this new way of life.

When Jesus called people to follow him, he said, *"The time is fulfilled, and the kingdom of God is at hand; repent and believe in the gospel."* (Mark 1:15) We discover a new life in the Kingdom when we *repent* by listening for Jesus' voice speaking to us through his teaching and *believe* by exercising the faith Jesus' words produce in our hearts. This happens as we ponder Jesus' Kingdom teaching, wrestle with his parables, and join in deep conversation with others who are helping us discern what God is saying and what he wants us to do. As we recognize what God is saying, the Spirit produces in us the faith we need to respond. This is the heart of discipleship, hearing the voice of our Shepherd and following his example one step of faith at a time.

Once when Jesus was teaching in the Temple courts during the Jewish festival of Tabernacles, he said to those who believed in him, *"If you abide in my word, you are truly my disciples, and you will know the truth, and the truth will set you free."* (John 8:31-32) Jesus' teaching is designed to set captives free. You can spend a lifetime studying his teaching and still not plumb its depths. But as you take time each day to read, reflect, discuss, and respond to his Word, Jesus will be speaking to you, the Holy Spirit will be planting faith in your heart, and the Father will show you the next step to take on your journey. This is the way of discipleship. This is the truth that sets you free. This is the life you were meant to live.

REFLECT AND DISCUSS
Read Matthew 5:1-12

1. How can I make seeking the Kingdom of God the central focus of my life?

2. How can I learn more about how things work in the Kingdom of God?

3. What does it mean for me to wrestle with the implications of Jesus' parables in my life?

4. What do I need to become not only a hearer, but also a doer of Jesus' Word?

5. God, what are you saying to me and what step of faith do you want me to take in response?

CHAPTER EIGHT

A KINGDOM OF POWER

SET FREE

As usual Mary lay staring at the ceiling. Sleep seemed to elude her every night. Moonlight streamed in from the window, illuminating the rich colors of the frescos on their bedroom walls. Her husband Boaz mumbled something incoherent and rolled away from her in the bed. Mary took the opportunity to slip quietly from underneath the fine wool blankets and go to the window. She looked down into their paved courtyard below and took a deep breath. *I love these starry skies and cool spring nights.* Their house was built on the gentle slope rising up beneath the towering Cliffs of Arbel. From their upstairs room, she could see out across the rooftops of Magdala down to the huge stone wharf where moored fishing boats blended into the shimmering darkness of the lake. Mary sighed. *Life has been good to us, but...* She quickly pushed away the dark thoughts that filled her mind, like unconsciously brushing off a pesky bug.

Magdala was the leading city on the Sea of Galilee, at least for now. Herod Antipas was building a new capital named after his patron, Caesar Tiberias, just four miles to the south. Mary knew it would soon overshadow her beloved hometown but she still loved Magdala's bustling waterfront, Roman-style baths, and the beautiful painted synagogue where they prayed on the Sabbath. Magdala was famous for the *tarichos,* the delicious Kinneret sardines which were caught in the lake, dried in wooden towers, packed in salted barrels, and shipped all over the Roman Empire. These little fish had made her and Boaz quite rich and very comfortable. *Well, as rich as you can be when the tax collectors are constantly pounding on your door!*

Mary of Magdala knew she had much to be thankful for, but a darkness still gnawed away at her soul. She had spent her whole life trying to forget what her father had done to her as a child, but every passing year the darkness inside her seemed to grow even darker. It was the curse of being "pretty," she supposed. By now she was used to turning away unwanted advances, but back then she didn't know how. She had tried everything to forget, even visiting the local fortune-teller and paying for her potions and spells, but it was like dark fingers had a hold on her and wouldn't let her go. Sometimes she took a sharp piece of broken pottery and cut the inside of her forearms in a vain attempt to muffle the pain in her soul. Even now she pictured how she could put an end to it all by jumping from the rooftop onto the hard stones below.

The sound of two men passing by on the street in front of the house brought her back to her senses. Her mind wandered to the news she had been hearing for weeks. They said a new rabbi from Nazareth was living in Capernaum and causing quite a stir. People who listened to him teach said he spoke with an authority they had never heard before. And it wasn't just his teaching; people said he touched lepers and they were made clean! He lifted lame beggars to their feet, and they walked! He spit on the eyes of the blind and they could see! Mary had heard of healers before, but they always seemed like charlatans, showmen who were greedy for her money and even for something more. But this sounded different. Mary decided it was time for her to go see this Jesus for herself.

After breakfast the next day, her slave girl came and passed on the news that Jesus was teaching outside of Capernaum. The sun was already climbing high in the sky, so Mary set out immediately on the Roman road to Capernaum to find the Nazarene. Her heart was racing, and she felt giddy inside. *I wonder if it is true that he can actually heal people.* She felt a dark shadow pass in front of her eyes but tried to ignore it as she had so many times before. Passing the second milestone, she rounded a bend and could see a crowd of people moving toward her, led by a man who was striking, not for his stature or physical appearance, but by the way he carried himself. She was sure it was none other than Jesus himself! She stopped and waited for them to reach her. As they drew near, she turned and joined the throng, ending up just a few steps behind the Rabbi. Excited voices surrounded her, and the people behind were pressing in, trying to get closer to Jesus. Trying not to feel claustrophobic, Mary's vigilance was heightened by the crush of people all around her. Then suddenly Jesus stopped in his tracks, and the crowd quickly bunched up around him as the ones behind bumped into those in front.

Looking around, Jesus said, "Who was it that touched me?" A chuckle rippled through the crowd as if he had told a joke. One of his disciples pointed out how senseless the question was when he said, "Master, the crowds surround you and are pressing in on you!" But Jesus said, "Someone touched me, for I perceive that power has gone out from me." Then there was a commotion as the crowd parted and a wretched woman collapsed at Jesus' feet. Mary remembered seeing her alongside the road when she was on her way. It was Veronica, a woman from Magdala with a continual menstruation, whom everyone avoided to prevent contracting ritual defilement, including her own family. Cringing, she cried, "It was me, Master. I was the one who touched you." The crowd gasped and immediately the murmurs started. *How could an unclean woman dare to touch a holy teacher?* Mary braced herself for the rebuke that was sure to come to this poor woman. But looking up at Jesus the woman continued in amazement, "And now I am healed!" Jesus took her by the hand, lifted her to her feet, looked into her eyes and said ever so gently, "Daughter, your faith has made you well; go in peace."

Mary felt tears welling up in her eyes, as astonishment shot through the crowd like a bolt of lightning. Before anyone could speak, a messenger arrived and addressed the man standing next to Jesus. It was then she realized the man was her next-door neighbor Jairus, one of the rulers of their synagogue. Mary remembered his 12-year-old daughter had been gravely ill with a fever for the past week. She couldn't hear what the messenger was saying, but she saw Jairus' knees buckle, and she didn't need to hear what had been said. More children died by the age of twelve than lived, so death was a painful reality they all had to face. Mary herself had lost two children who never reached the age of five. Then she heard Jesus' steady voice, "Do not fear; only believe, and she will be well." *What is he talking about? Can a dead child live again?*

Jesus and Jairus continued down the road toward Magdala with the crowd hot on their heels. Soon they were standing on her street in front of Jairus' spacious home, and they could hear the hired mourners praying and wailing inside in the courtyard. Jesus took three of his disciples and entered the house with Jairus, and soon the wailing stopped. Before long the mourners exited the house. "He is sending us home," one complained as she stomped off. The crowd started to disperse, and Mary was about to enter her own house, when Jairus stuck his head out of the door and motioned for her to come over. Drawing near, she could see wild joy on his tear-stained face. "You will never believe what just happened. I am not supposed to tell anyone, but he brought her back! She is alive!" He sobbed for joy and clasped Mary's hands so hard she thought they would break. "Now, the Sabbath will start soon, and the Rabbi cannot get back to Capernaum before sundown. We are full up with relatives. Can you and Boaz put Jesus and his disciples up for the night? I have convinced the Teacher to speak at the synagogue service tomorrow."

It took some skillful negotiation with Boaz and a lot of scurrying of the servants, but they prepared the guest room for Jesus and managed to find a place for each of his disciples to sleep as well. After sundown, the lamps in the courtyard were lit, Sabbath dinner was served, and the whole extended family reclined around the table with Jesus in the place of honor to the left of Boaz and Mary. Their son Abimelech asked Jesus to tell them some stories, and soon everyone was mesmerized by tales of seeds growing in secret, nets gathering both clean and unclean fish, and new wineskins being used to hold new wine. Mary suddenly realized how late the hour had grown and that the Rabbi was tired, so she brought the meal to an end, sending everyone to their respective beds.

The next morning, after some bread, olive oil, and figs, they all walked to the nearby synagogue for Sabbath prayers and took their place on the mosaic tile floor. Mary felt a surge of joy as she saw Jairus' daughter in perfect health sitting with her family. Jesus smiled at her and tousled her hair as he took his seat beside Jairus. One of the rabbis began the prayers, "Hear, O Israel: The Lord our God, the Lord is one. You shall love the Lord your God with all your heart and with all your soul and with all your might." As the congregation joined in the prayers and singing, Mary felt the darkness welling up inside of her. Reflexively she pushed it back down. It happened again, and again she tried to push it down.

It was as if an epic wrestling match was going on inside of her, but she tried to look as if nothing was wrong.

By this time the synagogue attendant had pulled a scroll from the cabinet and handed it to Jesus. He unrolled it on the ornately carved scroll table, read the reading, returned the scroll, and sat down on the Moses seat to teach. Mary couldn't make out what Jesus was saying because it was taking all of her strength now to hold down the darkness welling up inside of her. She felt as if she had swallowed a large stone and it was forcing its way back up her windpipe, choking her.

Mary never really knew exactly what happened next, but she heard yelling and shouting, and before she knew it, she was lying flat on her back on the floor. She was aware of Jesus standing over her, although she couldn't hear what he was saying. And then it was as if a mist lifted and she could see everything in vivid color and super-fine detail. She was weeping, and Boaz was holding her in his strong arms. Suddenly she realized everyone was looking at her, but somehow, she didn't care. Her throat felt raw, but it was as if a thousand-pound weight had been lifted off her chest. *The darkness is gone! The light has come!*

That afternoon they were back at her house seated around the three-sided table eating the midday meal and Jesus was telling more stories. Mary couldn't stop smiling, so much that her cheeks were starting to ache! It was all she could do to keep from leaping up from her cushion and dancing around the room. It was as if she had died and been reborn into a whole new kind of life. She looked at Jesus and realized she would spend the rest of her life trying to show him how grateful she was.[10]

JESUS THE HEALER

Of the many extraordinary characteristics of Jesus, the consistent reports of his miraculous healings and powerful deliverance of hurting and demonized people stand out as the most singular and unique trait of this builder from Nazareth turned rabbi. Of course, some Old Testament prophets healed, such as Elijah who revived the widow's son in Zarephath. (1 Kings 17:17-24) His disciple Elisha healed Naaman the Syrian military commander of his leprosy. (2 Kings 5:1-14)

[10] Based on Mark 5:21-43 and Luke 8:1-3

While these were exceptional events in the lives of the great Hebrew Prophets, miraculous healings seemed to be almost commonplace events in the ministry of Jesus. There were reports of other Jewish healers active around the time of Jesus, but unlike the Gospels, which were written by eyewitnesses within decades of the events they recorded, these reports of healing were written centuries later based on historically questionable hearsay. One such reputed Jewish healer was Rabbi Hanina ben Dosa, who was said to pray for the sick and then predict who would get well and who would die. Of course, this is a far cry from Jesus' countless miraculous healings of people suffering from nearly every kind of malady and spiritual oppression.

Even the ancient Greco-Roman world had its stories of healers, such as Apollonius of Tyana, but again these events were recorded hundreds of years later by those who were not even alive at the time and seem historically doubtful. The regular healings Jesus performed were often witnessed by his enemies, who conceded as a matter of fact that they actually happened. Some scholars even conclude that the third-century healing stories of Apollonius were created in order to compete with Jesus at a time when the followers of Jesus were rapidly multiplying across the Roman Empire. More often, healing in the Greek and Roman world came through participation in religious rites that were the forerunner of modern medical procedures.

Greeks and Romans believed the god Asclepius was capable of offering miraculous cures, and his shrines built for this purpose were very popular. People suffering from various diseases or injuries came to the Ascleipion where they took a cleansing bath and received a special diet meant to purge them of toxins and negative emotions. Then they made a financial offering, received a hallucinogenic drink, and fell asleep in a dark room or cave. They believed Asclepius would come to them in their drug-induced dreams and offer a cure. Afterward the patient told their dream to the priests, who interpreted them and administered the cure, often consisting of natural herbal remedies. Sometimes the priests performed surgeries on the patients while they were drugged and sleeping. These proto-medical treatments are categorically different from the healing miracles Jesus performed on a regular basis.

When Jesus first announced the Kingdom of God in Nazareth, he read from Isaiah 61 which declares the Messiah will give sight to the blind, set the oppressed free, and preach good news to the poor. (Luke 4:17-19) As Jesus began to carry out his ministry, John the Baptist, who had been imprisoned by Herod Antipas, sent some of his disciples to ask Jesus if he was the long-awaited Messiah. Jesus replied, *"Go and tell John what you hear and see: the blind receive their sight and the lame walk, lepers are cleansed and the deaf hear, and the dead are raised up, and the poor have good news preached to them. And blessed is the one who is not offended by me."* (Matthew 11:4-6)

The consistent testimony of those who were actually with Jesus is that he gave sight to the blind, made the deaf hear, made the mute talk, made the lame walk, cleansed lepers, rebuked fevers, cured dropsy, straightened bent backs, stopped continual hemorrhaging, and even restored the ear of the High Priest's slave Malchus which Peter struck off with a sword while his Rabbi was being arrested! (Luke 22:49-51; John 18:10) Some of these maladies were cured in connection with spiritual oppression when Jesus delivered people from demonization or when he declared the forgiveness of their sins. (Matthew 9:1-8, 12:22) The most dramatic of Jesus' healings were when he brought those who had died back to life. The power of death is the most inescapable of all the realities of a broken world, and Jesus demonstrated a power even greater than death itself. The most irrefutable of these resuscitations came when Jesus called Lazarus out of his tomb in Bethany in front of a large crowd even after his dead body had lain there decaying for four days! (John 11:38-44)

JESUS THE DELIVERER

In addition to physical healing, Jesus also set people free from spiritual oppression. Some people who encountered Jesus manifested signs of demons who were acting and speaking through them. Often, these demons seemed to react to Jesus' authority and try to gain control of Jesus by naming him as "Son of God" or "the Holy One of God." (Luke 4:34; 8:28) In the Bible, demons are understood to be angelic beings who were thrown down to earth from heaven with Satan when they rebelled against God. (Isaiah 14:12; Revelation 12:7-9) The Bible does not give us many details about the devil or demons but demonstrates demons are a real and malign force of the unseen spiritual world. It was commonly recognized that these evil or "unclean" spirits could tempt, influence, and even force people to do evil. The Greek word often translated "demon-possessed" in the New Testament literally reads "demonized" and can refer to a range of demonic influence over a person. Jesus delivered Mary of Magdala from seven demons. (Luke 8:2)

A Wealthy Family Home in Magdala, Hometown of Mary Magdalene

Just as some were reputed healers in the ancient world, even more were self-styled exorcists. Both pagan and Jewish exorcists relied on complex rituals, incantations and spells to try and gain control of demonic spirits. They utilized secret potions and magical objects to try and eradicate these unclean demons. The exorcist often chanted these magical formulas, danced, threw dirt into the air, and carried out dramatic acts to the delight of the onlookers. Archaeologists have discovered and translated many thousands of first-century documents written on papyrus, some of which record these complex magical spells. The first-century Jewish historian Josephus describes an exorcism in which an exorcist named Eleazar used a magical ring to pull out a demon through the nostrils of a demonized man.

By contrast to these sensationalist methods, both Jesus' healings and exorcisms were remarkably simple affairs. Often when Jesus healed someone, he simply touched them, or they touched him and were made well. Sometimes he told the lame to stand, and they stood. Occasionally he applied his own saliva to blind eyes, and they saw. Other times he asked them to do something like stretch out their hand or go and wash in a pool, and they were made well. Sometimes Jesus directly rebuked the sickness, and it disappeared. When Jesus cast demons out, most often he simply commanded them to go, and they left. Other times he engaged in brief dialogue with the demons before binding and expelling them.

When he delivered a deeply depraved Gentile man who was horribly demonized, Jesus demanded to know the demon's name and then cast a legion into a herd of pigs who promptly committed suicide! (Mark 5:1-20)

It was not by esoteric rituals or secret incantations that Jesus healed and delivered; it was simply by faith. First of all, it was Jesus exercising faith in the authority given to him by the Father to do the King's will on earth as it is in heaven. Secondly, it was the faith of those who received healing. Sometimes people approached Jesus with faith that he could heal them, and he did. Others were filled with doubt, but Jesus' word to them planted seeds of faith in their hearts. When they exercised those seeds of faith, they were healed. Often after healing someone, Jesus affirmed the role of their faith in the healing. He said to the hemorrhaging woman, *"Daughter, your faith has made you well; go in peace, and be healed of your disease."* (Mark 5:34) Conversely, a lack of faith proved to be a hindrance to healing, such as when he tried to minister to the resistant people of Nazareth and Matthew records, *"he did not do many mighty works there, because of their unbelief."* (Matthew 13:58) In all these instances, faith in Jesus' authority to heal released God's power to heal and deliver.

Four things stand out about Jesus' healing and deliverance ministry. The first is that Jesus was not trying to attract attention or gain notoriety like many so-called first-century healers and exorcists seemed to do. Jesus even went so far as to tell those he healed and delivered not to tell anyone what he had done! The second is that Jesus did not use any particular technique or ritual to heal and deliver; in fact, it seems as if Jesus did it a little bit differently every time to make it clear he was not using some kind of magic formula. The third is that Jesus healed everyone who came to him for healing and never turned anyone away regardless of their background. The fourth is that exercising faith and authority was the key to healing and receiving healing by the power of God.

JESUS THE PROPHET

In addition to his healings and exorcisms, Jesus was also known as a prophet because he did not rely on the authority of other teachers, but he spoke directly the words he received from God for others. While teaching in Jerusalem he told the crowds, *"For I have not spoken on my own authority, but the Father who sent me has himself given me a commandment—what to say and what to speak."* (John

12:49) Later Jesus said to the disciples privately in the upper room, *"the word that you hear is not mine but the Father's who sent me."* (John 14:24) Jesus simply spoke the words he received from the Father.

Sometimes Jesus knew what others were thinking before they spoke. When he forgave the paralytic in the house of Simon and Andrew, *some of the scribes were sitting there, questioning in their hearts, "Why does this man speak like that? He is blaspheming! Who can forgive sins but God alone?" And immediately Jesus, perceiving in his spirit that they thus questioned within themselves, said to them, "Why do you question these things in your hearts?"* (Mark 2:6-8) This supernatural insight into their objections led Jesus to heal the paralytic and so to demonstrate his authority to forgive sins.

Other times Jesus received personal knowledge about people he had just met and had no human way of knowing. When he was talking with the Samaritan woman at the well, he overcame her resistance by bringing up the subject of her husband. *The woman answered him, "I have no husband." Jesus said to her, "You are right in saying, 'I have no husband'; for you have had five husbands, and the one you now have is not your husband. What you have said is true." The woman said to him, "Sir, I perceive that you are a prophet."* (John 4:17-19) This insight led to her conversion and that of her whole village!

Jesus prophesied that the Temple would be destroyed some 40 years before the Romans tore down every building on the Temple Mount. (Mark 13:2) On three separate occasions Jesus foretold his coming suffering, and death in Jerusalem to the disciples. (Matthew 16:21, 17:22-23, 20:17-19) On their last night together Jesus privately told his closest disciples that one of them would betray him, that Peter would deny him, and that all of them would desert him. (Mark 14:17-31) All of these prophecies helped the followers of Jesus deal with major traumatic events that were to affect their lives and discern how God was leading them through these times.

Jesus demonstrated the Kingdom by doing God's will on earth as it is done in heaven. Jesus' prophetic knowledge was intrinsic to carrying out his Father's will. He knew his Father's will because he was always listening for and submitting to what the Father was doing and saying. When he was criticized for healing people on the Sabbath Jesus often answered them, *"My Father is working until now, and*

I am working." He went on to explain, *"Truly, truly, I say to you, the Son can do nothing of his own accord, but only what he sees the Father doing. For whatever the Father does, that the Son does likewise. For the Father loves the Son and shows him all that he himself is doing."* (John 5:17, 19-20) Prophetic knowledge and insights were the inevitable result of Jesus' intimate covenantal relationship with the Father, as was his power to heal and deliver. The same can be true for us as we follow Jesus' example.

JERUSALEM HEALINGS

Although most of Jesus' ministry was carried out in Galilee where he based his mission, John tells us Jesus and his disciples made regular trips down to Jerusalem to participate in the great festivals of Passover, Tabernacles, Dedication, and another unnamed feast. While he was there, Jesus centered his ministry in the huge courts of the Temple where he taught the crowds, debated with the religious leaders, and healed the sick. However, John records two healings that did not happen at the Temple, and these are of special interest because of what archaeologists have discovered about their settings.

In John 5 we read about the healing of the paralyzed man at the Pools of Bethesda, which means "house of grace" or "house of mercy." John seems to have more specific knowledge of Jerusalem than the other Gospel writers because he adds many geographical details not found in the other Gospels. He describes the setting of the healing this way: *Now there is in Jerusalem by the Sheep Gate a pool, in Aramaic called Bethesda, which has five roofed colonnades. In these lay a multitude of invalids—blind, lame, and paralyzed.* (John 5:2-3) The Sheep Gate is just north of the Temple Mount, where animals were brought into the city for use in the Temple sacrifices. The Pools of Bethesda are located just north of this gate. Before it was excavated skeptical scholars pointed out there are no examples in ancient architecture of a five-sided colonnade and so concluded John must be making this up. But once the archaeologists began to excavate this site, they discovered two large pools separated by a stone dam, measuring about 400 feet long, 165 feet wide, and 50 feet deep. In fact, these pools were surrounded by roofed porticoes, one on each of the four sides of the combined pools and one across the dam separating them for a total of five, exactly as John describes!

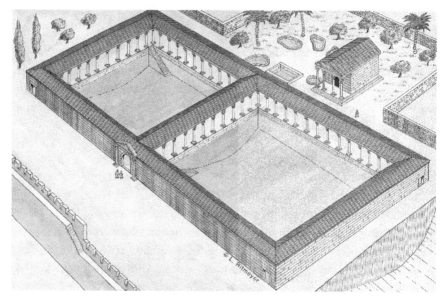

The Pools of Bethesda

Even more significant is that beside the pools the excavators uncovered an Ascleipion, a pagan healing shrine, which explains why so many sick and disabled people were gathered there. They discovered small caves, bathing pools, and pottery votive offerings representing the various body parts that needed healing. John tells us Jesus went to this healing site intentionally, not as he happened to pass by it. There he asked a paralyzed man who was lying in one of the porticoes around the pools, *"Do you want to be healed?" The sick man answered him, "Sir, I have no one to put me into the pool when the water is stirred up, and while I am going another steps down before me."* (John 5:6-7) Clearly the man was referring to the small bathing pools of the Asclepion, not the huge water storage pools which were nearly 50 feet deep with sheer sides. The amazing thing about this healing story is that, although the man expressed no faith and didn't even give Jesus a straight answer about his desire for healing, Jesus healed him anyway! It was an act of pure grace and mercy, which is the meaning of *Bethesda*, "house of mercy and grace."

In chapter 9 of John's Gospel, we read about the healing of a man who was born blind. As Jesus was leaving the huge Temple courts with his disciples, they passed by a blind man, presumably begging on the street. The fact he had been born blind caused the disciples to raise a thorny theological question, *"Rabbi, who sinned, this man or his parents, that he was born blind?"* (John 9:2) They were assuming the man's blindness was punishment for sin, but since he was born with this condition they wondered if it was his parents' sin that had caused it. Jesus dismissed both assumptions when he answered, *"It was not that this man sinned, or his parents, but that the works of God might be displayed in him."* (John 9:3) Then Jesus spit on the ground, made mud with his saliva, wiped it on the man's eyes and told him to go and wash in the Pool of Siloam.

The Pool of Siloam

The Pool of Siloam sits at the southern end of the ridge on which the original city of Jerusalem was built. This pool collects the cold, fresh water which flows from the Gihon Spring through a rock-cut tunnel which King Hezekiah built in the 8th century BC. In the time of Jesus a newly-built stepped street led from the Temple Mount down to the Pool of Siloam, and it was used by pilgrims and priests for religious processionals. This street has recently been discovered and is now being excavated so it is possible to walk on those very steps. For the blind man to go and wash in the pool meant he would have to navigate about 1,000 yards of steep steps and bustling crowds, but at Jesus' word he went anyway. When

Ancient Stepped Street to the Pool of Siloam

he got to the stepped pool, he knelt down by the water's edge, washed away the mud, blinked his eyes and found he could see for the first time in his life. It is hard to imagine the joy he must have felt as he bounded his way back up that stepped street to the Temple!

Both of these healings took place on the Sabbath day, which angered the religious authorities, and in both accounts, we hear of the healed men meeting Jesus again in the Temple courts. In the case of the paralyzed man healed at the Pools of Bethesda, he did not express gratitude or faith in Jesus but instead reported Jesus to the very authorities who wanted to kill him. In the case of the blind man healed at the Pool of Siloam, he defended Jesus' actions to the authorities, put his faith in Jesus and became a disciple. It is hard to imagine two more different responses to Jesus' healing mercy and it causes us to consider our response to Jesus' healing ministry today.

THE PURPOSE OF JESUS' HEALING MINISTRY

For those who have decided to follow Jesus, it is important to note how much time he spent healing broken people, delivering those in spiritual bondage, and speaking prophetically over others. Why did Jesus heal, deliver, and prophesy?

The most obvious answer is compassion. Once, when Jesus got into a boat and sailed to a desolate area to spend time alone, he arrived only to find a crowd there seeking him. Matthew describes his reaction, *When he went ashore he saw a great crowd, and he had compassion on them and healed their sick.* (Matthew 14:14) When a leper asked Jesus for healing, Mark describes his response this way, *Moved with pity, he stretched out his hand and touched him and said to him, "I will; be clean." And immediately the leprosy left him, and he was made clean.* (Mark 1:41-42) Jesus saw the Jews of Galilee as *"sheep without a shepherd"* and he responded to their needs by feeding them, teaching them, healing them, and delivering them. (Matthew 9:36)

But there is another reason Jesus healed and delivered. As we have seen, Jesus' central message was *"the Kingdom of God"* which he defined as God's will being done on earth as it is in heaven. (Matthew 6:10) Since there is no sickness in heaven, no blindness in heaven, no leprosy in heaven, and no demonic oppression in heaven, by healing and delivering people Jesus was showing them the Kingdom of God as well as telling them about it. He said, *"But if it is by the finger of God that I cast out demons, then the kingdom of God has come upon you."* (Luke 11:20) John describes Jesus' miracles as *"signs"* which were meant to point people toward faith in Jesus and the message he proclaimed. After Jesus turned water into wine at the wedding in Cana, John says, *This, the first of his signs, Jesus did at Cana in Galilee, and manifested his glory. And his disciples believed in him.* (John 2:11) Jesus' healings and exorcisms served as powerful demonstrations of the Kingdom he proclaimed and helped people to believe in him and enter into that Kingdom by faith.

However, when people in the crowds began demanding more of these supernatural signs from Jesus, he gave them exactly the opposite, *Then some of the scribes and Pharisees answered him, saying, "Teacher, we wish to see a sign from you." But he answered them, "An evil and adulterous generation seeks for a sign, but no sign will be given to it except the sign of the prophet Jonah."* (Matthew 12:38-39) The three days Jesus spent in the tomb before rising from the dead is the defining sign he would give to the world. After Jesus miraculously fed the crowds with five loaves and two fish, the people clamored for more miracles, *"Then what sign do you do, that we may see and believe you? What work do you perform?"* (John 6:30) Jesus refused to perform tricks for them and proceeded to increase the challenge of his teaching until most of the crowd had gone away except for his twelve closest disciples. The point is that Jesus' miracles were meant to help people trust and follow him, not feed an unhealthy dependence on him.

Many people assume Jesus was able to heal, deliver, and prophesy because he is divine. It is true Jesus claimed to be God, and the New Testament makes it clear Jesus is both fully human and fully divine. However, that was not the basis of his miraculous healings and deliverance. Back in Chapter 2, we noted that God *"emptied himself"* when he became fully human in Jesus and for about 33 years he chose to limit his divine power by operating in his full humanity while here on earth. (Philippians 2:5-8) The whole point of Jesus' life was to set an example for us to follow and show us the life we are meant to live. This is what it means to be a disciple: imitating everything Jesus did.

When we decide to follow Jesus by modeling our lives after his, it is tempting to gloss over his healings and assume we could never do the supernatural things he did. On the contrary, when Jesus was preparing his disciples to go out on mission, Matthew tells us, *he called to him his twelve disciples and gave them authority over unclean spirits, to cast them out, and to heal every disease and every affliction.* (Matthew 10:1) He gave them these specific instructions, *"Heal the sick, raise the dead, cleanse lepers, cast out demons."* (Matthew 10:8) He gave this challenge not only when he sent his inner circle of 12 disciples on mission, but also when he sent out the wider circle of 72 disciples. (Luke 10:9) These everyday men and women went out in faith that they could learn to do what Jesus did by his authority and they returned to report with amazement, *"Lord, even the demons are subject to us in your name!"* (Luke 10:17)

When we hear that Jesus-shaped discipleship includes doing the supernatural things Jesus did, our natural response is to object by pointing out we don't have the power to heal or cast out demons! Of course, it is true we do not have this power in ourselves, but Jesus shows us how to be a conduit of God's power to heal, deliver, and prophesy. As we have seen, Jesus was clear he was not doing this by himself, but was simply doing what he saw the Father doing and speaking the words the Father gave him to speak. (John 5:19; 12:49) As he followed his Father's direction and exercised that authority by faith, the supernatural power of God's Spirit flowed through Jesus to accomplish the King's will on earth as it is in heaven. This is what it means to live in the Kingdom of God. This is how Jesus could heal, deliver, prophesy, and perform miracles. This is how we can learn to do the same.

Jesus was very intentional about training his disciples to do everything he did. When Jesus miraculously fed the 5,000 with five loaves and two fish, he asked the disciples to participate in the miracle by distributing the impossibly inadequate supply of food to the huge crowd. (Matthew 14:19) It took faith for the disciples to wade into a hungry crowd with just a handful of food and believe it would be enough! Jesus taught them how to operate in supernatural power as he did by exercising faith. Jesus was also very clear that he was passing on to us the authority we would need to become conduits of God's power. On the last night he was with the disciples Jesus said, *"Truly, truly, I say to you, whoever believes in me will also do the works that I do; and greater works than these will he do, because I am going to the Father."* (John 14:12) After his death and resurrection, Jesus passed on the authority of the Father to those who would follow him: *"All authority in heaven and on earth has been given to me. Go therefore and make disciples of all nations, baptizing them in the name of the Father and of the Son and of the Holy Spirit, teaching them to observe all that I have commanded you. And behold, I am with you always, to the end of the age."* (Matthew 28:18-20)

To fulfill the Great Commission is to learn how to be a disciple who makes disciples by exercising the authority Jesus has given us to represent him and do his will on earth as it is in heaven. This includes feeding the hungry, welcoming the outcasts, healing the sick, and casting out demons. As we read in the book of Acts, the followers of Jesus continued operating in the supernatural power of the Spirit by exercising faith in the authority Jesus had given them. Peter and John went up to the Temple to worship and met a man with deformed feet begging at the Beautiful Gate, which leads into the inner courts of the Temple. Peter followed the example of Jesus by looking intently at the man and then acting in faith. He said to him, *"I have no silver and gold, but what I do have I give to you. In the name of Jesus Christ of Nazareth, rise up and walk!" And he took him by the right hand and raised him up, and immediately his feet and ankles were made strong. And leaping up, he stood and began to walk, and entered the temple with them, walking and leaping and praising God.* (Acts 3:6-7)

Acting and speaking *"in the name of Jesus"* means acting and speaking in the authority of Jesus. Peter and John were simply following the example of their Rabbi by faith, and the same power that flowed through Jesus flowed through them to do God's will on earth as it is in heaven. This became the normal pattern for those who followed Jesus. Ordinary people were empowered to carry out supernatural healings. (See Acts 14:8-10.) Prophecy became one of the normal functions of people in the body of Christ. (See Ephesians 4:11; 1 Corinthians 14:1-33.) This naturally supernatural way of life was critical to the advance of the Kingdom of God in the first centuries of Jesus' movement.

For much of my Christian life I simply assumed Jesus was able to operate in supernatural power because he was God. Since it is clear I am not God, I concluded that was not an example I was meant to follow. But as I came to understand Jesus and discipleship more biblically, I realized Jesus was showing me the life I am meant to live, even by the supernatural aspects of his life. I came to recognize that everyday men and women were empowered by the Spirit to do everything Jesus did. If the disciples were meant to do it, then I am meant to do it! Through discipling relationships with those further ahead of me on the journey, I began to believe in the authority Jesus has given me and started to learn how to exercise that authority by faith to do the will of God on earth as it is in heaven. Step by step I started to see the power of the Holy Spirit flowing through my life into the lives of others more effectively. I discovered God's presence and power in me was greater than the power of the enemy who stood against me. I began to learn how to discern what God was saying and appropriately speak that into the lives of others. I started to see people miraculously healed by the power of God at my hands, not every time, but more and more often as I kept practicing the way of Jesus and speaking in his name. I saw people miraculously freed from spiritual bondage and demonic oppression. I experienced a miraculous physical healing of my lower back after nearly a decade of constant pain. I saw more and better fruit growing in my life because I was living a more Jesus-shaped life.

If all of this sounds far-fetched or even crazy to you, I get it. It did to me too at first. But I encourage you to keep reading the Gospels, listening to what God is saying about this, and considering what it means for your next step of faith. I also encourage you to look for those who are ahead of you on the journey, especially in the area of living a more naturally supernatural life the way Jesus did, and asking them to help you learn to live a life that looks more like Jesus. This is how discipleship works.

REFLECT AND DISCUSS

Read John 9:1-41

1. Am I willing to believe that God's healing power can flow through me as it did through Jesus?

2. How can I learn to speak and act more effectively "in the name of Jesus"?

3. What are the uncomfortable risks I am willing to take in order to trust Jesus and follow his naturally supernatural example?

4. Who is ahead of me on this journey that I could imitate and ask to help me grow in healing, deliverance, and prophecy?

5. God, what are you saying to me and what step of faith do you want me to take in response?

CHAPTER NINE

UNCOMMON FRUITFULNESS

THE LAST RETREAT

John wiped the sweat from his brow and snapped at a mosquito with his handkerchief as the group came over a rise on the Roman road. *We must be near Lake Hulah... more like Swamp Hulah with all these bugs!* They were halfway through the second day of their journey, walking along the famous Via Maris which ran from Egypt in the south all the way to Damascus in the north. They had left Capernaum after breakfast the day before and headed north, planning to arrive in the region of Caesarea Philippi well before the sun set on that second day. A caravan of camels and an ox-drawn cart passed them going south. John nodded at the cart driver as he went by. *Probably spices and silks from the east, bound for the markets of Alexandria.* Simon was just ahead of him, talking with Jesus about something, and John tried to get closer so he could hear. His brother James was behind him, teasing Thomas loudly about buying something from the caravan for his wife.

John loved his life as a full-time disciple of Jesus. They were always going somewhere new and doing something exciting. It was very different from hauling nets every night. Listening to Jesus teach about the Kingdom of God and watching him minister to people with supernatural power never got old. And more recently they had been able to stretch their wings a bit when Jesus sent them out in pairs to do the things he had taught them. He wouldn't let them take extra gear or even any money when they went—they had to go by faith and simply look for new friends who would support them as they ministered. It was scary, but so amazing to see the power of God working through them, just as they had seen the Spirit working through Jesus so many times. John would never forget the first time he saw leprosy on a man's arm fade away as he declared healing in Jesus' name! He loved telling people of the Father's great love and repeating Jesus' stories of the Kingdom. When they had gathered together again back in Capernaum after their missional adventure, it was so encouraging to hear the testimonies of the other disciples. They were amazed to discover they could actually learn to do the things their Rabbi had modeled for them so many times.

Jesus and the disciples had spent a lot of time on the road these past few weeks and had seen God do amazing things, but this trip was different. They were not going somewhere to do ministry, but to get away and rest from all their work for a while. John was so looking forward to this down time. *I am so tired!* His legs were aching, and he could feel a sore spot on his left foot rubbing against his sandal. His whole life John had loved the weekly day of rest which his family observed, starting with the Sabbath dinner on Friday at sundown and continuing throughout the next day. He always found he was ready for the week of work ahead after he had enjoyed that day of rest with his family. But Jesus took this rhythm of rest and work to a new level. In addition to the weekly Sabbath rest, every morning they spent time in prayer with the Father before beginning their day refreshed and ready for the challenges that lay ahead. After a particularly busy season, Jesus would take them to Tabgha, the nearby place on the lake with seven springs, where they would spend an extra day or two resting and getting recharged in the lush grass under the shady trees.

Every once in a while, Jesus would take them away on a longer retreat, to get out of Galilee and away from the crowds who always seemed to recognize them and ask for more. Sometimes they went east into the area of the Decapolis, the ten Greek cities that lay mostly on the east side of the Sea of Galilee and the Jordan River, where no one knew who they were. John's favorite trips were when they went north and west, along the Mediterranean coast to the ancient Phoenician cities of Tyre and Sidon. He loved breathing the cool sea air and the feel of soft sand between his toes. This trip was one of those longer retreats, but now they were heading straight north to the ancient Greek city of Panias, famous for its shrine to the Greek god Pan. Situated at the base of Mount Hermon was a cave which was believed to be a gateway to the underworld. A strong spring flowed from this cave to feed the Jordan River, and several pagan temples were built there. John assumed they would not go to the actual pagan temple complex where all kinds of nasty things took place but would find a restful place in the area where they could unwind and reconnect.

As they drew near to Panias, John noticed Jesus was leaving the main road to follow a smaller path leading into a dense thicket. *I wonder where he is taking us now?* Before long, John realized the path was leading them down into a deep canyon, lush with bushes and trees. The air was growing cool and moist, almost like that Phoenician sea air John loved so much. *What's that sound?* In the distance John could hear a low hum that grew louder with every step. And then he saw it. *The Falls of Pan!* He had heard about this beautiful waterfall flowing from the nearby spring, but he had never seen it before. He stood there with the other disciples, mesmerized by the relentless flow and feeling the thick mist now billowing over his dusty face. John remembered how the Psalmist wrote, "As a deer pants for flowing streams, so pants my soul for you, O God... My soul is cast down within me; therefore I remember you from the land of Jordan and of Hermon, from Mount Mizar. Deep calls to deep at the roar of your waterfalls; all your breakers and your waves have gone over me." John wondered if one of the sons of Korah had stood here when he wrote that song.

They set up their camp in a hollow within the sound of the waterfall and spent the next couple of days resting and enjoying the cool, refreshing gorge. On the third day, Jesus began to engage them in deeper conversation. "Who do people say that the Son of Man is?" Jesus asked them. Various disciples called out their answers. "John the Baptist back from the dead!" "Elijah who was taken up in the fiery chariot!" "Jeremiah or one of the prophets!" Jesus smiled at them and asked, "But who do you say that I am?" Simon suddenly stood up and answered with his characteristic zeal, "You are the Christ, the Son of the living God." Everyone stared at Simon. His words seemed to hang in the air. *Is it true?* It was the question they had been asking themselves for over two years now but were afraid to answer. Jesus took Simon's hands in his, looked straight into his eyes and said, "Blessed are you, Simon Bar-Jonah! For flesh and blood has not revealed this to you, but my Father who is in heaven." They all breathed a silent sigh of relief and Simon grinned.

Jesus went on, "And I tell you, you are Peter, and on this rock I will build my church, and the gates of hell shall not prevail against it." *Peter! "Little Rock"? What kind of nickname is that?* Simon seemed like a pretty unstable stone to John. He knew the "gates of hell" was that opening in the pagan Cave of Pan, but wondered what Jesus was building? Jesus continued, "I will give you the keys of the kingdom of heaven, and whatever you bind on earth shall be bound in heaven, and whatever you loose on earth shall be loosed in heaven." John's head was spinning by now with too many thoughts to process. They all knew Jesus came from a family of builders in Nazareth, and he had entered into a fishing family in Capernaum. For over two years now they had been "fishing for people," as Jesus promised, but now they were going to start building with stones like Simon? And what were these keys that could bind and loose things in heaven?

Then Jesus got serious and motioned for all of them to draw close. He began to speak about their impending journey to Jerusalem for the Passover festival. He told them he would be arrested by the religious leaders, be executed, and then rise from the dead. *What are you talking about Jesus?!* If they weren't completely confused before, they certainly were now. Jesus was the most popular rabbi in generations. He drew huge crowds everywhere he went. The religious leaders wouldn't dare to touch him or there would be a riot. While John was pondering these thoughts, Simon pulled Jesus aside and they could see him gesturing as he spoke to the Rabbi. Jesus suddenly turned back to them, and spoke with full force to Simon, "Get behind me, Satan! You are a stumbling stone to me. For you are not setting your mind on the things of God, but on the things of man." Simon sat down heavily and hung his head. They all looked at the ground. Now Jesus was saying "Rocky" was not a building block, but rather a stumbling stone?

Jesus put his hand on Simon's shoulder as he spoke to all of them, "If anyone would come after me, let him deny himself and take up his cross and follow me. *Take up my cross!?* A shudder went down John's spine. He had never seen a man crucified, but he had heard his uncle Tobias describe it once. He would never willingly submit to this hated symbol of Roman oppression and torture! Jesus continued, "For whoever would save his life will lose it, but whoever loses his life for my sake will find it." It sounded like another one of Jesus' parables with a surprise ending. *Take up your cross and find your life?* It made no sense to John. But Jesus often said things that confounded them at first. John decided he would continue pondering the meaning of all this. As he fell asleep that night watching the embers of the fire fade away, he kept thinking about what it meant to be a building block rather than a stumbling stone and began to dream of Jerusalem.[11]

THE UNFORCED RHYTHMS OF GRACE

Jesus grew up in a religious family and by all accounts lived as a devout Jew, even though he eventually clashed with the religious leaders of his time. This means Jesus took a full night and day of rest every week, starting with sundown on Friday and finishing with sundown on Saturday. A typical Sabbath started with a special meal at sundown with your extended family and included lots of good rest, gathering at the synagogue to pray and hear the Word of God, playing games and telling stories. Jesus was not bound by all the legalistic rules of the rabbinical traditions, but he taught his disciples that the Sabbath was a precious gift given by God for the benefit of his children. He liked to say, *"The Sabbath was made for man, not man for the Sabbath."* (Mark 2:27) This weekly rhythm of taking a day of rest before every week of work was an essential rhythm in the life he modeled for his disciples.

Jesus also lived in a daily rhythm of working from his rest. Mark tells us, *And rising very early in the morning, while it was still dark, he departed and went out to a desolate place, and there he prayed.* (Mark 1:35) Each morning before stepping into his busy day, Jesus took time to be alone with his heavenly Father. He poured out his heart in prayer. He spent time listening for his Father's voice. Jesus did not depend on approval from others but was rooted every day in his intimate relationship with the Father. Jesus was not driven by the expectations and demands of his constituency; he was guided every day by the revelation and wisdom he received from his Father. This daily rhythm was the secret of his extraordinary strength and supernatural fruitfulness.

When Jesus and his disciples had completed a season of particularly demanding work, Jesus made a point of taking his disciples away to a nearby place for an extra time of rest. After the twelve disciples returned from their first mission trip

---

[11] Based on Matthew 16:13-28

without Jesus, he said to them, *"Come away by yourselves to a desolate place and rest a while." For many were coming and going, and they had no leisure even to eat. And they went away in the boat to a desolate place by themselves.* (Mark 6:31) These local retreats became an opportunity for them to rest, reconnect, and prepare for the next season of fruitful labor. It was a reminder that their strength came from their relationship with the Father and with each other, not from simply working harder and longer hours. Ancient tradition locates these local retreats in an area just west of Capernaum called Heptapegon, which means "seven springs." Known in modern times as Tabgha, these springs still flow today, creating a lush garden-like atmosphere where the cold springs waters flow into the lake. It is a perfect place to rest and be refreshed.

Heptapegon, Place of the Seven Springs

Every once in a while, after a busy season or before a particular challenge, Jesus took his closest disciples further away, completely out of the Jewish areas of Galilee. They went north along the coast into the area of the great Phoenician cities of Tyre and Sidon, or east into the region of the Decapolis, the ten Greek city-states which enjoyed relative independence under Roman rule. The point of going further away was anonymity, which was not always successful. Mark described one of these longer retreats when he wrote, *And from there he arose and went away to the region of Tyre and Sidon. And he entered a house and did not want anyone to know, yet he could not be hidden.* (Mark 7:24) In this instance a Syrophoenician woman figured out who they were and asked Jesus to heal her daughter. Jesus knew how important it is to completely unplug and disconnect from the demands of our normal life occasionally if we hope to find the deeper rest for our soul that is so desperately needed. But he was still watching for and listening to the Father, even in his times of rest, which is why he agreed to heal the Syrophoenician woman's daughter and consistently healed people, even on the Sabbath day.

Perhaps it was on one of these longer retreats that Jesus said to his disciples, *"Come to me, all who labor and are heavy laden, and I will give you rest. Take my yoke upon you, and learn from me, for I am gentle and lowly in heart, and you will find rest for your souls. For my yoke is easy, and my burden is light."* (Matthew 11:28-30) What clearer invitation could we have to intentionally take time to rest with Jesus and the people closest to us? I love Eugene Peterson's masterful paraphrase of these words: *"Are you tired? Worn out? Burned out on religion? Come to me. Get away with me and you'll recover your life. I'll show you how to take a real rest. Walk with me and work with me—watch how I do it. Learn the unforced rhythms of grace. I won't lay anything heavy or ill-fitting on you. Keep company with me and you'll learn to live freely and lightly."* (Matthew 11:28-30 in *The Message*)

Another benefit of retreat is revelation. Often, it is not until we get out of our familiar environment and disconnect from our normal routines that we are able to hear the still small voice of God more clearly. Near the end of his Galilean ministry, Jesus took his disciples on their final retreat to Caesarea Philippi, in the northernmost part of Israel. It is known in modern times as Banias, and archaeologists have discovered the remains of an extensive pagan worship site dedicated to the Greek god Pan, gatekeeper of the underworld. There is a large cave there from which, in ancient times, a strong spring flowed forming the headwaters of the Jordan River. The spring still flows there today, just below the cave, and the remains of several pagan temples are visible. Three quarters of a mile south of this cave the waters of the spring flow over the limestone lip of a gorge forming the beautiful Banias Falls.

Caesarea Philippi, The Cave of Pan

It was to this beautiful and refreshing environment that Jesus took his disciples for an extended time of retreat. While he was teaching and conversing with them, he asked, *"But who do you say that I am?"* Simon Peter replied, *"You are the Christ, the Son of the living God."* This is the clearest and most complete declaration of Jesus' true identity that we hear during the ministry in Galilee. Jesus explains the source of Simon's insight this way, *"Blessed are you, Simon Bar-Jonah! For flesh and blood has not revealed this to you, but my Father who is in heaven."* (Matthew 16:15-18) We need intentional times of retreat if we are hoping to receive significant revelation from our Father.

Here we see the secret of Jesus' amazing fruitfulness. He lived in intentional rhythms of rest and work: daily rhythms, weekly rhythms, seasonal rhythms, and occasional rhythms. On his last night with the disciples before being arrested, Jesus shared a beautiful picture of this fruitful rhythm as they walked through the Kidron Valley towards the Garden of Gethsemane. He said, *"I am the vine; you are the branches. Whoever abides in me and I in him, he it is that bears much fruit, for apart from me you can do nothing."* (John 15:5) The point of intentional times of rest and retreat is to reconnect to the vine. This is how we learn to abide more deeply in Jesus and depend on him for what we truly need. Just as the branch depends on the grapevine and draws nutrients from it in order to bear good fruit, so our connection to Jesus is what produces good fruit in our lives.

Banias Falls

Jesus explained how branches on the vine grow in their fruitfulness, *"Every branch in me that does not bear fruit he takes away, and every branch that does bear fruit he prunes, that it may bear more fruit."* (John 15:2) The skilled vinedresser prunes away those parts of the branch that are not essential so more of the nutrients can be put to work producing delicious grapes. Jesus shows us the same is true in our lives. We put so much time and energy into things that ultimately do not produce anything that is truly good or lasting. When we let our Father prune those parts of our lives back, it leads to growth that produces more and better fruit. This is what the Apostle Paul described when he wrote, *"the fruit of the Spirit is love, joy, peace, patience, kindness, goodness, faithfulness, gentleness, self-control"* (Galatians 5:22-23) As we learn to live in Jesus' unforced rhythms of grace, we will spend more time intentionally resting and learning to abide in him. This pattern will, in turn, teach us to keep in step with the Spirit as we follow Jesus. Good fruit that lasts flows naturally from the life of those who are walking in the way of Jesus by the power of his Spirit.

As Pam and I have decided to let the rhythms of Jesus' life shape our rhythms, we have seen more and better fruit naturally produced in our lives. We help each other be consistent in our daily rhythm of time alone with the Lord, in his Word and in prayer. We reinforce that with regular prayer together. We intentionally plan our week around observing a full 24 hours of rest and renewal on our designated Sabbath. We begin this in the evening, so we wake up already in the mode of rest and renewal for the rest of the day. We take extra days of rest before and after especially challenging seasons of fruitful ministry. We plan well ahead so we can have at least two significant times of rest and refreshment each year in a beautiful place with people we love. As we have followed Jesus' example in this way, we have become healthier people and our lives have become more fruitful with changed lives. What about you? What defines the patterns of your life? Will you let Jesus determine your rhythm and pace in order to bear more and better fruit?

MULTIPLYING THE FRUIT OF DISCIPLESHIP

The good fruit of Jesus' life was the changed lives of those who came to know and follow him. He was clear about his purpose, as he told the transformed tax collector Zacchaeus, *"the Son of Man came to seek and to save the lost."* (Luke 19:10) Jesus was not interested in building a religious institution or attaining a political position. He chose not to accumulate possessions or wealth. He never used his popularity to influence those in positions of power or to curry their favor. Instead, Jesus invested his time and energy in ordinary people who came from nearly every walk of life. Those who encountered Jesus were profoundly changed. Some feared his power and distanced themselves from him. Others were threatened by his authority and did everything they could to eliminate him. Still others were drawn to Jesus and committed themselves to learning his teachings and imitating his way of life. Those who drew near to Jesus were fundamentally transformed.

As we saw in Chapter 4, Jesus offered his friendship to people and invested in those who were responsive and reciprocated friendship. When it was clear Simon and Andrew were "people of peace" he spent time in their home, healed Simon's mother-in-law, shared a meal with them, and told them the Good News of the Kingdom. When Jesus called Matthew the tax collector, he immediately spent the rest of the day in Matthew's home, eating and conversing with him and his friends. If we hope to bear the kind of good fruit Jesus did, this will become the pattern of our lives as well. We will offer our friendship to even the most unlikely of people. We will invest in building relationships with those who are responsive and express their desire to be our friend as well. We will show them what the Kingdom of God looks like and then explain it to them. Looking for and investing in people of peace is the beginning of a fruitful life.

But Jesus didn't just look for friends, he also called followers. Simon showed Jesus he was a friend who would serve him by offering his boat. Jesus then decided to see if Simon would become more than a friend by challenging him to drop down his nets. When Simon went against his better judgment and did as Jesus asked, he demonstrated he was ready to become a follower who would submit to him. And so, Jesus challenged Simon, Andrew, James, and John to follow him and learn how to fish for people. (Luke 5:1-11) To be a disciple is to respond to both an invitation to friendship and a challenge to follow. Jesus gave his disciples access to his life so they could come to know what he knew and do what he did. He trained them by not only inviting them into a supportive Covenantal relationship, but also by challenging them to follow his example of living a Kingdom lifestyle. It was through this careful calibration of Covenantal invitation and Kingdom challenge that Jesus trained his disciples to do everything he did, even the supernatural things.

When Simon made his profession of faith on that final retreat in Caesarea Philippi, Jesus gave him a new name Peter, meaning "Rocky," and offered him the keys of the Kingdom, a symbol of authority. Jesus said it was with living stones like Peter that he would build his church. (Matthew 16:13-20) In modern culture we often signify the covenant of marriage by taking the same family name. In this covenant of marriage, we usually have the same keys on our key ring, reflecting the life we share together. In the Old Testament "the Rock" is often a name for God himself. (See Psalm 46.) By giving Peter this new name and these powerful keys, Jesus invited him into the intimate Covenant relationship of his Father's family with full familial authority! Jesus had entered Simon's family and transformed their family fishing business into a Kingdom business of fishing for people. Now Jesus invited Peter into his Father's family to join in their family business, which is the building of a whole New Creation. It is hard to imagine a more generous invitation!

Along with this amazing Covenantal invitation, Jesus brought a strong Kingdom challenge by telling them he was going to Jerusalem to suffer and die. When Peter resisted the call of the cross, Jesus challenged him to submit in the strongest possible terms, *"Get behind me, Satan! You are a hindrance to me. For you are not setting your mind on the things of God, but on the things of man."* (Matthew 16:23) The Greek word translated *"hindrance"* here is *skandalon,* which is a stone that causes you to trip and fall. Jesus was giving Simon a clear choice:

would he submit to the cross and become a building block in the Father's great construction project, or would he follow his own way and become a stumbling stone that causes others to fall? To become part of Jesus' family means joining the family business, which means being willing to surrender our lives. Jesus then addressed all of the disciples when he said, *"If anyone would come after me, let him deny himself and take up his cross and follow me. For whoever would save his life will lose it, but whoever loses his life for my sake will find it."* (Matthew 16:24-25)

If we are going to be more than simply friends who serve Jesus, we will submit and follow the example he has set for us. This means accepting both Covenantal invitation and Kingdom challenge. If we are going to be followers who submit to Jesus and are part of his Father's family, we will surrender to the family business, the family's mission. That means, like Jesus, we will look for people of peace and build friendships with those who reciprocate our invitation. We will call people to more than just friendship by challenging them to follow us as we follow Jesus. Disciples are meant to make disciples. As our lives become more Jesus-shaped, we in turn will become living examples for others to imitate. Our disciples are meant to make disciples. This is how good fruit multiplies. This is how the Kingdom of God comes. And ultimately, with these disciples we will build extended spiritual families which are focused on seeking and saving the lost; families on mission that are looking for people of peace and demonstrating the Kingdom of God.

This is the secret of Jesus' extraordinary fruitfulness. He invited friends, challenged them to become followers, and with them built a family surrendered to the Father's will. If we hope to bear good fruit that lasts, we will do the same. Jesus was clear this would cost us everything, just as it did him. The only way into this kind of fruitful, abundant life is by carrying a cross. To resist the cross is to be a stumbling stone. To surrender to the cross is to become a building block in the Father's great construction project, a new heaven and a new earth! Jesus is the master stone mason who is shaping stumbling stones like us into building blocks that can be used to build his Kingdom. This great adventure, this abundant life, is for all those who will lay down their lives, take up their cross, and follow Jesus all the way to Jerusalem and beyond.

REFLECT AND DISCUSS

Read John 15:1-10

1. How can I more intentionally live in rhythms of abiding and bearing fruit like Jesus did?

2. What are the areas of my life that need pruning in order to bear more and better fruit?

3. Am I bearing the Jesus-shaped fruit of changed lives by finding people of peace, making disciples, and building a family on mission?

4. What does it look like for me to take up my cross and follow Jesus wherever he leads me?

5. God, what are you saying to me and what step of faith do you want me to take in response?

CHAPTER TEN

CITY OF THE KING

A GIFT FIT FOR A KING

Light and laughter streamed out through the windows into the dark courtyard of Simon the Leper's house, where Mary was standing in the chill of the evening air. Ever since Jesus had called her dead brother Lazarus out of the tomb, the whole town of Bethany had been in an uproar. Too many people had seen him dead and buried for four days to deny the miracle. Plus, Lazarus was around to tell everyone what it was like to die and come back to life again!

When Simon the Leper heard Jesus was staying in Bethany on his way to Jerusalem for the Passover, he immediately invited the Rabbi to his home for a celebratory feast. Obviously, Simon no longer had a skin disease, or else no one would have accepted his invitation! Mary was reminded he was one of the many "used-to-bes" among Jesus' followers. Bartimaeus used to be blind. Mary of Magdala used to be demonized. Zacchaeus used to be a tax collector. This Simon used to be an outcast leper until Jesus touched him and made him clean. Mary smiled to herself. *No wonder he was so excited to throw this party in Jesus' honor!*

Mary heard her sister in the adjacent room barking orders to the girls who were serving the banquet. *Somehow Martha always manages to put herself in charge, even in someone else's house!* Now she heard her brother's voice coming from the dining room, telling his story again for the umpteenth time. Mary looked down and felt the smooth sheen of the alabaster vial in her hands. She recalled the day her dear father had presented this expensive perfumed oil on her thirteenth birthday as an addition to her dowry. He beamed as he said, "This will give scent to your unmatched beauty on the day you are joined to your beloved husband!" Sadly, he never lived to see that day. Tears began welling up in her eyes, but she blinked them away. Her sadness had been replaced with a new kind of joy. After meeting Jesus and answering his call to follow, Mary wondered if she would ever give herself to another. Everything else seemed trivial compared to sitting at the Master's feet and joining in the Kingdom he had begun.

Martha's strident voice in the courtyard shook Mary from her reverie, and she leaned back further into the shadows. She knew her sister would be furious with her for abandoning the kitchen once again. But Mary had more important things to do. She remembered Jesus' words to Martha in a similar situation, "Mary has chosen the better portion, which will not be taken away from her." *Master, I want to give you the better part this time.* Martha darted back into the kitchen with a stack of platters. Seizing the opportunity, Mary took a deep breath and stepped out of the shadows into the brightly lit dining room. About sixteen people reclined on pillows there, crowded around the outside of a low u-shaped table. Simon the Leper reclined near the end of the left side of the table in the host's place, with his wife to his right and Jesus to his left, in the place of honor. Servant girls came and went, bringing more food and clearing the empty bowls. No one paid any attention to Mary, supposing she was serving with the girls.

Making her way to the left side of the table, Mary knelt down behind Jesus, who was talking to Simon the Leper. Her heart was beating so hard she thought everyone must hear it by now. *Please don't be mad at me daddy. I am giving your gift to the One I love most!* Mary reached down and carefully snapped the slender neck of the alabaster jug. Immediately a powerful fragrance began to fill the room. Leaning forward, she poured half the contents on Jesus' head and began to gently wipe it into his hair. Now all conversation faded away and every eye in the room was on her. Jesus turned slowly to look at her and smiled. Mary shifted back on her heels and poured the rest of the oil on Jesus' feet. A collective gasp emerged when she unwound her hair from underneath her scarf and began using it to wipe the oil into her Rabbi's feet. Only the lowliest slave washed another's feet, and never with precious myrrh! Of course, a married woman never displayed her hair in public, but even for a single woman like Mary it was considered questionable, especially in the presence of a great Rabbi like Jesus.

Jesus' disciple Judas Iscariot, the keeper of the moneybag, broke the silence by protesting loudly, "Why was the ointment wasted like that? This ointment could have been sold for more than three hundred denarii and given to the poor." *He doesn't care a thing about the poor!* For some reason, Mary had never trusted Judas. Jesus put his hand on Mary's shoulder and said, "Leave her alone. Why do you trouble her? She has done a beautiful thing to me. For you always have the poor with you, and whenever you want, you can do good for them. But you will not always have me. She has done what she could; she has anointed my body beforehand for burial. And truly, I say to you, wherever the gospel is proclaimed in the whole world, what she has done will be told in memory of her."

Judas stalked out of the room as conversations resumed around the table. Jesus smiled at Mary again and said, "Daughter, you have no idea what this gift means to me." It was true, she didn't really understand what Jesus meant by anointing his body for burial, but she felt fully understood and deeply loved, both of which were new experiences for her. Glowing inside, she quietly retreated from the room, filled with anticipation for whatever this Passover holiday would bring.[12]

A DRAMATIC ENTRANCE

Although Jesus and his disciples traveled to Jerusalem to participate in the great festivals regularly over the roughly three years of his public ministry, they spent the majority of their time in Galilee with Capernaum as their home base. Jesus welcomed and engaged both Samaritans and Gentiles whenever they crossed his path, but he made it clear his intentional missional focus was on the everyday

---

[12] Based on John 12:1-8

Jews who lived in the towns and villages of Galilee. When he sent his disciples out on mission he said, *"Go nowhere among the Gentiles and enter no town of the Samaritans, but go rather to the lost sheep of the house of Israel."* (Matthew 10:5-6) In spite of this strategic focus on the north, Jesus knew his ultimate destiny lay far to the south in Jerusalem, the holy city of Israel's kings. While on that final retreat to Caesarea Philippi, he told his disciples of the suffering, death, and resurrection that awaited him there. From that point on, his focus shifted away from Galilee and he began to direct his attention southward. The way Luke said it was, *"his face was set toward Jerusalem."* (Luke 9:53)

It is always tricky to nail down a strict chronology of Jesus' ministry because the Gospel writers organized their accounts of Jesus' life more thematically than chronologically. We do know Jesus and the disciples did not travel directly from Caesarea Philippi to Jerusalem. In fact, in Luke's Gospel it takes 10 chapters for them to make the journey! But it is clear from that point on Jesus and his core disciples, including Mary Magdalene and a number of female followers, deliberately began to make their way south to Jerusalem, planning to celebrate the Passover there. They took several side trips and ministered to various people they encountered along the way. As they came into the ancient city of Jericho, Jesus healed the blind man named Bartimaeus and then invited himself over for dinner and to stay the night at the most unlikely place of all, the extended family home of the diminutive chief tax collector, Zacchaeus. (Luke 19:1-10) Right up to the end of his ministry on earth, Jesus continued to heal people, teach the Good News of the Kingdom, and transform lives by his radical welcome of outcasts and his unconditional love for everyone he met.

The next morning, Jesus and his disciples arose and began the final day's journey up through the Judean desert to Jerusalem, along the Roman road known as the Ascent of Adumim, an elevation gain of over 3,300 feet. This ancient trade route was the final leg of the pilgrim route to the holy city. As the Passover drew near, the road became increasingly crowded with pilgrims making their way up to Jerusalem for the festival. The final ascent of their journey climbed the eastern slope of the Mount of Olives, the ridge that runs north and south, just to the east of Jerusalem and the Temple Mount. Before cresting the Mount of Olives, they came to the village of Bethany, home of Jesus' beloved friends Mary, Martha, and Lazarus.

The Church in Bethany at the Tomb of Lazarus

In an earlier visit to their extended family home, Jesus scolded Martha for being so distracted by the meal preparations and affirmed her sister Mary for sitting at his feet, taking the deliberate posture of a disciple, unheard of for a woman in ancient times. (Luke 10:38-42) Sometime after that, Jesus and the disciples were summoned back to Bethany by Mary and Martha when their brother Lazarus fell deathly ill. By the time they arrived, Lazarus had already been dead four days, and his decaying body was sealed in the family tomb. To the shock of his family, the people of Bethany, and the religious officials in nearby Jerusalem, Jesus called Lazarus back to life from death, and he came stumbling out of his tomb! (John 11:1-44) In Bethany still today you can find a rock-cut tomb which has been identified since ancient times as the family burial site from which Jesus raised Lazarus back to life. Over the centuries it has changed form so much it is impossible to tell if it is the same tomb, but it is certainly the same area where all this happened. This irrefutable miracle of miracles, attested by countless eyewitnesses, convinced the religious leaders in Jerusalem the only way for them to retain their power was to put Jesus to death. (John 11:53)

It is clear the extended family of Mary, Martha, and Lazarus had become Jesus' spiritual family when he and the disciples visited Jerusalem, so it is no surprise they stayed in their home during this final Passover week. That night another resident of Bethany, a man known as Simon the Leper, invited Jesus and the disciples to a banquet in his home. Simon is most likely one of the many lepers Jesus had healed who wanted to show his gratitude by honoring Jesus with a special dinner. Mary of Bethany, as she is known to distinguish her from several other Marys who were disciples of Jesus, shocked everyone at this banquet with a lavish show of devotion. She took a very expensive vial of perfumed oil and poured it on Jesus' head and feet, wiping his feet with her hair. (John 12:1-8) While Judas and some of the other disciples criticized her, Jesus praised her for such a beautiful act and interpreted it as a symbolic anointing pointing forward to his impending death. (Matthew 26:6-13)

The next day Jesus and his disciples joined the throng of pilgrims making their final ascent over the Mount of Olives into Jerusalem. But Jesus intentionally planned to enter the holy city in a powerfully symbolic way. The prophet Zechariah predicted the Messiah would appear on the Mount of Olives riding on a young donkey, *Rejoice greatly, O daughter of Zion! Shout aloud, O daughter of Jerusalem! Behold, your king is coming to you; righteous and having salvation is he, humble and mounted on a donkey, on a colt, the foal of a donkey... On that day his feet shall stand on the Mount of Olives that lies before Jerusalem on the east.* (Zechariah 9:9, 14:4) Jesus had arranged for a friend in the nearby village of Bethphage to have a young donkey ready for this very moment. He sent two of

Jerusalem, Looking West from the Mount of Olives

his disciples to get the donkey, they brought it to Jesus, and he rode this little colt over the Mount of Olives and down the other side into the city of Jerusalem, just as Zechariah had foretold. Up until this moment, many rumors about Jesus circulated among the Jewish people. Jesus was intentionally circumspect about his true identity, not wanting the authorities to arrest him before he could fulfill everything the Father had planned for him to do. But now Jesus made it crystal clear to everyone exactly who he was and why he was coming to Jerusalem. The Messiah was the promised king descended from David who would come to save God's people and establish God's reign. When the crowds saw what Jesus was doing, they understood his message. They cut palm branches to lay in the road and even spread out their cloaks for him to ride over, as though they were rolling out the red carpet to honor the arrival of their King! They began to shout out a famous phrase from Psalm 118:25-26 which calls on the Messiah to save his people, *"Hosanna to the Son of David! Blessed is he who comes in the name of the Lord! Hosanna in the highest!"* (Matthew 21:9) The religious leaders were well aware of what Jesus was doing and why the crowds were reacting to him as they were. They tried to get Jesus to quiet the people, but Jesus replied, *"I tell you, if these were silent, the very stones would cry out."* (Luke 19:40)

The crowds were thrilled to see Jesus entering Jerusalem as Messiah, because they had waited so long for God to deliver them from their enemies. They assumed Jesus had come to establish a new dynasty to supplant the Herodians, raise up a great army of Israel, and defeat the Romans on the battlefield. Little did they know the true nature of their coming Messiah. Jesus wasn't coming to establish an earthly kingdom which would soon be conquered by the next invading army, but a heavenly Kingdom which continues forever. He was not destined to be just the King of the Jews, but King of the whole world. He was not coming to enact his will over the people, but rather so that the will of God would be done on earth as it is in heaven. His rule was not to be imposed at the point of the sword but would come through the most powerful act of all, by willingly laying down his life for the sake of the world. Although the crowds cheered for their coming King, they did not understand the nature of his Kingdom. Later that week Jesus would say it this way, *"you did not know the time of your visitation."* (Luke 19:44)

It is instructive to realize Jesus' closest disciples were nearly as clueless as the crowds about the nature of his Kingdom. Although Jesus had repeatedly warned them of the suffering and death that awaited him in Jerusalem, they too were caught up in the excitement of the moment and projected onto their Rabbi all their own expectations and desires of what they wanted Jesus to be for them. As followers of Jesus, we must always be aware of our tendency to seek first our own kingdom rather than God's. The essence of discipleship is submission and following. Jesus said, *"If anyone would come after me, let him deny himself and take up his cross daily and follow me."* (Luke 9:23) This means as disciples we are always learning to let go of our will in order seek God's will. It means we are choosing to lay down our plans so that we can discover God's plan. It means seeking the Kingdom Jesus is building, not trying to build our own. The path of discipleship does not lead us to the lavish Palace of Herod; it leads to the stark rock of Golgotha. It is only by taking up our cross and following Jesus that we will truly discover the Kingdom he died and rose to establish.

THE CITY OF DESTINY

Any pilgrim cresting the Mount of Olives with Jesus that day would have been awestruck by the view of the walled city of Jerusalem stretching out before them. Still today it is a breath-taking experience to walk through one of the seven gates in the walls of the Old City of Jerusalem and plunge into the unique sights, sounds, and smells of this ancient city. In the time of Jesus, the warren of stepped streets would have been crowded with residents, priests, pilgrims, merchants, donkeys, and pushcarts, much as it is today. The great Palace of Herod stood on the western ridge of the city, its highest point, overlooking the Temple Mount to the east. This is where the Roman governors, like Pontius Pilate, took up residence when they visited the Holy City for the Passover. Dropping down between these two huge structures was the Tyropoeon Valley where the Hasmonean Palace stood, home of the Jewish dynasty that predated Herod the Great. It was here that Herod Antipas took up residence when visiting Jerusalem for the great festivals. An ingenious water system fed a number of pools in and around Jerusalem, including the Pools of Bethesda and the Pool of Siloam.

Jerusalem in the Time of Jesus

Above all it was the massive Temple Mount that dominated the impressive skyline of Jerusalem and still does today. A large flat rock forms the tip of what came to be called Mount Zion, the ridge that runs north from the original city of Jerusalem. In the tenth century BC, a Jebusite named Araunah owned this flat rock and used it as a threshing floor until King David bought it as the site for the new *"house of the Lord."* (2 Samuel 24:18-25) David's son Solomon eventually built a beautiful Temple on the top of Mount Zion, with the flat rock serving as the floor of the

Holy of Holies, the innermost chamber of the Temple. Solomon built a square courtyard surrounding the Temple, with large retaining walls holding up the sides of that plaza. The Babylonians destroyed this impressive First Temple nearly four hundred years later when they invaded Jerusalem in 587 BC. Almost seventy years after that, when the Jewish exiles were allowed to return to Jerusalem under the Persian king Cyrus the Great, their appointed governor Zerubbabel directed the rebuilding of the Temple on the same site, which was completed in 519 BC. This humble Second Temple evoked both cheers of delight that the sacrificial system was restored and tears of sorrow that it was a mere shadow of the glory of Solomon's Temple. (Ezra 3:8-13)

Five hundred years later, after Herod the Great was declared "King of the Jews" in 40 BC by the Romans and won control of the land from various warring factions, he began an extremely ambitious remodeling and expansion of the Second Temple, around 20 BC. Herod completely rebuilt the Temple building itself, utilizing a thousand priests trained as stone masons so the sacrifices could continue uninterrupted. He dramatically expanded the Temple Courts and surrounded them with enormous colonnaded porticoes, over thirty feet high, forty-five feet wide, and extending for nearly a mile in length. This plaza contained a series of barriers surrounding the Temple itself, forming its inner courts and creating layers of increasing exclusion. Signs on a fence threatened death to any Gentile who approached closer to the Temple. Then there was the Court of Women into which only Jews could enter. Then there was the Court of Israel to which female Jews were forbidden entry. Beyond that lay the Court of the Priests which was reserved for the priests on duty, the Sanctuary of the Temple itself into which only the priest chosen by lot that day could enter, and then the Holy of Holies into which only the High Priest was allowed to enter once a year on Yom Kippur, the Day of Atonement.

Until you actually stand on the Temple Mount, it is almost impossible to imagine the size of the courtyard Herod built around the Temple; it equals the size of 25 American football fields! This courtyard required the construction of gigantic retaining walls, utilizing stones as big as 570 tons to hold back the fill that literally engulfed the mountain! At the southern end of this plaza Herod built a huge colonnaded building called "The Royal Stoa" that stretched nearly a thousand feet long and stood over a hundred feet tall. The first-century Jewish historian Josephus called it "a structure more noteworthy than any under the

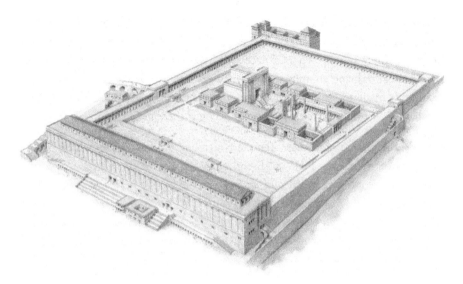

Herod's Temple Mount

sun." When Jesus and the disciples descended one of the massive staircases leading down from the Temple courts, they said, *"Look, Teacher, what wonderful stones and what wonderful buildings!" And Jesus said to him, "Do you see these great buildings? There will not be left here one stone upon another that will not be thrown down."* (Mark 13:1-2) And it was true! Some forty years later in AD 70, the Roman Legions invaded Jerusalem to put down the Jewish Revolt and tore down every single structure on the Temple Mount. They even tried to destroy the retaining walls of the plaza, but the stones were so massive that even the advanced Roman engineers couldn't obliterate it. That is why the platform of the Temple Mount still stands today in its original dimensions. Jesus knew his ultimate destiny lay here in Jerusalem and it was in this massive Temple complex that Jesus centered the final chapter of his mission.

PROVOKING THE POWERS

When Jesus and his disciples visited the Temple Courts, they ascended one of the monumental staircases from the south that fed underground tunnels leading to the Court of the Gentiles. There they saw the various tables of the money-changers who converted Jewish coins into the Tyrian shekel set up in the shade of the Royal Stoa. This was not surprising because it was a necessary function, since the annual Temple tax required of all Jewish men could only be paid in that foreign currency. They also saw the stalls of those selling animals for sacrifice. Likewise, this was expected as a necessary function for worshipers, since it was not practical to bring an animal from great distances to offer as a sacrifice at the Temple. It made more sense for many pilgrims to bring some extra money and purchase their unblemished pigeon or lamb right there in the Temple courts.

When Jesus first entered these Temple courts, he did something which deeply shocked everyone, even his own disciples. Mark says, *he entered the temple and began to drive out those who sold and those who bought in the temple, and he overturned the tables of the money-changers and the seats of those who sold pigeons. And he would not allow anyone to carry anything through the temple. And he was teaching them and saying to them, "Is it not written, 'My house shall be called a house of prayer for all the nations'? But you have made it a den of robbers."* (Mark 11:15-17)

This was one of the most radical things Jesus ever did, because he publicly challenged the authority of the religious leaders of Israel in the heart of their power base. Many people have assumed Jesus was reacting to a financial injustice in which the merchants were overcharging for their services. While it is true that Jesus quotes Jeremiah 7:11 which describes the Temple as *"a den of robbers,"* it is unlikely Jesus was trying to reform the financial practices of the Temple, because that would have required a much larger and more far-reaching act. Had Jesus turned over every table and driven out every animal from the Temple Mount, it would have caught the attention of the Roman military commander stationed in the Antonia Fortress, which was built onto the northwest corner of the Temple Mount. In response to such an act he would have sent Roman soldiers into the courts to quell the disturbance and arrest Jesus. (Compare what happened to Paul there in Acts 21:27-36.) The fact that Jesus' action doesn't evoke such a response tells us this was a more limited event in which Jesus prophetically announced judgement on the exclusive nature of Temple practice.

When King Solomon first dedicated the Temple, he prayed it would be a place where both Jews and Gentiles would come together to worship and pray. (1 Kings 8:41-43) Jesus quoted Isaiah 56:7, *"Is it not written, My house shall be called a house of prayer for all the nations'?"* This is the very passage in which Isaiah prophesied that both Jews and Gentiles will worship together in the Temple when the Messiah comes. (Isaiah 56:1-8) But the religious leaders had created a series of restrictive barriers excluding Gentiles, women, and those considered unclean from direct access to God's presence. Jesus was dramatically protesting these exclusive barriers the religious leaders had set up.

Jesus' shocking act of turning over the tables and driving out the animals looks like one of the symbolic acts the ancient prophets of Israel carried out in Jerusalem to make a powerful point. The Prophet Jeremiah tried to warn the religious leaders of Israel of the impending Babylonian invasion by smashing a clay pot in one of the gates of Jerusalem and declaring, *"Thus says the Lord of hosts: 'So will I break this people and this city, as one breaks a potter's vessel, so that it can never be mended.'"* (Jeremiah 19:1-15) Jesus' action in the Temple was a similar prophetic act of judgment, demonstrating that the religious leaders had forgotten the Temple was meant to be a place where people of every nation could come and encounter God.

This sounds much like the inclusive message of Jesus' opening sermon in the synagogue of Nazareth where he shockingly included the Gentiles in the Messianic promises. Jesus also foretold the impending destruction of the Temple and he promised after his death and resurrection the presence of God would now dwell in the hearts and lives of his followers through the outpouring of the Holy Spirit. (John 14:15-24) The Gospel writers point out that, in the moment Jesus died on the cross, the huge curtain separating the Holy of Holies from the Sanctuary of the Temple was torn in two from top to bottom. (Mark 15:38) About 40 years later every structure on the Temple Mount was destroyed by the Romans, just as Jesus predicted. (Mark 13:1-2)

After this prophetic act in the Temple courts, Jesus and his disciples returned to Bethany where they stayed with the extended family of Mary, Martha, and Lazarus. During this final Passover, they rose each morning and made the one and three-quarter mile walk over the Mount of Olives, through the Kidron Valley, into the walled city and up onto the Temple Mount. The Passover pilgrims crowded around Jesus in the Temple courts, presumably in the shade of the massive porticoes, listened to his teaching, and witnessed his miraculous healings. (Matthew 21:14-17) This is where the religious leaders started challenging Jesus publicly and began trying to provoke a pretense for his arrest and execution. Various religious and political factions who were normally at odds found common cause in trying to eliminate Jesus. The Pharisees and Herodians teamed up to try and trap Jesus with a politically charged question about paying taxes. The Sadducees tried to trap him by asking a thorny theological question. In every case, Jesus managed not only to escape their trap, but also made a brilliant point in the process! Matthew describes the reaction of the crowds to Jesus' insightful answers this way: *When they heard it, they marveled... they were astonished at his teaching.* (Matthew 22:15-33) This only left the religious leaders feeling more threatened by Jesus' popularity and more determined to destroy him.

Jesus' prophetic act against the Temple and his clashes with the religious leaders remind us not to become too comfortable with our own religious cultures. I am writing this as someone who has made his living working in the church my whole life. I am sorry to say I have seen the very same dynamics Jesus addressed in the Temple in every church I have served. I must confess I have seen these dynamics in my own life as well. There is a constant human inclination to use God for our own purposes. Religious leaders can slip into building their own kingdoms rather than leading people into God's Kingdom. Religious people can develop judgmental attitudes toward those considered outside their own community. Religious systems can become barriers that prevent people from experiencing the transforming power of God's presence. Every once in a while, we need Jesus to come into our temple courts, turn over some tables, and drive out some money changers. To follow Jesus is to tear down the man-made barriers that stand between lost people and a saving God who loves them. To follow Jesus is to confront Pharisaical legalism, Sadducean ritualism, and Herodian manipulation whenever we see it. Like Jesus, this won't necessarily earn us lots of friends in high places, but it will open the way for many who are far from God to enter past the torn curtain into the Holy of Holies and experience the life-changing power of a God who knows them intimately and loves them completely.

REFLECT AND DISCUSS

Read Matthew 21:1-13

1. How can I recognize Jesus as my true King by offering him the best I have?

2. In what ways do I confuse the kingdoms of this world for the Kingdom of God?

3. How can I tear down the barriers human religion builds between God and people?

4. Am I ready to take up my cross and follow Jesus all the way to Golgotha?

5. God, what are you saying to me and what step of faith do you want me to take in response?

CHAPTER ELEVEN

A FINAL PASSOVER

A PASSOVER LIKE NONE OTHER

"I bet I'll see him first!" Peter declared, slapping his friend on the back. John just smiled and continued studying the foot traffic passing by on the Siloam Road. They both had a competitive nature, and ever since they were young it seemed they were always trying to best each other at whatever they were doing. Jesus chose them to prepare for a special Passover dinner within the walls of Jerusalem that night, but they still didn't know where it would be held. The meal started at sundown, and they still had a lot to do. That morning Jesus had given them cryptic instructions, "When you have entered the city, a man carrying a jar of water will meet you. Follow him into the house that he enters and tell the master of the house, 'The Teacher says to you, "Where is the guest room, where I may eat the Passover with my disciples?"' And he will show you a large upper room furnished; prepare it there." Peter had replied, "Well, this man carrying a water jar shouldn't be too hard to find!" Everyone knew only women collected water.

While the morning sun was still low in the eastern sky, Peter and John had come over the Mount of Olives from Bethany, walked through the Kidron Valley, entered Jerusalem at the Spring Gate, and found a place to sit by the road where they could see all those who were coming up from the Pool of Siloam. Plenty of women passed by with water jars carefully balanced on their heads, but they saw no men doing women's work. Then they both cried out at the same time, "There!" Sure enough, a man was coming up the stepped street with a large water jar on his head. Based on his clothes, he looked like a slave from a wealthy family. He abruptly turned left off Siloam Street and began to climb one of the steep streets leading up to the Southwest Hill. Peter and John sprang to their feet. They didn't approach the man but followed at a distance. They both knew this road led up to the most sought-after neighborhood in Jerusalem where the rich and powerful priestly families of Jerusalem lived.

Once they had come nearly to the top of the hill, the man turned down a side street. They rounded the corner just in time to see him disappear through a well-made door into one of the large extended family houses. They knocked on the door, and a young man answered. He was not a slave, but clearly a member of the upper-class family that lived there. "Can I help you?" he asked politely. Peter replied with his carefully memorized password, "The Teacher says to you, 'Where is the guest room, where I may eat the Passover with my disciples?'" The teenager's face lit up, "Oh, we've been expecting you! Come in, come in!" As they entered the finely paved courtyard, they were amazed to see what a large home it was. The rooms surrounding the central court were built of large limestone blocks, two stories high.

"My name is John Mark," the young man continued. Peter and John introduced themselves and followed him up the stairs leading to the second floor. John Mark showed them the large guestroom which had been set up for them. A low u-shaped table was in the middle of the room, surrounded by cushions. John Mark gestured to shelves built into the far wall. "You should find everything you need is here." John replied, "This will be perfect, thank you!" and the young man left them to their work. After setting the table with dishes and the four cups, they rigorously swept out the entire room to make sure there was no leaven in any of the cracks or crevices. Once the room was ready, they departed on the long walk back down to the Temple to buy their Passover lamb for sacrifice. Before ascending the staircase leading to the Double Gate, they both took a mikveh immersion bath to ensure they were ritually pure before entering the Temple Courts.

Standing between the towering columns of the Royal Stoa, Peter bargained with a merchant for an unblemished year-old lamb. John took the lamb by the legs, placed it over his shoulders, and the two men set off for the Beautiful Gate leading to the inner courts of the Temple. As they passed through the 50-foot tall golden doors they saw a man with deformed feet begging. *He's been sitting here for as long as I can remember!* Peter thought to himself. Smiling at the man, Peter handed him the few coins left over from his purchase of the lamb before they entered the Court of Women.

Making their way through the crowded court, John joined the line of men waiting to ascend the fifteen semi-circular steps leading to the Nicanor Gate, giving access to the Court of the Priests which surrounded the Temple itself. He stared in awe at the Corinthian Bronze doors, aware they were more valuable than gold. When his turn finally came, a priest took the lamb out of his hands, carefully cut its throat and let the life blood drain into a special cup which was passed down a line of priests, the last of whom sprinkled the blood on the huge altar of sacrifice. Meanwhile, the first priest efficiently cleaned and skinned the animal. Before long John made his way back down the semi-circular steps carrying the wrapped carcass of the lamb.

John and Peter made their way through the crowds back to the house on the Southwest Hill. When they knocked on the door, this time they were greeted by Mary, the mother of John Mark and matriarch of the household. "Johnny told me you were making preparations! We are so honored to host you and the Teacher for this special holiday." They thanked her as she showed them the clay oven in the corner of the courtyard which was already full of hot coals. "You can roast the lamb here, and I have asked the servants to provide you with plenty of unleavened bread and wine." From the upper room, they saw the sun starting to dip low on the horizon as they took care of their final tasks and heard Jesus arriving with the rest of the disciples.

Oil lamps set in the wall niches flickered light across the faces of the disciples as they took their places, reclining on cushions around the u-shaped table. But then Jesus did something none of them could have imagined. He rose from the table, took off his robe, wrapped a towel around his waist, and picked up the foot-washing basin by the door. They were shocked to see their honored Rabbi lower himself in this way, but before they could object, he began to wash their feet. When Jesus got to the far end of the table, Peter blurted out, "You shall never wash my feet." Jesus answered him, "If I do not wash you, you have no share with me." After more protests, Peter finally relented along with the rest. When he was finished, Jesus put his robe back on and returned to the host's place near the left end of the table between Judas and John. He said, "Do you understand what I have done to you? You call me Teacher and Lord, and you are right, for so I am. If I then, your Lord and Teacher, have washed your feet, you also ought to wash one another's feet. For I have given you an example, that you also should do just as I have done to you."

While they were still reeling from this shock, Jesus began the Passover meal. As he recounted the story of God's deliverance of his people from bondage in Egypt, they drank from the first cup of wine called "the Cup of Sanctification." After eating unleavened bread with greens dipped in saltwater and bitter herbs, they refilled and drank from the second cup of wine, called "the Cup of Deliverance." Then came the main part of the meal in which they ate the roast lamb that had been sacrificed at the Temple. As they finished the lamb, Jesus took more of the unleavened bread in his hand and broke it as he offered the traditional blessing. But then he said something quite unexpected, "Take, eat; this is my body." Perplexed by this, they silently chewed their bread as Jesus picked up the third cup of wine, known as "the Cup of Redemption," and recited the traditional blessing over it. But then he said, "Drink of it, all of you, for this is my blood of the covenant, which is poured out for many for the forgiveness of sins. I tell you I will not drink again of this fruit of the vine until that day when I drink it new with you in my Father's kingdom." John suddenly remembered the time in the Capernaum synagogue when Jesus said, "I am the bread of life... Truly, truly, I say to you, unless you eat the flesh of the Son of Man and drink his blood, you have no life in you." *Is this what he meant by that?* John wondered.

None of them understood what all this meant, but Jesus went on to teach them as they asked questions. He said one of them would betray him. He said they would all desert him. He told Peter he would deny him. After the meal ended, Jesus continued with more mind-bending teaching about the role of the Holy Spirit. By this time their heads were spinning, and they couldn't think of any more questions to ask. Peter was fuming and John was trying to remember everything the Rabbi had told them. Jesus led them in one more song and they left the upper room, heading down into the Kidron Valley which was lighted by the full Passover moon. By now they could see the grove of olive trees called Gethsemane up ahead where they planned to spend the night. *I need a good night's sleep!* John thought to himself. Little did he know the events that were about to take place would shatter their dreams, turn their lives upside down, and change the world forever.[13]

THE LAST SUPPER

Ever since God delivered his people from slavery in Egypt through the blood of the lamb which was spread on the doorposts of their homes, the Jews had recounted their story of salvation every year on the 15th of Nissan by reliving the special meal they were commanded to eat that first night. Each part of the Passover meal had a symbolic meaning that allowed them to recall the narrative of God's saving grace. Covenant relationships were often ratified through a shared meal, and the Passover meal was the annual renewal of God's Covenant with his people. Although we don't know all the details of this meal in the first century, we know it did include a roast lamb which was sacrificed at the Temple, four symbolic cups of wine, unleavened bread, greens, bitter herbs, and the retelling of the Exodus.

Jesus explained how important this particular meal was when he told his disciples, *"I have earnestly desired to eat this Passover with you before I suffer. For I tell you I will not eat it until it is fulfilled in the kingdom of God."* (Luke 22:15-16) This is why Jesus went to great lengths to keep the location of this Passover meal secret, even from his own disciples. He knew one of his own was going to betray him, and he didn't want that to happen before he could reinterpret the Passover meal for his disciples, ratifying the New Covenant and giving his followers an opportunity to renew that relationship by remembering his death and resurrection as often as they gathered and shared this special meal. He told Peter and John to follow a man carrying a water jar and gave them a coded phrase to identify themselves to the owner of the house in order to keep the actual location secret. (Luke 22:7-13)

On the southwest hill of Old Jerusalem stands the traditional site of the Upper Room, known today as the "Cenacle" (Latin for dining room). Underneath this building archaeologists have discovered the foundations of a large first-century

---

[13] Based on Mark 14:12-31; Luke 22:7-34, John 13:1-39

Jewish home. Mark's Gospel describes a young man who woke up from his bed that night and tried to warn Jesus before his arrest in the Garden of Gethsemane. (Mark 14:51-52) Luke recounts a prayer meeting in the house of Mary the mother of John Mark, to which Peter went for refuge after his miraculous escape from prison. (Acts 12:12) Based on these references, I am convinced the remains underneath the Cenacle are the foundations of the very house of Mary and John Mark where Jesus arranged to share this Passover meal with his disciples.

Traditional Site of the Upper Room in Jerusalem

Jesus set the tone for this revolutionary night right from the start by doing the unthinkable. Although he was the person of greatest honor, he chose the position of greatest humility by washing his disciples' feet. Feet were considered the most unclean part of a person's body. Normally people would wash their own feet, or this task was reserved for the lowest slave of the household. Often a large basin, specially designed for foot washing, sat on the floor near the door. Jesus was clear about the implications of this revolutionary act when he said, *"If I then, your Lord and Teacher, have washed your feet, you also ought to wash one another's feet."* (John 13:1-20)

As with everything else Jesus did, he was setting an example for his disciples to follow, showing them that humility and serving others in love is his way of leadership. As if that weren't enough for one evening, Jesus went on to reinterpret the traditional Passover meal by pointing to himself as *"the Lamb of God who takes away the sin of the world"* as John the Baptist prophesied at his baptism. As the sacrificial lamb on their table had been broken and bled for their deliverance, Jesus was interpreting his impending death as the perfect sacrifice that saves the whole world from slavery to sin and death. Jesus explained this is the basis of his new covenant of grace when he said, *"This cup that is poured out for you is the new covenant in my blood."* (Luke 22:20)

Ancient Foot-Washing Basin

Jesus also said some things that were difficult for the disciples to hear that night. He foretold how someone in their inner circle would betray him to the religious authorities. John was seated to the right of Jesus, and Judas was to his left, which were the two seats of greatest honor. Peter seems to have been seated at the opposite end of the u-shaped table, which was the position of lowest honor. He motioned to John that he should ask Jesus who was the betrayer. When John leaned back and asked Jesus, he replied, "It is he to whom I will give this morsel of bread when I have dipped it" and he dipped his bread into the bowl and gave it to Judas. (John 13:21-30) By giving Judas the seat of honor to his left, it seems as if Jesus was trying to reach Judas right up to the very moment of his betrayal. But Judas did not change course. After Judas left to report his location to the authorities, Jesus went on to say, *"You will all fall away, for it is written, 'I will strike the shepherd, and the sheep will be scattered.'"* When Peter insisted that he would rather die than fall away, Jesus told him directly, *"Truly, I tell you, this very night, before the rooster crows twice, you will deny me three times."* (Mark 14:27, 30)

All of this was painful for the disciples to hear, but it also helped them accept their failure when it happened and receive the restoration Jesus was already offering them. The purpose of biblical prophecy is not primarily to foretell the future, but to prepare us for what is coming, help us understand what God is doing, and empower us to respond in faith. Jesus spoke a personal prophetic word to Peter that night, *"Simon, Simon, behold, Satan demanded to have you, that he might sift you like wheat, but I have prayed for you that your faith may not fail. And when you have turned again, strengthen your brothers."* (Luke 22:31-32) Jesus was preparing Peter to repent and be restored following the betrayal of his Rabbi. After his resurrection, when the risen Jesus served the disciples breakfast on the shore of the Sea of Galilee, he explicitly restored Peter to his leadership role when he said, *"Feed my lambs... Tend my sheep... Feed my sheep."* (John 21:15-19) In spite of his epic failure, Peter accepted his restoration and went on to lead the first church in Jerusalem and beyond!

As the evening went on, Jesus shared with the disciples some of his most insightful and powerful teaching. He gave them a new standard for their relationships with each other, *"A new commandment I give to you, that you love one another: just as I have loved you, you also are to love one another. By this all people will know that you are my disciples, if you have love for one another."* (John 13:34-35) Jesus told them he was going away, but not to worry because he was going to prepare a place for them in the Father's extended family household. When Thomas said he did not know the way to that place, Jesus said, *"I am the way, and the truth, and the life."* (John 14:6) Jesus said he would send the Comforter to be with them forever. He said he and the Father would make their home inside of them. As they left the upper room and made their way through the Kidron Valley to the Garden of Gethsemane, Jesus said, *"I am the vine; you are the branches. Whoever abides in me and I in him, he it is that bears much fruit, for apart from me you can do nothing."* (John 15:5) It is likely Jesus was pointing to a vineyard they were passing when he gave this powerful image of our fruitfulness flowing naturally from our connection to him.

THE FINAL TEST

The Garden of Gethsemane

When they arrived at the Garden of Gethsemane, the main group of disciples settled down to sleep, but Jesus asked his three closest disciples, Peter, James, and John, to come support him in prayer. There is still a grove of ancient olive trees at the base of the Mount of Olives, the location of the Garden of Gethsemane in which Jesus asked these disciples to pray with him. Nearby stands a beautiful church built over a large rock, marking the traditional location of Jesus' agonizing prayer and recreating the atmosphere of an olive grove on the night of a full moon. He said to these three closest disciples, *"My soul is very sorrowful, even to death. Remain here and watch."* Jesus himself went a stone's throw further, fell down on the ground, and began to pour out his heart to the Father, *"Abba, Father, all things are possible for you. Remove this cup from me. Yet not what I will, but what you will."* (Mark 14:32-36) Jesus' human survival instinct was telling him to do whatever was necessary to avoid the suffering and death he knew was coming. The Holy Spirit was telling him his destiny was to be found in submitting to the suffering and death which lay ahead. When he turned back to his closest friends for courage, he found they had fallen asleep. Twice more he prayed, and twice more his friends failed him. Luke tells us the pressure of this spiritual battle was so heavy it exacted a physical toll on Jesus' body; *being in agony he prayed more earnestly; and his sweat became like great drops of blood falling down to the ground.* (Luke 22:44)

"Gethsemane" means olive press, and it is no surprise archaeologists have discovered evidence of first-century olive oil production there. Huge, weighted levers applied tremendous pressure to crushed olives in order to squeeze out the oil. It is hard to imagine a more vivid image than squeezing oil from olives to describe what Jesus was experiencing. Back in Caesarea Philippi, Jesus had called out the satanic influence when Peter suggested he did not have to go to Jerusalem and die. (Matthew 16:21-23) Now Jesus was faced with the real temptation to slip over the Mount of Olives in the darkness and disappear into the Judean wilderness. He had spent forty days surviving in that desert and was well-acquainted with caves where no one would find him. Jesus was praying that night for the strength he needed to resist this temptation and the faith required to surrender his whole self to the Father, no matter what suffering was to come. After admitting the dread of what lay ahead but relinquishing his will to the Father, Jesus found the strength he needed to face his destiny and complete the final leg of his earthly journey from Gethsemane to Golgotha.

First-Century Olive Oil Press in Gethsemane

A very real struggle is constantly being waged in the heart and mind of every human being on this broken planet. Jesus summarized it when he said to his sleeping friends that night, *"Watch and pray that you may not enter into temptation. The spirit indeed is willing, but the flesh is weak."* (Mark 16:38) Our flesh is that very human part of us which wants to get our own way, serve our own ends, and do what we think is right. Our spirit is that part of us which can submit to God's Spirit, who empowers us to know and do the will of God on earth as it is done in heaven. There is a battle between our flesh and our spirit, and Jesus shows us the way to win that battle so the Spirit can have his way in us. It is through prayer. First, it is through brutally honest prayer, in which we pour out our raw hopes, fears, and desires to God. This is followed by the prayer of surrender, in which we deliberately choose to set aside our way and seek first the Kingdom of God. In the Garden of Gethsemane we learn how to take up our cross, die to ourselves, and fulfill the destiny God has for each of us. We would do well to learn from Jesus and imitate his honest prayer of surrender, so we can find the strength we need to relinquish our will and embrace God's will for our lives.

The Church of All Nations at Gethsemane

While Jesus poured out his heart and surrendered to the Father in prayer, Judas arrived with the soldiers who had been tasked by the religious leaders to arrest Jesus. Judas was one of his most trusted disciples, evidenced by the fact Jesus had entrusted him with their corporate money bag. (John 12:6) The painful irony of Judas' betrayal was complete when he identified Jesus to the soldiers by kissing his Rabbi's cheeks, using the greeting of a close friend or family member. None of this took Jesus by surprise. He knew what was coming but chose not to run. When Peter valiantly tried to fight back and defend his Master, cutting off the ear of the High Priest's slave Malchus, Jesus rebuked him saying, *"Put your sword back into its place. For all who take the sword will perish by the sword. Do you think that I cannot appeal to my Father, and he will at once send me more than twelve legions of angels? But how then should the Scriptures be fulfilled, that it must be so?"* (Matthew 26:52-54) The extraordinary level of Jesus' submission becomes apparent when we remember he continuously chose not to save himself by exercising the supernatural power that was always at his disposal.

At this point the Gospel writers report, to their own shame, that all of them fled in fear, abandoning Jesus in his hour of greatest need. However, Peter and John summoned up the courage to follow the soldiers at a distance and see where they took Jesus. When they saw the soldiers take Jesus into the large house of the High Priest Caiaphas, they even went so far as to access to the central courtyard of that house, where they tried to blend in with the servants who were warming themselves around a charcoal fire. Meanwhile Jesus was taken to a large upstairs room that looked down into the courtyard. There, Caiaphas had gathered the Sanhedrin, the Jewish religious council, to pass judgment on Jesus. Archaeologists have discovered a large first-century home on the wealthy southwest hill of Jerusalem where the priestly aristocracy lived. We don't know if it is the house of Caiaphas, but it was the home of a wealthy priestly family and it fits the descriptions we have in the Gospels. If it isn't the house where Jesus was tried by the Sanhedrin, it is very much like it.

Although they had arranged for various witnesses to give false testimony against him, the religious leaders still could not get two people to agree on what crime Jesus had committed. Jesus chose not to respond to the false accusations levied against him, but when Caiaphas finally asked him directly, *"Are you the Christ, the Son of the Blessed?"* Jesus responded, *"I am, and you will see the Son of Man seated at the right hand of Power, and coming with the clouds of heaven."* (Mark 14:61-62) This was enough for them to accuse Jesus of blasphemy and condemn him to death. Tearing their robes, they began to spit on him, mock him, and beat him.

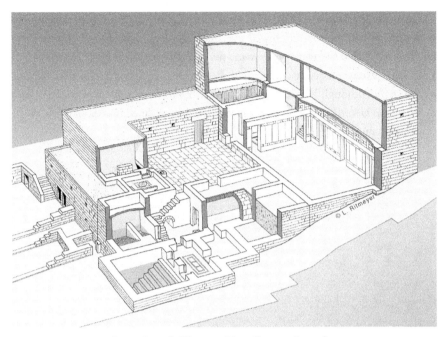

Large Priestly House in First-Century Jerusalem

In the oral traditions of the rabbis, which were written down in the Mishnah around AD 200, clear rules govern trials carried out by the Sanhedrin. Capital cases were to be tried during daylight hours and were not to be carried out on the eve of a Sabbath festival day. Capital cases were to begin with reasons for acquittal rather than reasons for conviction. Verdicts of acquittal could be reached on the same day, but verdicts of conviction were to be confirmed after a night's sleep. Condemnation required the evidence of two witnesses who agreed, otherwise their evidence was thrown out. The Sanhedrin was to carry out trials in the Chamber of Hewn Stone, part of the inner Temple courts, not in the house of the High Priest. We don't know if all these rules were in effect in the first century, but it is clear from the Gospel accounts that this proceeding, which violated all these standards, was anything but a fair trial. All along the religious leaders had been trying to come up with an excuse to get rid of Jesus, and now they had manufactured their excuse.

Meanwhile, Peter huddled around the charcoal fire in the courtyard down below, where he was recognized by a servant girl as a follower of Jesus. His Galilean accent gave him away, but he denied even knowing Jesus. A rooster crowed in the distance.

Twice more Peter was identified with Jesus, but he denied it even more vehemently each time. When the rooster crowed a second time *Peter remembered how Jesus had said to him, "Before the rooster crows twice, you will deny me three times."* (Mark 14:72) Luke tells us Jesus made eye contact with Peter at that moment *and he went out and wept bitterly.* Although he had promised Jesus, *"Lord, I am ready to go with you both to prison and to death,"* when the chips were down Peter failed his Rabbi in the worst way imaginable. (Luke 22:33, 62)

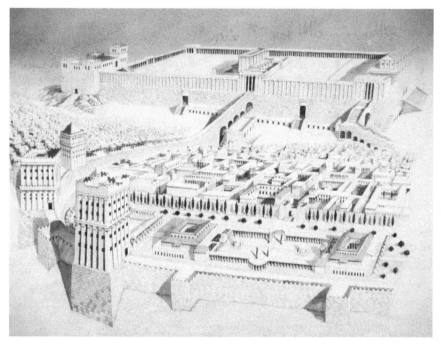

Herod's Palace in Foreground with Temple in Distance

At that time the Romans had not authorized the Sanhedrin to carry out executions, so early the next morning they formalized their decision and then took Jesus to the nearby Palace of Herod where the Roman governor Pontius Pilate was holding his daily court while visiting Jerusalem for the Passover. Herod's Palace was an enormous complex consisting of three huge towers guarding two large multi-story buildings which stood at each end of a great plaza known as *the gabbatha*, meaning "pavement" in Aramaic. The second-story balcony overlooking this pavement served as the Governor's *"judgment seat*" from which he made proclamations and passed judgment on cases brought before him. (John 19:13) The religious leaders had gathered a crowd sympathetic to their political goals in this large plaza and brought Jesus to Pilate on the judgment seat. Since Pilate couldn't care less about the Jewish charge of blasphemy, Caiaphas brought a different accusation against Jesus, *"We found this man misleading our nation and forbidding us to give tribute to Caesar, and saying that he himself is Christ, a king."* (Luke 23:2) Since Pilate's main job as Roman governor was to maintain order by putting down revolution and keeping the people subject to Caesar, this pushed all his political buttons.

Pilate had always been driven by political expediency, but his instinct for self-preservation was even more heightened at this time since his primary political benefactor back in Rome had recently been sent into exile, leaving Pilate particularly vulnerable to suspicion. When he realized Jesus was from Galilee, Pilate tried to pass the buck by sending Jesus to Herod Antipas, the ruler of Galilee who was also visiting Jerusalem for the Passover. But when Jesus refused to perform tricks for Herod, Antipas sent him back to Pilate. After Pilate cross-examined Jesus further he said to Caiaphas, *"You brought me this man as one who was misleading the people. And after examining him before you, behold, I did not find this man guilty of any of your charges against him. Neither did Herod, for he sent him back to us. Look, nothing deserving death has been done by him. I will therefore punish and release him."* (Luke 23:6-13) Pilate was politically savvy enough to tell this was a set-up, and also his wife told him of a dream she had that night warning him not to condemn this righteous man.

Pilate decided to try another tactic to remove himself from this political pickle. There was a custom at Passover for the Roman Governor to pardon a popular prisoner to help placate the crowds, so Pilate offered to release Jesus. But the religious leaders stirred up the crowd to ask for a murderous insurrectionist named Barabbas instead. *The governor again said to them, "Which of the two do you want me to release for you?" And they said, "Barabbas." Pilate said to them, "Then what shall I do with Jesus who is called Christ?" They all said, "Let him be crucified!" And he said, "Why? What evil has he done?" But they shouted all the more, "Let him be crucified!"* (Matthew 27:20-23) Then Pilate had Jesus scourged, a terrible lashing that literally ripped the flesh from the victim's back. He hoped this would satisfy the blood lust of the crowd, but they still cried, *"Crucify him! Crucify him!"* After more weak protests, Pilate caved in to the political pressure and condemned a perfectly innocent man to death for a crime he knew Jesus did not commit.

Aside from Jesus, no one is blameless in these terrible events. The religious leaders falsely accused Jesus, Judas betrayed him, the disciples abandoned him, Peter denied him, Herod mocked him, the crowds turned against him, and Pilate condemned him. Perhaps we can find ourselves in this painful story as well. The simple truth is that some of us resist Jesus because he threatens our self-serving autonomy. Others of us avoid publicly identifying with Jesus for fear we will be ridiculed and rejected as he was. Still others of us affirm things we know to be lies about Jesus for our own perceived benefit. It is difficult to stand with Jesus and seek his Kingdom when the world tries to exert its own rule over us. And let us not be naïve and ignore the fact that the kingdoms of darkness were arrayed against Jesus, seeking to destroy him and all he stands for through people in power and the systems of which they were part. The same is true today.

Like those first disciples, we have all fallen short and failed to be true to Jesus, our true Lord and King. Like them, we are up against spiritual powers that are far greater than ourselves. The Good News is Jesus' New Covenant of grace is for used-to-bes who have failed spectacularly like Peter but are humble enough to receive the gift of forgiveness and restoration. The Good News is Jesus' Kingdom is where we receive his authority and power to overcome all the forces that seek to keep us from fulfilling God's will on earth as it is done in heaven.

We are invited to Jesus' table, where we can receive the Lamb who takes away the sin of the world. We are called to the Garden, where we can learn in prayer to choose God's will over our own. And we are invited to the *gabbatha,* where we see the truly innocent one take on the condemnation we rightly deserve. Wherever you find yourself right now, take heart and do not give up. Although the disciples despaired and thought all was lost at this moment, in fact God was at work in all these terrible events to bring about his good purpose, better than they could have imagined! The same is true in our darkest night when it seems there is no hope. No matter how badly you have failed or what injustices have been done to you, the only way forward is through the cross which is the next and most difficult step on this journey. Don't give up and turn back now.

REFLECT AND DISCUSS

Read Luke 22:14-62

1. How can I consciously renew my participation in Jesus' New Covenant when I receive Communion?

2. Am I willing to overcome the temptation to serve my flesh by surrendering in prayer to the Spirit?

3. What are some of the ways I betray, deny, and abandon Jesus in the normal course of my life?

4. How have I fallen into the trap of using Jesus to achieve my own purposes rather than take the risk of standing with him no matter what the cost?

5. God, what are you saying to me and what step of faith do you want me to take in response?

CHAPTER TWELVE

CATASTROPHE!

A LIVING NIGHTMARE

My son! My beloved son! It seemed like a bad dream from which she couldn't awaken. Mary of Nazareth stumbled over a stone on the stepped road, tears blurring her sight. The crowd raged and surged through the narrow city streets, carrying her along like a branch in a swollen river in springtime. She desperately tried to hold on to Mary Magdalene, the only thing keeping her afloat in this sea of pain and despair. A Roman soldier screamed obscenities as he lashed Jesus' back with his cruel whip. Her son tripped and fell under the weight of the large crossbeam they had tied across his shoulders. The whip cracked again. More swearing and shouting from the soldiers, but Jesus could no longer bear the weight of the timber. Finally, one of the soldiers grabbed an African bystander from the crowd and strapped the beam on his shoulders. And the grisly parade lurched forward once again.

Ever since Jesus was first conceived, she knew beyond a shadow of a doubt he was special. At his birth the angels, the shepherds, the mysterious wise men all confirmed her son was the one who would save his people. *But now this! How can it be?* Mary's mind raced back over the events of these past few years. When Jesus left home to meet her nephew John, who was baptizing at the River Jordan, Mary's hopes had soared. When he turned the water into wine at Cana, she knew it was finally happening! But then came Jesus' fateful sermon in the synagogue of Nazareth. She couldn't understand why he included the Gentiles in God's promises to his people. It broke her heart when Jesus disappeared, but she truly believed he was wrong. When she heard reports of the things her son was saying and doing, she feared for his sanity. So, she and her other sons went to Capernaum and knocked on the door of Simon's house, hoping to bring Jesus home and help him regain his right mind. Jesus' reply, that his family were those who do the will of God, only confirmed her worst fears—he really was crazy.

But as the months and years went by, something started to change inside of Mary. Although Jesus' brothers ridiculed him, Mary was drawn to the things she heard about her son. People repeated the parables he taught, and she could feel her heart stirring. People recounted the things he did, and she was amazed. Mary met people who had been miraculously healed by him and was deeply moved by their testimonies. During this Passover in Jerusalem, she had come to the Temple courts every day, standing at the edge of the crowd, to hear her son's profound teaching. Slowly she began to believe all the promises were finally being fulfilled in her beloved son Jesus. But early this morning she had awakened with a start to the sound of Mary of Magdala pounding on the outer door of the house where she was staying with the extended family. Magdalena told her the religious leaders had arrested her son in the night and were now petitioning Pilate to put him to death. As the two women made their way to Herod's Palace, they were suddenly swept up in this crowd following Jesus as he carried his crossbeam to Golgotha.

Now the crowd squeezed through the Garden Gate in Jerusalem's northwestern wall and spilled out into the bright morning light that bathed the open countryside. Mary blinked at the brightness. She knew where the soldiers were taking him. A knot tightened in the pit of her stomach at the sight of the ancient quarry-turned-cemetery in the distance, with the grisly rock of Golgotha hulking like a monster in the manicured garden. *No Lord, no! Not the Place of the Skull!* The spire of uncut stone in the quarry left behind by the Temple builders had become the Roman's chosen place of public crucifixion, being just outside the city walls and beside the well-traveled road to Jaffa. Her mind was a blur, unable to process the horrific sight unfolding before her. Jesus was stripped naked, laid down on the crossbeam, arms stretched out tight and wrists nailed to the rough wood with iron spikes. The sharp crack of hammer on metal pierced her heart with every blow. The crossbeam was lifted and hung up on one of the vertical posts protruding from the top of the 20-foot-high rock. Magdalena covered Mary's eyes as his ankles were nailed in place, but Mary's legs buckled, and the two women held onto each other as they went down together on their knees. From the crowd came shouts of derision and mockery. Even one of the murderers being crucified alongside Jesus swore at him.

Now everything seemed to spin around her as a distant memory floated back into Mary's mind. She remembered when Jesus was just over one month old, they brought him to the Temple for his dedication and were met by a prophet named Simeon. He foretold that Jesus would fulfill God's promise of salvation and then, as he blessed them, he said to Mary, *"a sword will pierce through your own soul also."* (Luke 2:22-35) Mary could feel that sword now, like a hot iron deep in her soul, as she watched her bleeding son struggling against the nails for every breath. Then she felt a gentle hand on her shoulder. Looking up she saw it was John the son of Zebedee, one of Jesus' closest disciples. The sorrowful kindness on his face broke the fragile dam inside of her and she began to weep violently and uncontrollably while he held her tight.

Mary lost all track of time, but she could see the sun had risen overhead by now. Her head was still swimming with grief. The smell of blood and sweat hung heavy in the air. Jesus seemed to fade in and out of consciousness as he periodically pulled himself up on his bleeding arms, filling his lungs with air. He was slowly drowning in his own fluids as his strength slipped away. In spite of it all, he quoted Psalm 22 while crying out to God in lament. He promised salvation to the other criminal hanging beside him. Incredibly, he offered forgiveness to the very soldiers who tortured him. And now, through cracked and blood-stained lips, Jesus spoke directly to her.

John and Magdalena lifted Mary to her feet, and the three of them moved closer to the rock. Jesus looked at her and then at John, saying, "Woman, behold, your son!" Then he looked from John back to her and said, "Behold, your mother!" Instantly Mary knew what was happening. She had rejected Jesus' vision and mission back in Nazareth. She had spurned his invitation in Capernaum to become part of his new family. But now he was welcoming her as a member of this extended spiritual family that does the will of God on earth as it is done in heaven! Mary could see the tears welling up in John's eyes as he held her hand even tighter. She could feel Magdalena's arm around her shoulders. Mary knew that whatever happened, from this day on she would always have a place in the family of her son, the crucified Messiah.[14]

THE WAY OF SUFFERING

Before Pilate sentenced Jesus to crucifixion, he had him scourged. Roman law prescribed scourging as a precursor to crucifixion. Mark tells us this was another attempt by Pilate to satisfy the crowd and avoid crucifixion, but it didn't work. The scourge was a whip made of a short handle to which were attached strips of leather. A Roman scourge typically included sharp pieces of bone or metal embedded in the ends of these strips. According to historians, Roman scourging tore the flesh from the victim's back, exposing bones and organs. Often this brutal punishment was enough to kill its victims. Following this horrific beating, the Roman soldiers taunted Jesus, dressing him like a king in a purple robe with a crown of thorns and a reed for a royal staff. *Kneeling down before him, they mocked him, saying, "Hail, King of the Jews!" And they spit on him and took the reed and struck him on the head.* (Matthew 27:29-30) Little did they know they were abusing the true King of kings and Lord of lords before whom one day they would bow in speechless awe and wonder.

After this they dressed Jesus again in his own blood-soaked robe, they laid the horizontal beam of a cross on his shoulders, and led him out to the place of crucifixion. The Roman practice was to force the condemned man to carry the crossbeam on which he was to be crucified through the city streets to the place of execution, a dramatic announcement for all to see of the terrible sentence being carried out. Jesus was so weakened from his all-night interrogation and the blood loss from his severe scourging that he was unable to carry the crossbeam very far before collapsing. Roman soldiers claimed the right to force any subject person to carry their load one mile, so they conscripted a Jewish pilgrim named Simon who had come to Jerusalem for the Passover from Cyrene on the north coast of Africa. Placing the cross beam on Simon's shoulders, the soldiers pulled Jesus to his feet and drove them both forward toward Golgotha. In a literal sense, this unsuspecting man from Cyrene answered Jesus' call to take up his cross and follow. Because Mark includes the detail that Simon was the father of Alexander and Rufus, we can conclude he and his sons became followers of Jesus and part of the community to whom Mark was writing. (Mark 15:21) Something about drawing so near to Jesus in his darkest hour moved this pilgrim to put his trust in Jesus rather than reject him as a condemned criminal.

[14] Based on Luke 8:1-2, 40-56

We don't know how many of the male disciples were aware of what was happening to Jesus and were with him on the way to Golgotha, but we do know many of the women disciples followed Jesus to his place of crucifixion. A crowd of both men and women filled the streets, crying out in grief and lamenting this miscarriage of justice. Despite a culture which devalued women, Jesus spoke directly to them saying, *"Daughters of Jerusalem, do not weep for me, but weep for yourselves and for your children. For behold, the days are coming when they will say, 'Blessed are the barren and the wombs that never bore and the breasts that never nursed!' Then they will begin to say to the mountains, 'Fall on us,' and to the hills, 'Cover us.' For if they do these things when the wood is green, what will happen when it is dry?"* (Luke 23:27-31) We see how Jesus, in the midst of unimaginable distress and pressure, still focused on the needs of others rather than concern for himself.

Since ancient times, pilgrims in Jerusalem have sought to retrace the path on which Jesus carried his cross, from the place of his condemnation to the place of his execution. In the Middle Ages this pilgrim's route came to be called "the Via Dolorosa," meaning the way of suffering. They assumed the Antonia Fortress, built onto the northwest corner of the Temple Mount, was where Pilate tried Jesus, since it served as the barracks of the Roman Legion in Jerusalem. For this reason, the traditional Via Dolorosa, followed by throngs of pilgrims still today, begins in the northwest part of the city and winds its way to the ancient Church of the Holy Sepulcher, marking the site of Jesus' crucifixion and resurrection. However, the first-century Jewish writers Philo and Josephus both tell us Pilate stayed at Herod's Palace on the western edge

The Via Dolorosa in Jerusalem

of the city and it was there, in the huge plaza, that he passed judgement and imposed punishment. For this reason, we now know the historical route on which Jesus carried his cross began on the southwest hill of Jerusalem where Herod's Palace is located and made its way outside the northwest wall of the city through the Garden Gate, to an ancient quarry-turned-cemetery where the Church of the Holy Sepulcher sits today, now inside the northwest quarter of the city.

Whether you follow the streets of the traditional Via Dolorosa or walk the more historically accurate route to Golgotha, it is a powerful experience to retrace the way of Jesus' suffering, as we do regularly on the pilgrimages we lead. But it must have been so much more impactful for the disciples who were brave enough to join the crowd that was following Jesus, beaten and bleeding, through the streets of Jerusalem on that fateful Friday. Some, like Jesus' women disciples, were there by choice. Their love and devotion to their Rabbi gave them courage not to turn away from Jesus in this dark hour, but to draw near and share in his suffering. Others, like Simon of Cyrene, were swept up in events beyond their control, but were transformed by their encounter with the suffering Jesus nonetheless. Since Mary Magdalene, John the son of Zebedee, and Mary the mother of Jesus were all at the foot of the cross, we can assume they also followed Jesus as he carried his cross along the way of suffering. These brave disciples stand as an example for us who seek to take up our cross and follow Jesus today.

The Remains of Herod's Palace in Jerusalem

Jesus was clear his way is not the easy way. He said, *"Remember the word that I said to you: 'A servant is not greater than his master.' If they persecuted me, they will also persecute you."* (John 15:20) He warned the disciples, *"they will deliver you up to tribulation and put you to death, and you will be hated by all nations for my name's sake."* (Matthew 24:9) It is true that harsh persecution came to many who followed Jesus in those early centuries and most of Jesus' core disciples were ultimately executed for their faith in him. It takes great faith and determination to follow Jesus down the Via Dolorosa, but there is no other way to be his disciple.

While we may or may not see overt physical persecution in our lives today, the way of Jesus is the way of self-sacrifice where we are called to lay down our lives for others. The way of Jesus will always lead us into conflict with the kingdoms of this world because they are under the influence of the kingdom of darkness. Jesus invites us to join him on this way of suffering to confront whatever forces may seek to keep us from extending the Kingdom of God, because paradoxically this is the road that leads to the truly abundant life. As Jesus promised in his Sermon on the Mount, *"Blessed are those who are persecuted for righteousness' sake, for theirs is the kingdom of heaven. Blessed are you when others revile you and persecute you and utter all kinds of evil against you falsely on my account. Rejoice and be glad, for your reward is great in heaven, for so they persecuted the prophets who were before you."* (Matthew 5:10-12)

THE DEATH BLOW

Both the traditional Via Dolorosa and the more historically accurate route on which Jesus carried his cross, lead to the Church of the Holy Sepulcher. To the visitor today, this ancient church appears, at first, a somewhat ramshackle warren of dark chapels covered by gilded domes and filled with soot, oil lamps, and crowds of religious tourists. The present remains of the church are a far cry from the awe-inspiring beauty and scale of the original building built by Queen Helena, mother of Constantine the Great, in 335 AD. Many western Protestants who visit this site do not find it an uplifting experience because the layout of the church is confusing, the religious rituals feel alien, and the decoration seems overdone. However, it is a place worth exploring and understanding because all the historical and archaeological evidence points to this as the actual location of the rock of Golgotha where Jesus was crucified and the nearby rock-cut tomb where he rose from the dead.

Archaeologists have discovered the remains of an ancient rock quarry underneath the Church of the Holy Sepulcher. Large limestone blocks were cut away from the hillside there to rebuild the Temple following the return of the exiles from Babylon at the end of the sixth century BC. The site was abandoned for centuries and in time became overgrown. In the first century BC, the old quarry was transformed into a cemetery by planting a garden and cutting fine tombs into the rock walls. By the first century AD, Joseph of Arimathea, a wealthy member of the Jewish Sanhedrin, purchased a plot in this cemetery and had a new family tomb cut in its rock walls. Although this area is now enclosed inside the city walls in the heart of what is known as the Christian Quarter of Jerusalem, in the first century it was located just outside the northwestern city wall, near the "Gennath" or Garden Gate, alongside the road leading from Jerusalem to Jaffa on the coast.

In one area of the hillside, the limestone was unstable and unsuitable for building, so the stonemasons simply cut around that section, leaving a twenty-foot-high rocky outcropping in the midst of the quarry. Because it was just outside the city wall and next to a heavily used road, the Romans chose this rock as their place of execution. It came to be known as "Golgotha," meaning place of the skull. Crucifixion was the most horrific form of Roman capital punishment, designed to terrify a subject population. This is why they typically chose the most visible site they could find outside the city. John tells us that Jesus went out, bearing his own cross, to the place called The Place of a Skull, which in Aramaic is called Golgotha. He also wrote, the place where Jesus was crucified was near the city. (John 19:17, 20) Mark tells us, those who passed by derided him, wagging their heads and saying, *"Aha! You who*

Ancient Rock Quarry Outside Jerusalem

would destroy the temple and rebuild it in three days, save yourself, and come down from the cross!" (Mark 15:29-30) These descriptions that Jesus went out, was crucified near the city, and was mocked by those who passed by are all consistent with the location of this rocky outcropping outside the city walls and next to a major road.

The Top of the Rock of Golgotha in the Church of the Holy Sepulcher

Crucifixion was developed by the Assyrians and the Persians as a brutal form of execution, then adapted by the Romans to make it even more excruciating. The goal was to maximize the pain while prolonging suffering in as public a way as possible. The arms of the victim were stretched out and tied or nailed with iron spikes to the crossbeam. While carefully avoiding major arteries, the spikes were driven through the wrists, since a nail through the palms could not support the weight of a body. When John recounts the risen Jesus inviting Thomas to touch his wounds, the Greek word he used for "hand" refers to the lower arm and hand, so it is consistent with nailing through the wrist. (John 20:27)

Once the victim was nailed to the crossbeam, it was then lifted up and affixed to an upright post, often just a little higher than a man. Jesus' cross probably stood a bit taller since the soldiers put a sponge of sour wine on a reed in order to extend it to his lips. (Mark 15:36) The victim's heels were then nailed into the upright post. Sometimes the vertical post extended above the crossbeam and served as a place to affix a sign stating the crime for which this person was being executed. John tells us, *Pilate also wrote an inscription and put it on the cross. It read, "Jesus of Nazareth, the King of the Jews."* The religious leaders were upset with this affirmation of Jesus as King and told Pilate he should change it to *"This man said, I am King of the Jews." Pilate answered, "What I have written I have written."* (John 19:19-22) This ironic statement of truth was a very different charge than the crimes committed by the two insurrectionists who were being crucified alongside Jesus or the murderer Barabbas who was pardoned by Pilate instead of Jesus. (Matthew 27:15-26)

As the weight of the victim's body hung on their outstretched arms, the muscles around their rib cage constricted so the lungs couldn't expand with air and expel the bodily fluids which naturally accumulate in them. The victim had to pull his body up with his arms and push up with his legs in order to take a breath. The pulling and pushing caused excruciating pain in the wrists and ankles. As the victim slid up and slumped back down the scourging wounds in his back grated against the rough wood of the cross. Survival instinct drove the victim to continue pushing and pulling to catch each breath, no matter how painful it was. The cross was essentially a crude kind of torture machine operated by the victim on himself. But ever so slowly their lungs filled with fluid, reducing their lung capacity. As each excruciating breath became shallower and shallower, they slowly drowned in their own fluids until they could not push themselves up anymore. According to the first-century historian Josephus, some victims of Roman crucifixion lasted up to three torturous days on the cross. Mercifully, Jesus was already so weak that he died about three o'clock in the afternoon, after some six hours on the cross. (Mark 15:25, 33-34)

Although there are many references to Roman crucifixion in ancient writings, only two sets of human remains have been discovered that include physical evidence of Roman crucifixion. The first was discovered in Jerusalem in 1968—a Jewish man from the first century who was nailed to a cross through the heel bone. Normally the nails used for crucifixion were removed from the body and reused. In this case, because the tip of the five-inch iron spike was bent, the Romans left the nail in the heel bone when they buried him, to be discovered nearly 2,000 years later. The second set of crucified remains was discovered in Gavello, Italy, in 2007 and also dates to the first century. While the spike is missing from this burial, a round hole in each of the heel bones is consistent with Roman crucifixion. These discoveries confirm what we know about Roman crucifixion and support the Gospel accounts of Jesus' death on the cross.

First-Century Heel Bone and Spike of Crucified Man from Jerusalem

Understanding how excruciating the torture of Roman crucifixion was, it is surprising Jesus could say anything at all, but the Gospels record seven distinct interactions while he was dying:

1. **Forgive Them:** After Jesus was nailed to the cross by the four Roman soldiers, he prayed for them, *"Father, forgive them, for they know not what they do."* (Luke 23:34) Jesus taught his disciples to love their enemies and pray for those who persecute them, and that is exactly what he did from the cross. It is hard to imagine a greater act of grace than begging forgiveness for those who are in the very act of torturing you to death.

2. **Today in Paradise:** One of the criminals being crucified next to Jesus railed at him, saying *"Are you not the Christ? Save yourself and us!"* The criminal

being crucified on the other side defended Jesus and then said, *"Jesus, remember me when you come into your kingdom."* Jesus responded with the most powerful promise that can be spoken to a condemned and dying man, *"Truly, I say to you, today you will be with me in paradise."* (See Luke 23:39-43.) We see the grace of Jesus' New Covenant is enough to save anyone who would express even a mustard seed of faith, even with their final breath.

3. **Mother and Son:** Although Jesus' mother Mary had rejected his vision, considered him crazy, and declined to join his new family, now she stood with Mary Magdalene and the other women disciples at the foot of the cross. Apparently, John was the only male disciple who was with them that day. Jesus publicly affirmed Mary's place in the extended spiritual family he had established when he entrusted her to John's care, saying *"Woman, behold, your son!" Then he said to the disciple, "Behold, your mother!"* (John 19:26-27) No matter how we have ignored, rejected, or resisted Jesus in the past, he demonstrates there is always a place for us in the family of his Father.

4. **I Thirst:** As Jesus hung on the cross, he gave voice to the profound dehydration his overnight imprisonment, scourging, and now crucifixion had produced in his body when he simply said, *"I thirst."* (John 19:28) We are reminded Jesus' divine nature did not shield him from the horrific pain he suffered as a vulnerable human being, but that he had to drink this bitter cup of suffering to the very dregs.

5. **Forsaken:** Around 3 PM, near the end of his crucifixion, Jesus cried out, *"My God, My God, why have you forsaken me?"* (Matthew 27:46) Here we see the full humanity of Jesus on display as he lamented the forsakenness of his suffering and impending death. He quoted Psalm 22, the first half of which describes many of the terrible things he was experiencing and the second half of which offers thanks and praise for God's deliverance. Jesus shows us the way to overcome crushing despair is by openly expressing our feelings of abandonment, but at the same time by faith claiming God's promise of redemption.

6. **It is Finished:** As Jesus neared the end of his earthly life, he said, *"It is finished."* (John 19:30) In persistently submitting to the Father, Jesus knew his final breath would bring him across the finish line and complete the work he was sent to do. Because Jesus willingly died on the cross, his perfect sacrifice completes the work of our redemption. There is

literally nothing we can add to or take away from the salvation Jesus has accomplished for us.

7. **My Spirit:** Despite his very human feelings of abandonment and the growing weakness of his tortured body, with his final breath Jesus chose to entrust himself to his heavenly Father, *calling out with a loud voice, "Father, into your hands I commit my spirit!"* (Luke 23:46) Jesus shows us what it means to live and die by faith in the Father who loves us and will never forsake us.

With this final declaration of faith, Jesus breathed his last and died shortly after 3 o'clock in the afternoon. The Gospel writers report that from noon to 3 o'clock, the sun was darkened in the sky, an apparent solar eclipse. At the moment of his death, an earthquake struck, and the huge curtain separating the Holy of Holies in the Temple was torn in two from top to bottom. This was a powerful sign that Jesus' death has opened the way for everyone who puts their faith in him to draw near to the living presence of God without fear. Matthew even describes a number of people who were dead and buried coming back to life, perhaps emerging from the tombs in the cemetery surrounding Golgotha. (See Matthew 27:52-53.) It was a beautiful sign that Jesus' death means life for us. The Roman centurion overseeing the crucifixion was so moved by all he had witnessed that he declared Jesus innocent and said, *"Truly this man was the Son of God!"* (Mark 15:39)

LOVE SO AMAZING

The death of Jesus on a Roman cross is one of the most indisputable historical facts of his life and also one of the most significant. As John the Baptist prophesied at the very beginning of Jesus' public ministry, Jesus was destined to become the perfect sacrifice for all people, *"the Lamb of God who takes away the sin of the world."* (John 1:29) Although the priests of Israel continuously sacrificed animals on the huge altar in front of the Temple, it never seemed to be enough. In the covenant of the Law there was always a striving to do more, to work harder in order to become holy. It seemed the rabbis constantly established more rules and created new rituals in a never-ending attempt to earn God's forgiveness and merit his favor. By contrast, beginning with the outpouring of the Father's unconditional love at his baptism, Jesus inaugurated a New Covenant of preemptive grace for any who are genuinely open to receiving it. God's unconditional love and total acceptance is the starting point of this relationship. As we have seen, Jesus welcomed outcasts, forgave sinners, and invited people into an intimacy with God as their very own loving Father. At the final Passover meal, he explained to the disciples that this New Covenant of grace is ratified in his broken body and shed blood.

Ever since the people of Israel were saved through the blood of the lamb on the doorposts of their house, they understood the importance of a sacrifice to atone for their sins and make it possible for them to live in relationship with the God who created all things. Jesus' death on the cross is the ultimate sacrifice of atonement, because he is the only human being who lived in perfect harmony with the will of his heavenly Father and did not sin. By willingly offering himself and surrendering to the violent hatred of sinful human beings, Jesus has paid a price for us that we could never afford to pay. He has taken upon himself the guilt and shame of our sin and has absorbed in his own body the punishment of death we rightly deserve. In doing this, Jesus surprisingly won the ultimate victory over sin, death, hell, and the devil. Paradoxically, the very moment the devil thought he had won by snuffing out the Light of the world was the precise moment when Jesus triumphed over all the powers of evil and vanquished the kingdom of darkness. This victory has won freedom from everything that would prevent us from fulfilling our destiny and assures us God's ultimate purpose for all of creation will be fulfilled. Given all Jesus accomplished in his death, it is little wonder the cross stands as the central symbol of this New Covenant Jesus inaugurated and the Kingdom of God he established!

When we enter into a personal Covenant relationship with God by trusting Jesus and begin to follow him into a new life in his Kingdom, all the benefits of Jesus' death become ours. We are forgiven all our sins, guilt and shame are washed away, and we are restored to our rightful identity as the daughters and sons of God. By faith in Jesus, we are given authority to represent our Father the King, filled with the power to carry out his will on earth as is in heaven, and assured of his ultimate victory over the devil and his final weapon, death. But we must not think of all this as some kind of cold metaphysical transaction. At the heart of all these realities is a love so great and so powerful that we cannot comprehend it, because God is love. All Jesus did and said was an expression of the Father's great love for us. As Jesus said to the disciples, *"Greater love has no one than this, that someone lay down his life for his friends."* (John 15:13) Jesus' willingness to suffer and die on our behalf is the ultimate expression of this boundless love of God for us his children. This love is not just for some, but for all. It is too costly to be earned by legalistic effort or religious rituals; it can only be accepted by faith as a free gift of grace. The Good News of the cross is *God so loved the world, that he gave his only Son, that whoever believes in him should not perish but have eternal life.* (John 3:16)

In receiving this great love, we are empowered to love in return. Receiving the unconditional and inexpressible love demonstrated on the cross and poured into our hearts by the Holy Spirit produces in us an overflowing love for the God who created us, redeemed us, and restored us to himself. This sacrificial love also produces in us a stubborn and unconditional love for those around us. The disciple John, after a lifetime of learning this way of Jesus, said it so simply, *"We love because he first loved us."* (1 John 4:19) This is not a love that only responds to those who love us, but an irrational, other-worldly love for strangers, for outcasts, for the lost and the broken. Even a love for our enemies.

When Jesus was asked what our highest priority should be, he replied, *"The most important is, Hear, O Israel: The Lord our God, the Lord is one. And you shall love the Lord your God with all your heart and with all your soul and with all your mind and with all your strength.' The second is this: You shall love your neighbor as yourself.' There is no other commandment greater than these."* (Mark 12:29-31) The very heart of love is the willingness to sacrifice what we want for the good of another. That is why the cross stands as the ultimate expression of true love. When we receive that love we are changed and empowered to love in return. That is why Jesus said, *"If anyone would come after me, let him deny himself and take up his cross and follow me."* (Matthew 16:24) By taking up our cross and laying down our lives for the sake of others, we discover the power to live the most extraordinary life of Jesus.

Although I was generally aware of these concepts growing up, it wasn't until I was a teenager that this Good News came alive for me. Having lived overseas as a child, as an adolescent I didn't fit in socially with my peers in rural Washington State. I didn't have many friends and was consistently ridiculed and bullied at school. But my immediate family members loved me and were the safe harbor in this storm I was enduring. That is, until I discovered my parent's marital problems were causing them to consider divorce, and my world began to fall apart. In this moment, through some wonderful people in my church, I came to realize God's great love for me was the most important reality in the universe. I began to understand the meaning of Jesus' death on the cross, the perfect sacrifice that wiped away everything that was keeping me from receiving and living in the perfect love of the Father. As I opened my heart to God and put my trust in Jesus, the Holy Spirit began pouring that love into me, and everything changed. I discovered my true identity as a beloved son of God that nothing in this world could match or take away. I discovered a spiritual family where I was loved and accepted as I am. And I began to embrace a purpose beyond myself, a calling that was bigger and better than my wildest dreams. For over forty years now, every day on that journey has brought greater fulfillment and fruitfulness, even through trials, pain, and loss.

At the foot of Jesus' cross we discover a love so great it overcomes everything keeping us captive to sin and death. There is no other way to live the extraordinary Jesus-shaped lives for which we are created, except by coming to the cross and laying everything down at the feet of our crucified Lord. Whether this is the first time you have understood the Good News of Jesus, or it is a message you have embraced your whole life, right now the Holy Spirit is calling you back to the foot of the cross… to be forgiven purely by grace as were the very soldiers who crucified Jesus… to ask, as that criminal did, *"Jesus, remember me when you come into your kingdom"*… to hear that, like Mary, you have a place and a purpose in the family of God. Jesus invites you to trust him and calls you to follow him. There is no other way to answer that call except through the cross. As Jesus said, *"For whoever would save his life will lose it, but whoever loses his life for my sake will find it."* (Matthew 16:25) Come to the cross and let go of your old life, so you can take the next step of faith, following Jesus into the new, abundant, extraordinary life God has in store for you!

REFLECT AND DISCUSS
Read Mark 15:1-39

1. What would it look like to be honest about my doubts, fears, and pain while trusting the Father at the same time?

2. How can I receive the forgiveness and new life that Jesus' death on the cross makes possible?

3. What does it mean for me to take up my cross and follow Jesus on his way of suffering in order to become more like him?

4. How can I live more consistently in the sacrificial love of Jesus that empowers me to love others sacrificially?

5. God, what are you saying to me and what step of faith do you want me to take in response?

CHAPTER THIRTEEN

A NEW CREATION

THE DAWNING

As she hurried through the darkened streets of Jerusalem, Mary of Magdala looked back and just made out the forms of the other women disciples following her. She sensed the dawning day before she could see it, with a dim light beginning to emerge as they exited the city walls through the Garden Gate. Mary paused to let the others catch up, saying as loudly as she dared, "Hurry, we need to be there when the sun comes up!" As they approached the old quarry, long since converted into a garden cemetery, they saw the hulking outline of the rock of Golgotha, the place where the Romans carried out their most gruesome executions. The women shuddered as they hurried past the bloody rock. Mary blinked back the tears pooling in her eyes.

Even in the gray light of the dawning day, there was no mistaking the nearby tomb in which Jesus' body had been laid. It was newly cut in the rock wall of the quarry and fitted with an expensive rolling stone. On Friday afternoon the women had watched carefully as Joseph and Nicodemus pried loose a wedge holding the massive stone back, allowing it to roll down in its carved slot and seal Jesus inside with a dull thud. Ever since then Mary had heard the sick finality of that sound echoing in her mind over and over again.

"Do you still have the spices?" Mary asked Joanna. Joanna held up the expensive package to show Mary nothing was missing. The men had done their best to anoint Jesus' body for burial, but they were rushed by the setting of the Sabbath sun. Now the female followers of Jesus were determined to honor their Rabbi by finishing the job, regardless of the risks. Mary's eyes strained in the early morning gloom, as she looked for the squad of Roman soldiers who had been dispatched to guard the tomb. She had no idea how they would convince these hardened men to break the seal and roll back the stone, but if there was one thing she had learned from Jesus, it was to trust God for what seemed impossible.

As the morning dawned imperceptibly, they now saw the outline of the tomb more clearly. "Where are they?" whispered Salome, her voice betraying the fear she felt at the thought of confronting the soldiers. None of the women answered because the Romans were nowhere to be found. But that was not the biggest surprise. The women were soon dumbfounded to discover the tomb's stone had already been rolled back.

"Who did this?" gasped Mary the mother of James. Mary Magdalene bent over and looked inside the low doorway. In the growing light, she could just make out the shelf carved into the wall of the tomb where Jesus' body had been laid. A jolt of shock ran through her body as she realized the shelf was empty, save for a linen burial shroud. Mary let out a cry of horror as she came to the obvious conclusion. "Someone has stolen his body!"

Who was it? Why would they take him? What have they done with his body? Leaving the other women to keep watch at the empty tomb, Mary quickly retraced their steps to the home of Mary the mother of John Mark, in order to tell the other disciples what they had seen. The rest of the disciples rubbed sleep from their eyes and tried to comprehend what Mary was saying. "It's a trap," said Thomas. "I'm not going out there!" Finally, John and Peter decided to see for themselves. After running to the tomb, they arrived, crouched down, and went inside. They stared at the empty stone shelf and the oddly arranged grave cloths. Leaving the tomb, arguing as usual, Peter and John made their way back to the house, confirming the women's report of the empty tomb to the rest of the disciples.

All the women could do now was wait outside the tomb and pray. They didn't even have a body to anoint. Mary's head pounded as she leaned against the cool limestone wall of the ancient quarry. The early morning sun continued spreading its light in this dark place, and she began to weep, great sobs welling up from deep within. *Lord God, who would do such a terrible thing?*

Horrible images flashed through her mind like flickering flames from the watchman's fire: Judas' kiss in Gethsemane. Torches and soldiers. Swords and shouts. Caiaphas tearing his robes. The crowd shouting "Crucify him!" Pilate washing his hands. It was like a bad dream that wouldn't end. Mary fought back the sick feeling creeping up from the pit in her stomach. She desperately tried to blot out the excruciating memories of Jesus nailed to that bloody cross, crying out to his Father. It was as if those old familiar demons were trying to claw their way back in.

But something began to stir in Mary. She looked up. *What was that sound?* Wiping away her tears, she bent over once again to look inside the rock-cut tomb. And there, on either end of the burial shelf, sat two angelic messengers. Mary fell to her knees in terror, then heard the divine message: "Do not be afraid, for I know that you seek Jesus who was crucified. He is not here, for he has risen, as he said. Come, see the place where he lay." In her shock, these angelic words were simply too much for her to comprehend.

Stumbling out of the tomb, overwhelmed and confused, Mary bumped into a man she assumed to be the cemetery caretaker standing there. She pleaded, "Sir, if you have carried him away, tell me where you have laid him, and I will take him away." But then Jesus' voice cut through the jumbled maze in her heart and mind, suddenly making sense of it all. "Mary." She blinked, hardly able to believe what she heard. *Could it really be him? It is him!* She turned and said to him in Aramaic, "Rabboni!" An inexpressible tidal wave of joy washed over her, filling the bottomless pit of despair in her soul!

Falling at Jesus' feet, she clung to him, as did the other women, weeping still but now for joy. *I will never let go of him. I will never let go!* Jesus said to her, "Do not cling to me, for I have not yet ascended to the Father; but go to my brothers and say to them, 'I am ascending to my Father and your Father, to my God and your God.'" And then he was gone! Talking excitedly among themselves, the women hurried back arm in arm into the walled city and through the streets to the upper room. Mary Magdalene burst through the outer door into the courtyard and announced to the disciples, "I have seen the Lord!"[15]

---

[15] Based on John 20:1-18

THE EMPTY TOMB

It is hard to imagine the devastation the followers of Jesus experienced when their Rabbi was crucified and died. They had put all their hopes in him as Messiah. They assumed Jesus would establish his royal rule in Jerusalem, liberate them from the oppression of the Romans, restore the kingdom of Israel, and usher in a new era of peace and prosperity. Every one of these hopes was crushed when Jesus breathed his last breath on the cross and the rolling stone sealed his tomb shut with a thud. During that final week in Jerusalem, nothing had gone as they had imagined. Jesus did not do what they thought he would. He did not say what they expected him to say. Their horror at the plotting of the religious leaders and their shock at the brutality of the Romans must have been mingled with confusion and even anger at Jesus himself for not treading more lightly with the authorities or, on the other hand, for not raising an army. Although Jesus had repeatedly told them he was going to Jerusalem to suffer, die, and rise again, the disciples' presuppositions were so strong they seemed unable to comprehend what he was telling them. We all hear what we want to hear sometimes, don't we?

Jesus died on the cross about 3 o'clock on a Friday, just a few hours before sundown when the Sabbath would begin. The Romans often left corpses hanging on the cross for weeks, or until that cross was needed again, to maximize the deterrent factor of crucifixion. However, the Jews were scrupulous about burying people on the day they died, even in the case of someone who was crucified. (Deuteronomy 21:22-23) For that reason, sometime after 3 o'clock, the soldiers broke the legs of the two criminals who were crucified with Jesus, preventing them from pushing themselves up and thus ensuring their deaths before the Sabbath began. When they came to break Jesus' legs, they discovered he was already dead, which was confirmed by piercing his ribcage and witnessing the flow of both blood and the clear fluid that had filled his lungs. Not breaking Jesus' legs and piercing his side fulfilled Old Testament prophecies, as did so many aspects of Jesus' death. (John 19:31-37)

Joseph of Arimathea, a wealthy man who was a respected member of the Sanhedrin council, approached Pilate shortly after that, requesting permission to remove Jesus' body from the cross and bury him. As Mark says, this *took courage* because he was publicly aligning himself with a controversial leader who had just been executed for treason. (Mark 15:43) John tells us Joseph was a disciple of Jesus, but secretly for fear of the negative impact it could have on his standing with the Sanhedrin. (John 19:38) Another prominent member of the council, Nicodemus, who had come to Jesus with questions in the dark of night, joined Joseph in anointing Jesus' body for burial. (John 3:1-2, 39) Presumably, he also was concerned about the negative impact his association with Jesus could have on his political standing.

But something about the death of Jesus shook both of these men out of their complacency and moved them to step from the shadows of secrecy into the full light of publicly identifying as a follower of Jesus, even in his darkest hour. Sometimes we do exactly the same thing. We keep our faith in Jesus hidden to prevent anyone thinking less of us or to make sure it doesn't impede our social standing or professional progress. Joseph and Nicodemus showed us a more courageous path of integrity when they decided to take the risk of being counted with their Rabbi. Jesus said, *"So everyone who acknowledges me before men, I also will acknowledge before my Father who is in heaven, but whoever denies me before men, I also will deny before my Father who is in heaven."* (Matthew 10:33-34)

The preferred burial method for Jews in the first century was to be sealed in a rock-cut tomb designed for an extended family. If they could not afford this, some Jews were buried in pits dug in the ground. The body was anointed with perfumed oil and spices to mask the smell of decay, and a linen shroud was draped around the body from head to toe. Then the shroud was secured by wrapping the entire body in strips of cloth, with a special cloth covering the face. The body was placed in the tomb, either on a rock shelf or a horizontal shaft cut into the wall of the tomb, and the low entrance was sealed with a stone. The most expensive tombs featured a wheel-shaped rolling stone set into a narrow channel which allowed the stone to roll down and seal the door of the tomb. The body was left in the sealed tomb to decay for one year. On the anniversary of the person's death, the extended family gathered at the tomb to remember their loved one, collected the bones into a small stone box called an *"ossuary,"* and carefully place it in one of the shafts of the tomb. In this way the members of an extended family were buried in the same tomb for multiple generations, much as they lived in their extended family *oikos* houses.

First-Century Rolling Stone Tomb

Since the Sabbath was to begin soon, Joseph and Nicodemus quickly anointed Jesus' body for burial. There was no time to transport Jesus' body back to his family tomb in Nazareth or procure a tomb for him there in Jerusalem, so Joseph offered his own family tomb which was newly cut into the walls of that ancient rock quarry just outside the northwest city wall. People often assume the burial must have been located in a completely different place than the crucifixion, but in fact John tells us, *"Now in the place where he was crucified there was a garden, and in the garden a new tomb in which no one had yet been laid. So because of the Jewish day of Preparation, since the tomb was close at hand, they laid Jesus there."* (John 19:41-42) Amazingly, just as archaeologists have identified the rock of Golgotha underneath the Church of the Holy Sepulcher, so they have also discovered the rock-cut tomb of Joseph of Arimathea nearby!

While Joseph and Nicodemus anointed Jesus' body, Mary Magdalene and a number of other women disciples sat and watched them from a distance. When they sealed Jesus' body in the tomb, the women carefully noted which tomb it was because they planned to come back after the Sabbath had passed to finish the hurried anointing job carried out by the men. (Luke 23:55-56) After they discovered the tomb empty on that Sunday and encountered the risen Jesus, the empty tomb became a place of pilgrimage where the local community of Jesus' followers gathered on Sunday mornings to celebrate his resurrection. The tomb became well known as a place of Christian worship and was marked with etchings in the rock identifying it as such. One hundred years later, when the Roman legions were crushing the second Jewish revolt, the Emperor Hadrian demonstrated Roman sovereignty over Jerusalem by building pagan religious shrines over the places of Jewish worship. Because the empty tomb had already become known as a place of worship, Hadrian had his engineers fill in the rock quarry, burying the tomb and the rock of Golgotha, and built a temple to the goddess Venus directly over the tomb.

The Church of the Holy Sepulcher in Jerusalem

Two hundred years after that, when the Roman Emperor Constantine had converted to Christianity, his devout mother Helena came to Jerusalem to build churches in the most significant sites from Jesus' life. When she inquired of the local Christian community about the location of the rock of Golgotha and the empty tomb, they told her it was buried underneath the ruins of the pagan temple to Venus. Sure enough, when Queen Helena's workmen cleared away all the fill from the rock quarry, they discovered the rock of Golgotha and the empty tomb of Joseph, just as they had been told! When Helena built the new Church of the

Holy Sepulcher, she incorporated the free-standing rock of Golgotha into the courtyard of the church. She also cut away the hillside on three sides of the tomb, leaving a free-standing cube of rock with the tomb inside of it, so she could then build a round domed building over the tomb, protecting it and incorporating it into her magnificent church.

Sadly, that church has been destroyed multiple times by war, fire, and earthquakes over the past two millennia, greatly marring its original beauty. It is even more tragic that in the eleventh century an extremist Muslim ruler tore down the entire church and ordered his soldiers to destroy the tomb itself with pickaxes. As a result, only the base and part of the walls of the original rock tomb is in place, but the form of the tomb has been reconstructed over that base and is still a place of Christian worship and pilgrimage today. Recently an international team of experts undertook a detailed study of the tomb inside the Church of the Holy Sepulcher, dismantling, cleaning, and reinforcing structures dating back to the time of Queen Helena. The results of their study confirm the presence of the original tomb that was cut into the walls of the ancient rock quarry and identified by the early Christians as the tomb of Jesus. It is remarkable that we can still visit both the actual rock of Golgotha where Jesus died on a cross and the very stone tomb of Joseph of Arimathea where his body was laid to rest!

The Tomb of Jesus Inside the Church of the Holy Sepulcher

TRANSFORMING ENCOUNTERS

After Jesus was buried and the sun had gone down, it was both the Sabbath and the Passover holiday, so nearly every Jew stayed inside, resting and celebrating. Many of the followers of Jesus were likely staying at the large home of Mary, the mother of John Mark, on the southwest hill of Jerusalem where they had celebrated the Passover the night before. However, that Friday night and the Saturday that followed, they were not celebrating but rather hiding and mourning. Their Rabbi was dead, their hopes were crushed, and they were now identified with a convicted traitor. As planned, the women disciples procured perfumed oil and burial spices so they could show their devotion to the Master one last time. With Mary Magdalene leading the way, they rose before dawn on Sunday, the day after the Sabbath had ended, and made their way through the Garden Gate and outside the city walls to the tomb of Joseph in the quarry cemetery. We don't know how they planned to negotiate access with the squad of Roman soldiers who were guarding the tomb, but when they arrived the soldiers were nowhere to be found. Instead, they found the stone rolled away and the tomb empty.

The House of Mary, the Mother of John Mark

Naturally, they assumed someone had stolen the body. John tells us Mary Magdalene went back to report this to the male disciples, who were presumably still hiding out in the upper room at the home of Mary, the mother of John Mark. Peter and

John came to inspect the empty tomb and saw the grave cloths curiously lying on the stone shelf inside, exactly where Jesus' body had lain. They left with more questions than when they arrived but knew something strange had happened in that tomb. Then Mary and the women encountered two angels who asked, *"Why do you seek the living among the dead? He is not here, but has risen. Remember how he told you, while he was still in Galilee, that the Son of Man must be delivered into the hands of sinful men and be crucified and on the third day rise."* (Luke 24:5-7) While they were still trying to make sense of all this, Mary Magdalene encountered the risen Jesus, but mistook him for the gardener. When he spoke her name, suddenly she realized it was Jesus! She hugged him, and the other women fell at Jesus' feet to worship him, but Jesus sent them to tell the rest of the disciples he had risen and was going to meet them in Galilee. The women went back to the upper room where the male disciples were still hiding and Mary Magdalene was the first to announce the Good News of Easter, *"I have seen the Lord!"* (John 20:18)

We would expect the men who followed Jesus to trust the testimony of their spiritual sisters, but Luke tells us their cultural bias got the best of them. *Now it was Mary Magdalene and Joanna and Mary the mother of James and the other women with them who told these things to the apostles, but these words seemed to them an idle tale, and they did not believe them.* (Luke 24:10-11) A number of details in the Gospel accounts of Jesus' resurrection point to the accuracy and authenticity of these eyewitness reports. In the first-century women were not even allowed to give testimony in a court of law because, in that patriarchal setting, they were considered unreliable witnesses. Just as no one in that culture would make up a story about their leader being subjected to the shame of crucifixion, so no one would make up a story of resurrection in which women were the primary heroes and witnesses. However, that is exactly what we find in the four Gospels of the New Testament. It is notable that the male disciples, some of whom wrote the Gospels, are described as cowards who fled when Jesus was arrested, went into hiding, and, except for John, were apparently not even present at his crucifixion. It is also notable that it is to his female disciples the risen Jesus first appeared. These reports have all the hallmarks of historically accurate eyewitness testimony rather than a concocted conspiracy story!

Later that evening, two disciples from Emmaus came to visit the male disciples in Jerusalem, who had locked themselves in the upper room, and reported that the risen Jesus appeared to them while they were walking home and he even ate dinner with them! By that time Jesus had appeared to Peter as well. Then Luke tells us, *As they were talking about these things, Jesus himself stood among them, and said to them, "Peace to you!" But they were startled and frightened and thought they saw a spirit. And he said to them, "Why are you troubled, and why do doubts arise in your hearts? See my hands and my feet, that it is I myself. Touch me, and see. For a spirit does not have flesh and bones as you see that I have." And when he had said this, he showed them his hands and his feet. And while they still disbelieved for joy and were marveling, he said to them, "Have you anything here to eat?" They gave him a piece of broiled fish, and he took it and ate before them.* (Luke 24:36-43) Jesus was alive! They saw he was not a ghost, and this was not some kind of vision or apparition. They could touch him and eat with him. They saw the wounds of his crucifixion and knew this was the same Jesus who had been nailed to the cross and killed on Friday, but was now gloriously alive, never to die again!

The only one of the core group of male disciples who was not present that night was Thomas. When he returned to the upper room, they told him, *"We have seen the Lord,"* but he could not bring himself to believe it was true. Thomas said, *"Unless I see in his hands the mark of the nails, and place my finger into the mark of the nails, and place my hand into his side, I will never believe."* One week later, they were still behind locked doors and Jesus appeared among them again. He came to Thomas, held out his arms and said, *"Put your finger here, and see my hands; and put out your hand, and place it in my side. Do not disbelieve, but believe."* Thomas answered him, *"My Lord and my God!"* Jesus gave Thomas exactly what he needed in order to believe. Jesus pointed out not everyone would have this luxury but would have to believe based on the disciples' eyewitness testimony. He said, *"Have you believed because you have seen me? Blessed are those who have not seen and yet have believed."* (John 20:25-29)

Meeting the risen Jesus was the turning point from which the disciples would never look back. It was not a product of wishful thinking or a carefully constructed lie. They had seen him with their own eyes and touched him with their own hands, and they knew beyond a shadow of a doubt Jesus really did die and come back to life again. This meant everything they had witnessed him say and do was true. For three years they had followed Jesus, listened to his teaching, seen countless miracles, and yet still they misunderstood his mission and misconstrued who he really was. When the chips were down, they deserted him and went into hiding. But once they met the risen Jesus everything changed. They were transformed from confused cowards to spiritual leaders unafraid to pay for their testimony with their own lives. No one in history had ever conquered death, until that moment. They now knew Jesus is the Messiah; he is the King of kings and Lord of lords! They knew him as a man, but now they knew he was also God in flesh, and they worshiped him. Soon they would be filled by the Spirit and empowered to change the world, even if it cost them their very lives, which for most of them it did.

RESURRECTION POWER!

It is impossible to overstate the significance of Jesus' resurrection. That Jesus of Nazareth died and rose again confirms his identity as the God who became fully human to show us life as it is meant to be lived, who established the New Covenant by his sacrificial death on the cross, and who fulfilled all the Messianic promises by inaugurating the Kingdom of God. The resurrection is the greatest of all Jesus' many miracles, not just because he came back to life again, but because he was transformed into a whole new kind of indestructible life that is the first fruits of the new creation to come. Even Lazarus eventually got sick and died again, but Jesus was now alive never to die again! Jesus' promise of eternal life is not a nice religious idea or optimistic wishful thinking, but the sure and certain promise that those who are in Covenant relationship with him by faith will share in this same indestructible fullness of life that continues forever in God's eternal Kingdom.

The eyewitness accounts are clear that Jesus did not simply return to his previous state of being when he rose from the dead. His wounds proved he was unmistakably the same man they had known who died on a cross, but Jesus was now profoundly changed. He was different enough that his own disciples who knew him intimately often did not initially recognize Jesus in his risen state. Although they could touch him and he could eat food with them, Jesus could also appear and disappear from locked rooms. He was physical, but it was a whole new kind of physicality. Ever since Adam and Eve sabotaged God's good purpose in creation, the Creator of all things has planned to recreate a new heaven and a new earth and restore all things according to his perfect design. The resurrection of Jesus is the beginning of that new creation and the down payment which assures all those who trust and follow him that they too will be part of this eternal Kingdom.

The risen Jesus made it clear to the disciples they were not going back to the way things were before. When he appeared to the women at the tomb, he told them not to hold on to him because he was ascending to his original place at the right hand of the Father. (John 20:17) At the Last Supper, Jesus told the disciples he was going away to prepare a place for them in his Father's extended family home. Jesus told them things were going to work in a whole new way now. He explained, *"I will ask the Father, and he will give you another Helper, to be with you forever, even the Spirit of truth, whom the world cannot receive, because it neither sees him nor knows him. You know him, for he dwells with you and will be in you."* He said, *"If anyone loves me, he will keep my word, and my Father will love him, and we will come to him and make our home with him."* (John 14:16-23) When the risen Jesus appeared to them three days later in that same upper room, he breathed on them and said, *"Receive the Holy Spirit. If you forgive the sins of any, they are forgiven them; if you withhold forgiveness from any, it is withheld."* (John 20:23) From now on, the disciples would not be following Jesus around Judea and Galilee. Now they would be speaking and acting as the Father's representatives on earth. They would be filled with the Holy Spirit, and Jesus himself would take up residence inside of them to continue teaching them, shaping them, and guiding them as they took the Good News of the Kingdom beyond the land of Israel to the very ends of the earth.

We have seen that the textual record of Jesus' resurrection in the four Gospels bears all the marks of genuine eyewitness accounts. These are not mythological tales or a cobbled together conspiracy theory, but reliable historical records of real events. We have also seen that the physical evidence strongly corroborates these eyewitness accounts. We can touch the rock of Golgotha and visit the remains of Joseph's tomb outside the first-century walls of Jerusalem, just as they are described in the Gospels. But of all the evidence that supports the historical truth of Jesus' resurrection, the transformed lives of the disciples themselves is most convincing. Prior to the resurrection, these ordinary men and women were confused and self-serving, seeking a position in Jesus' palace, and ready to desert him at the first sign of trouble. After meeting the risen Jesus, these same women and men became fearless leaders who were ready to lay down their lives for their testimony that they had seen Jesus die on the cross and then met him gloriously transformed and fully alive. History tells us that eleven of the twelve disciples, along with many other followers of Jesus, were ultimately tortured and killed for this testimony, but did not recant their testimony.

It is hard to imagine more convincing evidence pointing to the truth of Jesus' resurrection than the changed lives and unwavering courage of these men and women. Even in the face of death, they held true to this transforming reality that Jesus had conquered sin, death, hell, and the devil, and they were certain of their future destiny in God's eternal Kingdom. The resurrection of Jesus produced in them an unshakable faith and empowered them to follow Jesus no matter what came against them. Can we say the same? As Jesus pointed out to Thomas, most people do not have the privilege of being able to touch his wounds and see the physical evidence as did those first disciples. But Jesus pronounced a blessing on those of us who would not be able to see with our eyes yet would still exercise faith in our hearts. Remember that faith not only comes from seeing, but also from hearing the word of Christ. (Romans 10:17) Thomas saw the wounds and believed, but we get to hear the testimony of those who saw.

We also get to see the fruit of changed lives still today. If we are listening to the Word of God, open to the work of the Holy Spirit producing the fruit of faith in our hearts, and willing to exercise that faith one step at a time, we will discover the power to live the extraordinary life of Jesus as those first disciples did, no matter what comes. The first followers of Jesus changed the world because of their faith in the resurrected Jesus. Jesus said all it takes is a mustard seed of faith to move a mountain. (Matthew 17:20) Are you ready to exercise your mustard seed of faith by taking the next step on this journey of following Jesus, your crucified and risen Lord?

REFLECT AND DISCUSS

Read John 20:1-23

1. Mary Magdalene and the women disciples of Jesus took significant risks in order to show their devotion to Jesus. What risks am I willing to take?

2. What evidence have I seen that helps convince me Jesus really did rise from the dead and became the first fruits of the new creation?

3. How can the resurrection of Jesus change my life as it did the first followers of Jesus?

4. Am I willing to share the Good News of Jesus' resurrection with others, even if it brings persecution in my life?

5. God, what are you saying to me and what step of faith do you want me to take in response?

CHAPTER FOURTEEN

TO THE ENDS OF THE EARTH

SKUNKED AGAIN

Simon sat on the aft seat of the family fishing boat, hunched over the gunnel, trailing his hand in the water and watching the first streaks of light break over the eastern ridge. It had been years since he spent a night hauling nets on the Sea of Galilee, and he could feel it in his aching back and shoulders. It would be nice if he and his six friends had something to show for all their work, but they had caught nothing and now dawn had come. But his mind drifted away. It seemed like his head had been swimming ever since that Sunday morning Mary Magdalene woke them up with her mad pounding on the outer door. Simon could hardly remember all the unexpected things that had happened in the days that followed. *Who could have ever imagined it all!* Yet he was clear about the one undeniable truth he had experienced—the crucified Jesus was in fact alive again and was the same person they had known, physically present again yet gloriously transformed.

Simon was shaken from his pondering by a voice calling to them from the shore, "Children, do you have any fish?" Thomas frowned and simply replied, "No," with a disdainful tone that warned the stranger not to rub salt in their wounds. The man on the shore said to them, "Cast the net on the right side of the boat, and you will find some." They all had the same thought. *Who has the audacity to tell us how to fish?!* But a memory stirred in Simon's mind. He caught John's eye. "Quick, help me with this casting net!" He gathered the circular net from his end of the boat, handing it to John, who spun the net out over the side while the others watched. The perimeter weights of the net started sink, but it was barely out of sight before the ropes began to pull tight. "Help him with the line!" Simon gestured wildly to the others. He could see the net was already full of fish. It was so full, the seven of them couldn't even lift it into the boat!

Something like this had only ever happened one other time in his life, a few years earlier in a cove just a mile east of here. John must have remembered the same thing, because at that moment he grabbed Simon by the shoulders, pulled his face up close, and blurted out, "It is the Lord!" Before he could think twice, Simon wrapped his cloak around his waist and jumped into the water, swimming toward the stranger on shore. Wading out of the water, his waterlogged clothes dragging him down, Simon's excitement suddenly gave way to shame. He was the one who had boasted he would never deny Jesus, yet that is exactly what he had done. Three times. He had failed to live up to the name Jesus had given him. *Peter, so-called "Rocky." More like lake mud than a rock,* he thought as he emerged from the water with the shoreline sucking at his sandals.

Awkwardly, Simon turned and waited for the others who were rowing the boat to shore, towing the bulging net full of fish behind them. By this time, they could smell the charcoal fire Jesus had built on the beach. "Bring some of the fish that you have just caught," Jesus said, "Come and have breakfast." Simon pulled the boat ashore and then helped them haul the massive catch onto the beach. It turned out to be 153 large fish, a record haul for a single casting net! Now they were all thinking of what happened the last time Jesus gave them fishing advice.

As they sat around the fire, no one knew what to say, and Jesus sat silently, watching the fish sizzling on the hot stones. Simon avoided making eye contact and tried in vain to shut out the memories. *"Come follow me and I will make you fish for people." How could a screw-up like me ever catch people?* It wasn't just the miraculous catch that gave him déjà vu. It was the smell of that charcoal fire, just like the one in the courtyard of the High Priest's house on that fateful night Jesus was arrested. Now the memories came crashing back like a rockslide. *"You will all fall away because of me this night." "Though they all fall away because of you, I will never fall away." "Truly, I tell you, this very night, before the rooster crows, you will deny me three times." "This man was with Jesus of Nazareth." "I do not know the man."* Simon looked down and blinked back the tears. This is why he went back to fishing for fish. He knew he had forfeited the right to fish for people. He knew he had become a stumbling stone and was no longer worthy to be a building block in Jesus' new family.

They ate without speaking, until Jesus finally broke the silence. "Simon, son of John, do you love me more than these?" Simon replied haltingly, "Yes, Lord; you know that I love you." Jesus said, "Feed my lambs." Simon could hardly believe his ears. *Feed my lambs?! What is he saying?* Jesus repeated the question while looking him straight in the eye, "Simon, son of John, do you love me?" He returned the stare and said to him more forcefully, "Yes, Lord; you know that I love you." Jesus said to him, "Tend my sheep." *Tend my sheep? Does he mean what I think he means?* A third time Jesus looked at him and repeated the question, "Simon, son of John, do you love me?" A pang of guilt shot through him like a Roman spear. Three questions for three denials. He cried out, "Lord, you know everything; you know that I love you!" Jesus said to him, "Feed my sheep."

Looking around the fire, Simon could see smiles growing on the faces of his friends. James slapped him on the back. They all understood what Jesus was saying. Peter was being restored as the leader of their family. *How is it possible? Shouldn't it be John? I am not worthy.* Now Peter could see the smile on Jesus' face, and he knew it was true. *I am Peter. It is not just a name; it is a calling. This is who God created me to be. To lead. To love. To lay down my life, just as my Master did.* Peter felt the shame melting away and faith taking its place. Jesus' words rang in his ears, giving him the confidence that he could do what he was being called to do. Now Peter knew his failure was behind him and a whole new life stretched out ahead of him.

When Jesus got up from the fire, Peter jumped up feeling a thousand pounds lighter. As he walked along with his Rabbi in that familiar way, Jesus' tone turned serious. *"Truly, truly, I say to you, when you were young, you used to dress yourself and walk wherever you wanted, but when you are old, you will stretch out your hands, and another will dress you and carry you where you do not want to go."* Instantly Peter knew what Jesus' was referring to, and he shivered. He remembered Jesus' words to them on their final retreat up in Caesarea Philippi, *"If anyone would come after me, let him deny himself and take up his cross and follow me."* Peter understood what Jesus was saying. His cross would be a literal one.

Suddenly he was taken back to that moment in the upper room a few weeks earlier when the risen Jesus had said to them, *"Peace be with you. As the Father has sent me, even so I am sending you."* And then he leaned over, breathed on them and said, *"Receive the Holy Spirit."* Peter realized this was the sending. They were to continue to do the things Jesus had trained them to do no matter what, even if it meant their fate would be the same as Jesus' fate. The Holy Spirit would give them the faith and courage they needed to face this challenge and complete this calling. When Jesus had breathed on them, Peter felt a tingling run through his whole body. He felt that same tingling now, running up his spine. Jesus stopped, turned to Peter, looked him in the eye and said, "Follow me." In that moment Peter knew he would never deny his Lord again. He would never look back. In the authority of Jesus' name and by the power of his Spirit, he would fish for people. He would make disciples. He would be a building block in God's new family. He would shepherd the sheep entrusted to him. No. Matter. What.[16]

PASSING THE BATON

For forty incredible days, the risen Jesus appeared to the disciples and taught them from the Scriptures about the Kingdom of God. These must have been some of the most powerful times the disciples had with Jesus. On one of those occasions Jesus said, *"These are my words that I spoke to you while I was still with you, that everything written about me in the Law of Moses and the Prophets and the Psalms must be fulfilled."* Then he opened their minds to understand the Scriptures, and said to them, *"Thus it is written, that the Christ should suffer and on the third day rise from the dead, and that repentance for the forgiveness of sins should be proclaimed in his name to all nations, beginning from Jerusalem. You are witnesses of these things. And behold, I am sending the promise of my Father upon you."* (Luke 24:44-49) The disciples were gaining supernatural insight into all they had experienced with Jesus, and he was preparing them for the next stage of their journey.

Following their initial encounters with the risen Jesus in Jerusalem, once the eight days of Unleavened Bread were completed, the disciples traveled to Galilee as their Master had instructed, presumably back to their homes in Capernaum. Jesus did not appear to them right away, so Peter decided he was going back to fishing, perhaps because he felt he was disqualified as a spiritual leader due to his triple

---

[16] Based on John 21:1-19

denials. Six of the disciples came with him. After catching nothing that night, they all had a major déjà vu at dawn when a stranger called to them from the shore and told them to put down their nets one more time. This is what Jesus had done when he first called them to follow him full time. Soon their nets were bulging with another miraculous catch, and they knew it was Jesus. It was as if he were calling them to follow him all over again in this new post-resurrection world.

Jesus built a charcoal fire on the beach and was cooking them a fish breakfast. Sitting with the others around the fire, Peter had a painful déjà vu of his own. The only other *"charcoal fire"* mentioned in the Gospels is the one that Peter sat around in the courtyard of the High Priest when he denied Jesus three times. (John 18:18) Now Jesus recalled that moment by using his old name *"Simon, son of John"* and asking him three times, *"Do you love me?"* Jesus answered each of Peter's affirmative responses by saying, *"Feed/tend my sheep/lambs."* (John 21:1-19) A large rock on the shore of the Sea of Galilee, just a few miles west of Capernaum, was identified in the fourth century as the location where this happened. Steps were cut into the rock to give easier access to the flat top, and eventually a church was built there, using the rock as part of the floor of the church. Today a small black basalt stone chapel known as "The Primacy of Peter" stands there. We don't have any archaeological evidence to confirm this as the actual site for this encounter, but it could well be accurate, and regardless is a beautiful spot to reflect on this interaction between Jesus and Peter.

The Church of the Primacy of Peter on the Sea of Galilee

As much as it must have hurt Peter for Jesus to remind him of his failure, it was a necessary act of healing to bring his shame into the light. Jesus took him back to that moment and addressed the shame Peter felt, not with condemnation but with forgiveness. Three times Peter had denied him, but now Jesus gave Peter the opportunity to reaffirm his love for Jesus three times. Three times Peter had failed him, but now three times Jesus restored him to his role as shepherd of the disciples. What an amazing act of grace that Jesus not only offered forgiveness and healing but even more renewed Peter's calling to lead. And Peter did go on to lead the first church in Jerusalem, eventually going out on mission to extend the movement of Jesus across the Mediterranean world! The truth is we are all like Peter. We have all failed and denied our Lord. The question is, will we sit down at the charcoal fire and let Jesus bring our shame into the light where it can be wiped away? Will we love Jesus enough to receive his gracious restoration and answer the call to become a sheep who learns to shepherd others?

Toward the end of their time in Galilee, Jesus took them up on a mountain and gave them their new commissioning, *"All authority in heaven and on earth has been given to me. Go therefore and make disciples of all nations, baptizing them in the name of the Father and of the Son and of the Holy Spirit, teaching them to observe all that I have commanded you. And behold, I am with you always, to the end of the age."* (Matthew 28:18-20) From the very beginning they had been amazed by Jesus' authority, how he spoke directly as a representative of God and acted on God's behalf to do his will on earth as it is done in heaven. Jesus had shown them and taught them how to exercise that same authority as daughters and sons of their Father the King. The followers of Jesus were amazed that the power of God flowed through them to heal and cast out demons as they had seen their Rabbi do so many times. Now Jesus formally handed over this authority, given to him by the Father, for his disciples to teach and pass on to others. When Jesus said, *"Go therefore..."* he passed the baton to them. What Jesus passed on to them was the authority to make disciples just as he had discipled them.

We have seen that the heart of discipleship is a relationship in which disciples come to know what their rabbi knows and learn to do what their rabbi does, so they become like the rabbi and call disciples of their own. This is exactly what the risen Jesus commissioned the disciples to do in his absence. Through their Covenant relationship with Jesus, he taught them about the Kingdom of God and trained them to live out that Kingdom in their lives. Here the baton was officially passed and the disciples were recognized as the rabbis. Now it was their turn to do with others what Jesus had done with them. Specifically, they were to welcome more and more people into the New Covenant family of God through the gracious entry rite of baptism, where they would receive their identity as children of God. Then they were to teach these new followers not only the content of Jesus' teaching by their words, but also to show them the way of Jesus by their own example. None of this was to be done in their own wisdom and power; rather, Jesus would be with them every step of the way through the empowering presence of the Holy Spirit who was about to fill them and would continually guide them.

This final commissioning Jesus gave his disciples is our commissioning as well. If you have put your faith in Jesus and decided to follow him, then you have begun the journey toward becoming a rabbi who calls and trains other disciples. It begins by receiving the gracious love of the Father who declares over us, as he did over Jesus, "This is my beloved son, in him I am well pleased" and "This is my beloved daughter, in her I am well pleased." The journey continues as you study the teaching of Jesus and all that the Bible teaches us about Jesus. At the heart of the journey is deciding to intentionally pattern your life after Jesus, seeking to live as he did in an extended spiritual family that is seeking those who are lost and learning to abide in him regularly so that you bear good fruit that lasts. It is critical to have someone in your life who is ahead of you on the journey that you can learn from, ask questions of, and follow their example as they model the example of Jesus for you. (1 Corinthians 11:1) This is not always possible, but it is a door that is worth knocking at until you find someone who can disciple you.

Soon, this will be your role with others. You will become the one who invites others into your life, opening your family and your home, and modeling Jesus for them. Of course, we all feel inadequate to this task and are painfully aware of our many imperfections. The good news is we don't need to be a perfect example. We already have that, and his name is Jesus! What people do need is a living Jesus-shaped example, and we can offer that, imperfect as we might be, because Jesus is alive in us through the power of the Holy Spirit. We stand in a long line of those who have received the baton from someone ahead of them on the race and have passed it on to us. Now it is our turn to pass the baton on to others as we help them learn to run this race with us.

SENT AS WITNESSES

By the end of those heady forty days with the risen Jesus, the disciples had made their way back to Jerusalem, and he led them up onto the Mount of Olives. Jesus told them, *"You will receive power when the Holy Spirit has come upon you, and you will be my witnesses in Jerusalem and in all Judea and Samaria, and to the end of the earth."* (Acts 1:8) Witnesses are not experts who have all the answers. They are not professionally trained public speakers or high-pressure salespeople. Witnesses are simply those who tell what they have seen and heard. Witnesses share their experiences with others. Very few of Jesus' core disciples were particularly well educated, well connected, or well off. They were basically ordinary men and women, most of whom came from what we would think of as lower- or middle-class backgrounds and blue-collar professions. But Jesus sent them out as his witnesses. The word "apostle" means "sent ones," and these men and women became the first Apostles because they were sent out of their normal context to extend the movement of Jesus and bring the Good News of the Kingdom to more people. Their calling was to give testimony to what Jesus had done in their lives and to tell others what they had heard and seen.

Jerusalem from the West, Mount of Olives in the Distance

Jesus described the geographical strategy that would unfold as they followed the leading of the Holy Spirit and learned to live as witnesses. First, they would give witness within the walls of Jerusalem and multiply families of disciples who were following Jesus and living on mission together there. Then the movement would overflow the walls of Jerusalem and spread through the surrounding Jewish region of Judea. Then they would break through the tricky cultural and religious barriers that stood between them and their cousins the Samaritans, who typically hated and were hated by Jews. Once that dividing wall of hostility was broken down, then they would become witnesses to the pagan Gentile world that was filled with foreign gods and rife with immoral practices. This process would ultimately lead them across the globe to the very edges of human civilization until the whole world receives the witness that Jesus has risen and the Kingdom of God is at hand. Just as with the final commissioning, this sending was not only for the first disciples, but is for us as well. We are all sent as witnesses to demonstrate and articulate the Good News of Jesus for those who don't yet know him and are not yet part of his family. Some of us are sent to our Jerusalem, some to our Judea, others to our Samaria, and still others are sent all the way to the ends of the earth!

But Jesus was clear none of this would be possible until the Holy Spirit filled them with the power they needed to answer this calling. Jesus led them a little further up the Mount of Olives, and then he ascended into heaven and left them looking up into the sky wondering what had just happened. Two angels appeared to them and said, *"Men of Galilee, why do you stand looking into heaven? This Jesus, who was taken up from you into heaven, will come in the same way as you saw him go into heaven."* Then they remembered Jesus told them to wait in the city for the Spirit to be poured out, so they returned to the upper room in the house of Mary, the mother of John Mark, to pray and wait. Luke tells us about 120 men and women disciples gathered there. (Acts 1:11-15) About ten days later, during the festival of Pentecost, they were all together in one place when the Holy Spirit was poured out upon them. They heard the sound of a mighty rushing wind and saw something that looked like flames of fire on each of their heads, and each of them was filled with the Holy Spirit. Surprisingly, they found they were able to speak in foreign languages that they had never studied before! (Acts 2:1-13) This wasn't a random spiritual phenomenon, but rather empowering by the Spirit to go into the streets of Jerusalem and share the Good News of Jesus with people who had come to Jerusalem from many different countries in their own native languages. The Holy Spirit was equipping them beyond their own abilities to be Jesus' witnesses in Jerusalem to people who came from the ends of the earth!

Modern Buildings Built Over the Upper Room in the House of Mary,
the Mother of John Mark

This was the beginning of the movement of Jesus that has changed countless lives and altered the course of human history. It began on that day of Pentecost in Jerusalem when the Holy Spirit empowered Peter to preach his first sermon, and 3,000 people came to faith in Jesus and were baptized! (Acts 2:14-41) It continued as followers of Jesus began to gather in homes to function as spiritual families on mission and the apostles taught the crowds in the Temple courts, just as Jesus had done. Miraculous signs and wonders happened as ordinary people learned to exercise the authority of Jesus by the power of the Holy Spirit. Before long the religious leaders were so threatened by all of this that they initiated persecution which drove many of the followers of Jesus out of Jerusalem and into Judea and Samaria. (Acts 8:1-3)

Next, the Apostles saw Samaritans coming to faith in Jesus, and then the Roman centurion Cornelius and his extended family embraced Jesus and were filled with the Spirit! (Acts 8, 10) The movement began to take root in major Gentile cities like Antioch, and from there the former persecutor Saul was sent on a series of missional journeys that brought the Good News of the Kingdom across Asia Minor and into Greece. (Acts 13-19) The movement of Jesus continued to spread both east and west as disciples made disciples and formed extended spiritual families who were living on mission, seeking and saving the lost by the power of the Spirit, just as Jesus had done. For centuries the church had no public buildings but met in extended family homes and carried out their mission in the public marketplace, meeting lost people where they lived and worked. By the time Christianity was adopted as the official religion of the Roman empire in AD 323, the movement of Jesus had spread as far east as it had west, and the world would never be the same.

BUILDING A NEW CREATION

It would be a mistake for us to assume this movement was created by men and women who were building the church for Jesus. Remember, on that final retreat with his disciples in Caesarea Philippi, Jesus said he is the one who will build his church. But he also said he will use stones like Peter (aka "Rocky") to build it. When Peter resisted the cross, Jesus made it very clear he could either submit as a disciple and become a rock shaped by Jesus into a building block, or he could follow his own way and become a stumbling stone that causes others to trip and fall. (Matthew 16:13-23) During his final week in Jerusalem, while he was teaching in the Temple courts, Jesus reiterated this theme when he predicted his impending death outside the city walls and then quoted Psalm 118:25, *"Have you never read in the Scriptures: 'The stone that the builders rejected has become the cornerstone; this was the Lord's doing, and it is marvelous in our eyes'"*? (Matthew 21:42)

I wonder when Peter realized Jesus' crucifixion was a quite literal fulfillment of this prophecy from Psalm 118. If you remember, the builders of the Temple who cut limestone blocks from that ancient quarry carved around a section of rock that was not suitable for building, leaving a 20-foot-tall rocky outcropping which the Romans chose as their place of crucifixion. That means Jesus was killed on what was literally *the stone that the builders rejected!* Some weeks later, Peter and John were arrested in the Temple courts for healing a lame man and sharing the Good News of Jesus. When they were examined by the Sanhedrin, the very council that had condemned Jesus to death, Peter said to them, *"Jesus is the stone that was rejected by you, the builders, which has become the cornerstone. And there is salvation in no one else, for there is no other name under heaven given among men by which we must be saved."* (Acts 4:11-12) Peter realized when Jesus literally died on the stone that the builders rejected, he laid the cornerstone of his new church. When Jesus rose from the dead, he demonstrated this church was the means by which he would extend the New Covenant to all people. And now, by the power of the Holy Spirit, Jesus was using living stones like Peter and John, like Mary and Martha, to build his church into a movement that was literally going to change the whole world into a new creation defined by the Kingdom of God!

Many years later, Peter had become an Apostle who was sent to the ends of the earth and saw countless people come to faith in Jesus as the movement spread across the Mediterranean with hundreds of churches planted in extended family homes. While composing a letter to the churches for which he was responsible, Peter wrote, *As you come to him, a living stone rejected by men but in the sight of God chosen and precious, you yourselves like living stones are being built up as a spiritual house* [oikos], *to be a holy priesthood, to offer spiritual sacrifices acceptable to God through Jesus Christ.* (1 Peter 2:4-5) Still today Jesus is using *"living stones"* to build a *"spiritual oikos,"* an extended spiritual family that is living on mission to reach the lost and make disciples who make disciples. These families are meant to function like a new kind of Temple, filled with the Holy Spirit, where lost people are welcomed into the transforming presence of the God who loves them without measure. This is what it means to say that Jesus is building his church and using ordinary people, disciples just like you and me, to do this extraordinary thing. This church is not a building but a Covenant family who are living out the Kingdom mission of God in order to see a whole new creation born.

We have seen that Jesus the builder from Nazareth who was conceived by an unmarried mother, fled as a refugee to Egypt, and lived most of his life in obscurity, went on to live the most extraordinary life this world has ever seen. What makes Jesus so extraordinary is not just the incredible teachings he left us, or the countless miracles he performed, or even the fact that he died and rose from the dead. The most extraordinary thing about Jesus is that he multiplied this abundant life in the lives of 120 men and women, who in turn multiplied that life into thousands of people, and they passed it on to hundreds of thousands, so that this life spread across the world to transform the lives of literally billions of people two thousand years later! What makes the life of Jesus so extraordinary is that it has the power to keep changing lives and thus to change the world.

No matter how ordinary you feel, your destiny is to live an extraordinary Jesus-shaped life. You may live in obscurity and never be known to those outside your immediate circle, or you may have far-reaching impact on people you have never even met. Either way, Jesus' invitation to follow him is your call to an extraordinary life; a life in which you freely give the unconditional love you freely receive from your heavenly Father; a life in which you lay down what you want and take up what God has for you; a life in which you welcome outcasts and embrace the unclean; a life in which you invite others to follow you as you follow Jesus; a life in which you live as part of a spiritual family that seeks and saves the lost; a life in which you do the will of God on earth as it is in heaven. As you pattern your life on the Way of Jesus and fill your heart and mind with the Truth of Jesus, his extraordinary Life will grow in you and be multiplied through you! This is the extraordinary life that has been growing in me, despite my failures, and in my family, my church, and those in whom I have been blessed to invest my life. I cannot imagine a better life to be living and I want that same life for you!

Jesus is building his church, a global family of spiritual families made up of disciples who are putting their trust in him, being filled with his Spirit, and following his example by the power of that same Spirit. The risen Jesus is breathing his Spirit into you right now. As you put your trust in Jesus, I challenge you to receive the Holy Spirit and ask him to fill you, empower you, and guide your steps. I encourage you to find someone who is ahead of you on the journey who can be a living example of Jesus in your life. I urge you to join an extended spiritual family that is living on mission together. This is how you can learn to invest your life in others by being a living example of Jesus to them. By keeping your eyes on Jesus and continuing to surrender to the Spirit, you too will become a living stone in the spiritual *oikos* Jesus is building. Like Simon Peter and Mary Magdalene and so many other living stones who have come before, you will come to know the deep joy and lasting peace of living this extraordinary life and will become part of the great cloud of witnesses who cheer others on, until Jesus returns and fully establishes the Kingdom of God in his new creation. God bless and keep you as you take one step of faith at a time on this incredible adventure of following Jesus!

REFLECT AND DISCUSS

Read Acts 2:1-13

1. How can I let Jesus bring my failures into the light so I can be restored and empowered to fulfill my calling?

2. What does it mean for me to listen to what Jesus is saying and wait for the Holy Spirit to fill me and guide me?

3. How can I allow the Holy Spirit to empower me to tell people the Good News of Jesus in a way they can understand?

4. Who am I willing to invest my life in and set an example of Jesus for, in order to see God's Kingdom spread to more and more people?

5. God, what are you saying to me and what step of faith do you want me to take in response?

MORE RESOURCES BY BOB ROGNLIEN TO HELP YOU FOLLOW JESUS

FIND THEM ALL AT
WWW.BOBROGNLIEN.COM

❖ Book | *Recovering the Way: How Ancient Discoveries Help Us Follow the Footsteps of Jesus*

➢ A longer, more in-depth treatment of Jesus' life, including the background of the world in which he lived, his birth, and his boyhood. Includes over 100 photos, reconstruction drawings, and maps. Excellent for serious students and teachers who want to go deeper.

❖ Video | **Recovering the Way: The Video Series**

➢ An in-depth video teaching series that illuminates the life of Jesus with thousands of full color photos, reconstruction drawings, and animated maps. The twelve 40-minute episodes correspond to the twelve chapters in the book, *Recovering the Way* (see above) and will bring the Way of Jesus to life for you.

❖ Trip | **The Footsteps of Jesus Experience**

➢ A 14-day journey through Israel and Palestine, following the life of Jesus from birth to resurrection. We keep the group relatively small, stay in unique Christian guesthouses, drive ourselves in vans, do lots of walking off the beaten path, focus on the historically verifiable sites, and keep an intentionally spiritual focus. It is not a tour, but an intensive pilgrimage.

❖ **Books | Footsteps Every Day: A Journey Through the Gospels (4 vols: Matthew, Mark, Luke, John)**

➢ Daily Gospel readings and reflections on the Way of Jesus, illuminated by insights from history, archaeology, and culture. These four books of daily devotions will take you through all four Gospels in one year.

❖ **Podcast | The Footsteps Podcast with Bob Rognlien and Matt Switzer**

➢ In each episode Footsteps Experience leaders Bob and Matt take you on a journey to a significant site in the Holy Land and show how the discoveries there bring a specific biblical passage to life with new insights and applications.

❖ **Trip | The Footsteps of Paul Experience**

➢ A 15-day journey from Antioch to Corinth through Turkey and Greece, following the missional journeys of the Apostle Paul and his disciples. We keep the group relatively small, stay in boutique hotels with historical and cultural charm, drive ourselves in vans, go off the beaten path, focus on the historically verifiable sites, and keep an intentionally spiritual focus. It is not a tour, but an intensive pilgrimage.

❖ **Book | A Jesus-Shaped Life: Discipleship and Mission for Everyday People**

➢ A practical guide to putting the Way of Jesus into practice in your everyday life with the people who are closest to you. It tells the story of how Bob and Pam learned to pattern their lives and their family more intentionally after Jesus. It also offers practical tools, vehicles, and strategies to make discipleship and mission a part of your daily life.

❖ **Book | Empowering Missional Disciples**

➢ A resource for leaders who want to help those they lead to live a life that looks more like Jesus and produces more of the fruit he produced. Includes lots of field-tested tools and vehicles for multiplying missional disciples.